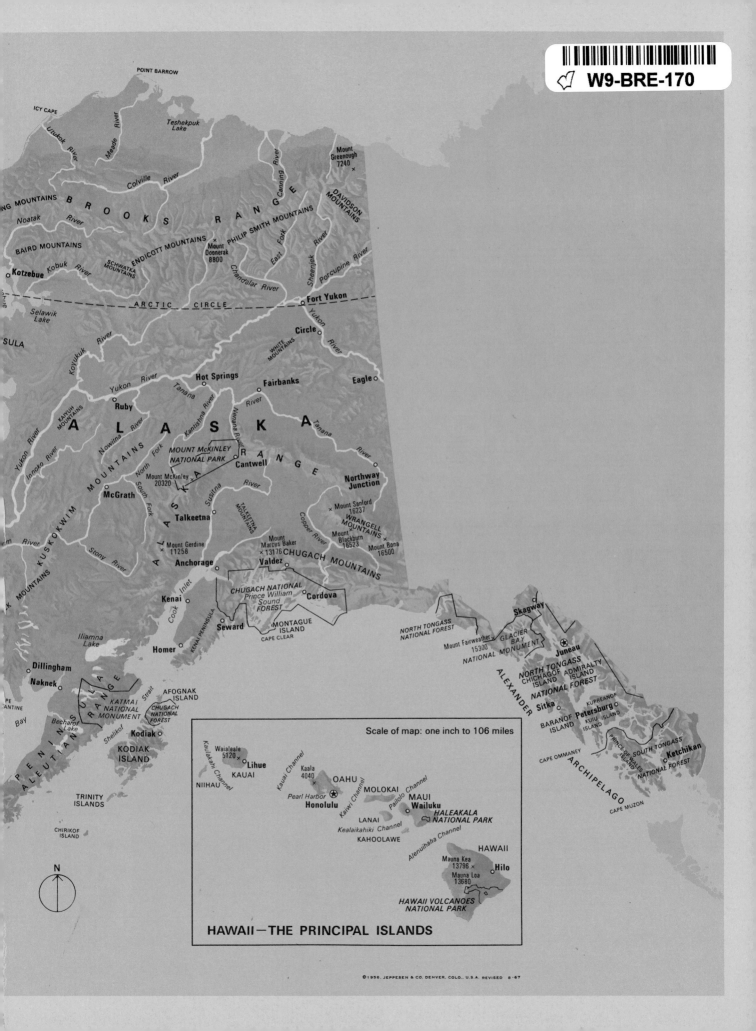

POINT BARROW

ICY CAPE

Teshekpuk Lake

Ulukok River

Meade River

Colville River

NG MOUNTAINS

B R O O K S   R A N G E

Canning River

Mount Greenough 7240 ×

DAVIDSON MOUNTAINS

Noatak River

BAIRD MOUNTAINS

ENDICOTT MOUNTAINS

PHILIP SMITH MOUNTAINS

East Fork

Sheenjek River

Porcupine River

SCHWATKA MOUNTAINS

Mount Doonerak 8800 ×

Kobuk River

Kotzebue

Chandalar River

SULA

Selawik Lake

ARCTIC   CIRCLE

Fort Yukon

Koyukuk River

Yukon River

Circle

Yukon River

WHITE MOUNTAINS

KAYUH MOUNTAINS

Yukon River

Tanana River

Hot Springs

Fairbanks

Eagle

Innoko River

Ruby

River

Nowitna River

A L A S K A

Kantishna River

Nenana River

Tanana

North Fork

Yukon River

K U S K O K W I M   M O U N T A I N S

MOUNT McKINLEY NATIONAL PARK

Cantwell

R A N G E

Tanana River

Mount McKinley 20320 ×

McGrath

South Fork

Susitna River

River

Northway Junction

Stony River

Talkeetna

TALKEETNA MOUNTAINS

A L A S K A   R A N G E

Mount Sanford 16237 ×

WRANGELL MOUNTAINS

Mount Gerdine 11258 ×

Copper River

Mount Blackburn 16523 ×

Mount Bona 16500 ×

River

Anchorage

Mount Marcus Baker × 13176

CHUGACH MOUNTAINS

Valdez

K MOUNTAINS

Cook Inlet

CHUGACH NATIONAL Prince William Sound FOREST

Cordova

NORTH TONGASS NATIONAL FOREST

Skagway

Kenai

KENAI PENINSULA

Seward

MONTAGUE ISLAND

Mount Fairweather 15300 ×

GLACIER BAY NATIONAL MONUMENT

Juneau

Iliamna Lake

Homer

CAPE CLEAR

ALEXANDER

NORTH TONGASS CHICHAGOF ADMIRALTY ISLAND ISLAND

Dillingham

Sitka

NATIONAL FOREST

Naknek

A L E U T I A N   P E N I N S U L A   R A N G E

Becharof Lake

Shelikof Strait

AFOGNAK ISLAND

KATMAI NATIONAL MONUMENT

CHUGACH NATIONAL FOREST

BARANOF ISLAND

KUPREANOF ISLAND

Petersburg

KUIU ISLAND

ARCHIPELAGO

PE ANTINE

Bay

Kodiak

KODIAK ISLAND

CAPE OMMANEY

PRINCE OF WALES ISLAND

SOUTH TONGASS

Ketchikan

TRINITY ISLANDS

CHIRIKOF ISLAND

CAPE MUZON

NATIONAL FOREST

N

Scale of map: one inch to 106 miles

Waialeale 5120 ×

Lihue

Kauaiakahi Channel

Kauai Channel

Kaala 4040 ×

Paliolo Channel

KAUAI

OAHU

MOLOKAI

NIIHAU

Pearl Harbor ✪

Honolulu

Kaiwi Channel

MAUI

Wailuku

HALEAKALA NATIONAL PARK

LANAI

Kealaikahiki Channel

KAHOOLAWE

Alenuihaha Channel

HAWAII

Mauna Kea 13796 ×

Hilo

Mauna Loa 13680

HAWAII VOLCANOES NATIONAL PARK

HAWAII—THE PRINCIPAL ISLANDS

The Frontier
States

TIME
LIFE
BOOKS ®

LIFE WORLD LIBRARY
LIFE NATURE LIBRARY
TIME READING PROGRAM
THE LIFE HISTORY OF THE UNITED STATES
LIFE SCIENCE LIBRARY
GREAT AGES OF MAN
TIME-LIFE LIBRARY OF ART
TIME-LIFE LIBRARY OF AMERICA
FOODS OF THE WORLD
THIS FABULOUS CENTURY
LIFE LIBRARY OF PHOTOGRAPHY

TIME-LIFE Library of America

The Frontier States

Alaska Hawaii

By Richard Austin Smith
and the Editors of
TIME-LIFE BOOKS

TIME-LIFE BOOKS, New York

The Author: Richard Austin Smith has been a professional writer since his days at Duke University in the 1930s. A military correspondent in Europe at the end of World War II, he shortly joined Time Incorporated, where, after a stint in the Washington Bureau, he wrote a total of 75 major stories for FORTUNE magazine. These included studies on both Alaska and Hawaii, profiles of such people as the Rockefeller Brothers and the Sheik of Kuwait, examinations of cities like Los Angeles and Dallas, and special reports on such topics as the price-fixing conspiracy in the electrical industry. This last story laid the groundwork for the investigations by Senator Estes Kefauver's antitrust subcommittee and earned Smith the University of Connecticut's prestigious Loeb Award for "distinguished reporting of business and financial news" in 1962. He is the writer or co-author of several books on U.S. and international business, including *Corporations in Crisis,* a study of decision making in American industry. His novel, *The Sun Dial,* won a Knopf Literary Fellowship award in 1940. The father of two sons, he lives with his wife in a 250-year-old house on the Connecticut shore at Noank.

The Consulting Editor: Oscar Handlin, Charles Warren Professor of American History at Harvard University and director of the university's Charles Warren Center for Studies in American History, is one of America's foremost social historians. His work on U.S. immigrants, *The Uprooted,* won the Pulitzer Prize in 1952.

Frontier States Consultants: George William Rogers, consultant for this book's chapters on Alaska, is the author of *Alaska in Transition* and *The Future of Alaska.* A University of California graduate with a doctorate from Harvard, he is a professor of economics at the University of Alaska.

    Harry V. Ball, consultant on Hawaii, is a professor of sociology at the University of Hawaii. He is an expert on the sociology of law, especially as it pertains to race relations.

The Cover: On the Hawaiian island of Maui, black lava rocks, spewed from an ancient, now quiescent volcano, frame an inlet touched with gold by the rising sun.

TIME-LIFE BOOKS

Editor
Jerry Korn
Executive Editor
A. B. C. Whipple
Planning
Oliver E. Allen

Text Director	**Art Director**
Martin Mann	Sheldon Cotler

Chief of Research
Beatrice T. Dobie
Picture Editor
Robert G. Mason
Assistant Text Directors
Ogden Tanner, Diana Hirsh
Assistant Art Director: Arnold C. Holeywell
Assistant Chief of Research: Martha T. Goolrick
Assistant Picture Editor: Melvin L. Scott

Publisher
Joan D. Manley
General Manager: John D. McSweeney
Business Manager: John Steven Maxwell

Sales Director: Carl G. Jaeger
Promotion Director: Beatrice K. Tolleris
Public Relations Director: Nicholas Benton

TIME-LIFE Library of America

Series Editor: Oliver E. Allen
Editorial Staff for *The Frontier States:*
Assistant Editors: David S. Thomson, Peter M. Chaitin
Picture Editor: Robert W. Bone
Designer: John Newcomb
Assistant Designer: Jean Lindsay
Staff Writers: Tony Chiu, Frank Kendig, Victor Waldrop, Peter Wood
Chief Researcher: Clara E. Nicolai
Text Research: Clare Mead, Ruth Silva, Evelyn Hauptman
Picture Research: Nancy J. Jacobsen, Myra Mangan, Linda Ferrer, Toby Solovioff, Victoria Winterer, Vista Grayson

Editorial Production

Production Editor: Douglas B. Graham
Quality Director: Robert L. Young
Assistant: James J. Cox
Copy Staff: Rosalind Stubenberg, Patricia Miller, Florence Keith
Picture Department: Dolores A. Littles, Marquita Jones
Art Assistants: Mervyn Clay, Patricia Byrne, Jean Held

The text chapters of this book were written by Richard Austin Smith, the picture essays by the editorial staff. Valuable aid was provided by these individuals and departments of Time Inc.: LIFE staff photographers George Silk and Ralph Crane; Editorial Production, Robert W. Boyd Jr.; Margaret T. Fischer; Editorial Reference, Peter Draz; Picture Collection, Doris O'Neil; Photographic Laboratory, George Karas; TIME-LIFE News Service, Murray J. Gart; Correspondents Joan Abramson (Honolulu), Robert N. De Armond (Juneau), Jane Estes (Seattle), Joseph Rychetnik (Anchorage), Robert Weaver (Fairbanks).

Contents

Introduction

Any book on Alaska and Hawaii faces two challenges. One is to overcome the many preconceived notions about both states, notions that can be evoked, full-blown as it were, by simply saying their names. Mention of Alaska conjures up images of the great log on the fire and the great gray wolf at the door, the kayak moving through the ice floes, leaping salmon, crashing timber, silent blue glaciers—a flashing impression of gold rushes and last chances, of indomitable men and unconquerable wilderness. Mention of Hawaii is likely to evoke another instant panorama: wind in the high palms, surfers on the curving sea, brown maidens enchained in flowers—effortless euphoria in a tropical sanctuary that is free of tension, flooded with warmth, secure in the ancient Island ways.

Such images, however, are more nostalgic than real. Today's Alaska is still a rugged wilderness, to be sure, and will remain so under the inexorable dictates of climate, but it is one with access to the advances and conveniences of modern America. Oil-drilling platforms now stand among the salmon in its tidal waters, the snowmobile is replacing the dog sled, jet aircraft have shrunk the old dimensions of the Great Land. Indeed, any harking back to the times Jack London wrote of in his bravura tales about the Frozen North is known derisively among sophisticated Alaskans as the "malamute syndrome." By the same token, Hawaii is no somnolent Pacific "paradise," but a bustling American state. Some 80 per cent of its people live in one metropolitan area, Honolulu, instead of a scattering of grass huts and taro patches, and lead urban lives with many of the pressures common to the U.S. mainland.

The second challenge is to show that these two states belong naturally in one book. At first glance it seems odd to put the nation's biggest state and the fourth-littlest one, an arctic landmass and a tropical archipelago, cheek by jowl in the same volume. Actually, treating Alaska and Hawaii together was done for compelling reasons, though they may not be apparent on the surface. Both states are still frontiers. Alaska's proud distinction is that it has remained a frontier, in the wild, physical meaning of the term, at a time when the older states would consider themselves backward if they had not long ago outgrown such a designation. Indeed, they were *predestined* to outgrow it if Frederick Jackson Turner's classic, *The Frontier in American History*, is to be believed. For the very existence of a frontier had the effect of breeding in Americans the qualities that led to its obliteration. When they turned to with their frontier-developed "coarseness and strength combined with acuteness and inquisitiveness . . . [their] restless nervous energy [and] dominant individualism," the frontier was inexorably transformed into farms, villages and cities. But with Alaska it was different, and not because its citizens have been any the less "American" in the qualities Turner observed. Four factors—topography, climate, history and the nature of the Alaskans themselves—have combined to give Alaska a unique pattern of development.

With Hawaii, the frontier designation is warranted partly because the Islands are still in the process of being physically created. A volcanic archipelago, they were built of lava from submarine eruptions begun millions of years ago and continuing today. The volcanic mountains of Mauna Loa and Kilauea have been steadily adding to the mass of the island of Hawaii, while in the abyss off its southern shores submarine volcanoes are slowly thrusting potential islands toward the surface. But the state is also a frontier in the sociological sense. Made up of Japanese, Caucasians, Chinese, Filipinos and part-Hawaiians, along with a sprinkling of Koreans, Negroes and other races, the state has been breaking new ground in racial relations. Not only is Hawaii the nation's first truly multiracial state, but also it is the only one where a majority of the citizens are of non-Caucasian extraction. How they have managed to get along together with a remarkable degree of forbearance and cooperation is a heartening example to the U.S. and, just as importantly, to the watchful nations of Asia.

In addition to their being "frontier states," Alaska and Hawaii have some other surprising things in common. They are united by a paradox, for the Pacific makes islands of Hawaii, while climate makes Alaska insular. Both are dominated by one city; in the case of Alaska, Greater Anchorage has between 35 and 40 per cent of the total population. The two states have almost no snakes, but an insect is the bane of each: swarms of mosquitoes come with the Alaskan summer, sometimes killing bears; termites attack Hawaiian houses on the wing, burrowing into woodwork high above the ground. Both states are dependent on government expenditures to a remarkable degree, and both must import between 80 and 90 per cent of the necessities of life. Each is trying to preserve an intrinsic mood or spirit, Hawaii the warmth and hospitality of the Aloha spirit, Alaska the excitement and drive of the gold rush. Both have formidable problems with land, Alaska because it contains so much that is unexplored and so much whose ownership is contested by the aboriginal "owners," the Eskimos, Indians and Aleuts; Hawaii because so much acreage is concentrated in the hands of so few owners that a land monopoly exists. Each is struggling to overcome a common barrier to the education of its aboriginal citizens, for both the native Hawaiians and the Eskimos share a reluctance to excel, to stand out from the crowd. Finally, both states are in the grip of sweeping change—economically, culturally, socially—and change can be expected to take place on a more compressed time scale than elsewhere in the U.S. One aim of the present book has been to examine these changes, to spot the significant trends that will dictate the way of life in the two states five or 10 years down the road.

Six years elapsed between my first visit to Hawaii and those necessary for the writing of this volume, and a decade passed in the case of Alaska; yet time did not seem to have affected the initial impression each left on me. With Alaska, it was the feeling that danger and beauty walk hand in hand over the Great Land. Outside the few and scattered cities, one soon senses that a man's first mistake could easily be his last, with never a mark on the wilderness conceding he had even existed. So powerful is this feeling of nature putting men on their mettle that even a sojourner takes away with him a special feeling of comradeship for those who

remain in Alaska: you and they have been through the "war" together. From time to time an urge to return to Alaska occurs—to see at first hand how the battle goes. Yet once there, one's sensation is again of mile after mile of wilderness rolling by without the least human trace upon it, save that as one turns away, groping for the meaning of some snow-clad summit, the heart seems to hear a horn blowing in the distance, lonely—and mocking.

With Hawaii, my recurring recollection was one of warmth, as much spiritual as climatic. But there was another feeling about Hawaii, mysterious, exciting, awesome: the sense of being in the power of the volcanoes. On Oahu the russet bulk of Diamond Head serves as a constant reminder that a volcano could thrust itself hundreds of feet into the Hawaiian sky, as this one probably did, in a few days or weeks. On the island of Hawaii the mark of the volcanoes, both active and extinct, is everywhere upon the land. The lava flows have the impersonality of an elemental force, blindly destructive—until one hears they are the handiwork of Pele, volcano goddess of the ancient Hawaiians. Then little instances of design, of capriciousness, begin to suggest that Pele is indeed still around. I remember visiting the smoldering town of Kapoho just after its destruction by an eruption in 1960 and seeing there how the river of fire rock had come to the edge of some graves, then unaccountably flowed around them, leaving the little cemetery an island in the sea of molten lava. I also remember the jocular warning of a volcanologist at Kilauea crater in 1967 that I should not have given my wife some lehua pompons, Pele's flower, without first offering one of the blood-red blossoms to the goddess herself. My wife and I thought nothing more of the matter until hours later, dressing for dinner in Hilo, 60 miles from Kilauea, we suddenly felt the whole hotel rock in the kind of earthquake Hawaiians describe as "Pele knocking." The single strong shock registered four on the Richter Scale of 10. From then on it seemed only natural to offer the first lehua blossom to Pele.

In addition to the awareness of the volcanoes' power, there is an indefinable something else about Hawaii. Even among the pleasure domes of Waikiki, one gets the feeling that at night the catamarans of the ancient Polynesians are just beyond the surf line, waiting for the first torch to bring them in to the beach. The feeling is unshakable that the old gods are still up in the mountains, deep in the volcanoes or brooding over the ocean.

And they may very well be.

—Richard Austin Smith

In the dim light of the low winter sun, shown in a multiple exposure
as it rises and sets in barely five hours, Fairbanks lies quietly under
a blanket of snow. As winter temperatures drop, sometimes to 50
degrees below zero, city life becomes more and more confined indoors.

1

ALASKA

The Great Land

The prospector, a stocky man in his middle forties, surveyed the scene with disgust. To be sure, there was still plenty of gold in the ruby sands of that stream roiling along behind his cabin, and it would likely be no harder than before to pan $5,000 worth during the brief Alaskan summer, then pack it out for shipment at the nearest settlement, 40 miles down the beach. Nor was there any shortage of game; his private joke was that he would not even bother with moose that did not come into camp and stand directly under his butchering rack. But a scant mile away, where the glowing blue ice of the glacier rose like another sea above the littoral, an oil well was being drilled. Its crew had scrambled ashore from an old landing craft when the prevailing wind had unaccountably changed for 24 hours, blowing the icebergs out of the bay. Now an airstrip ran in front of his cabin door, and every few days a big plane roared in bringing barrels of drilling mud, crates of fancy groceries—and more men. The number had risen to 40, roughly the bear population of the area, and the ramparts of silvery driftwood, the thin, green curtain of spruce, had gone down before a line of prefabricated buildings.

"I'll be pulling out any day now," he said. "Too damned many people around here."

But where would he go, if even Alaska had gotten too crowded for him?

"Oh, back in the mountains of Oregon," replied

the prospector. "I hear there's pockets there that never saw a white man."

Whatever surprises this little episode may hold for Oregonians, who consider their state quite well settled with nearly 20 people per square mile, it illustrates the incongruities that beset one on every hand in Alaska. For if Oregon has "pockets" of virgin land, the Alaskan areas where whites have never ventured are so vast they could swallow up an entire state the size of Oregon. Alaska has 586,400 square miles of territory; it is bigger than Texas, California and Montana, the next largest U.S. states, all put together. Within this enormous area live only some 270,000 people, 100,000 fewer than live in Oregon's largest city, Portland. Four time zones lie within Alaska's borders, and so far westward does it reach that a portion of it lies in the *Eastern* Hemisphere. Why, with so much space to roam in, should a man seeking solitude ever consider leaving for points south? The answer is, of course, that so much of this vast expanse is very nearly uninhabitable. The cold, wild interior is forbidding, even for such rugged types as old prospectors. The coast is far more habitable and an overwhelming proportion of Alaska's people live on it. Alaskan civilization is, in fact, little more than a series of toe holds on the perimeter of an enormous wilderness.

Alaska is a square block of land, some 750 miles to a side, with two long arms, the Aleutian Islands curving southwestward and the Panhandle running southeast. The state is so huge that if a map of Alaska were superimposed on one of the "Lower 48"—the slightly barbed term Alaskans use in referring to the coterminous states of the Union— the Panhandle would dip into the Atlantic at Charleston, South Carolina, the Aleutians would breach the U.S. border with Mexico and continue on into the Pacific at a point between Los Angeles and San Francisco, while the northernmost tip of Alaska, Point Barrow, would thrust up into Canada, above Duluth.

The nickname the Alaskans have given this enormous chunk of real estate also seems incongruous in 20th Century America. The "Last Frontier" suggests a preoccupation with the past at a time when the nation as a whole has become more future-oriented than ever. Frontiers, at least in their historic sense of being the cutting edge of civilization brought to bear on areas of free, unsettled land, are things the Lower 48 have long since left behind. Alaska, however, has not only remained a frontier but is a very different sort of frontier from any that ever existed in the Lower 48. Four factors

have combined to give Alaska a unique pattern of development: topography, climate, history and the nature of the Alaskans themselves. Any one of them could become the starting point for an examination of what is so special about the 49th state, but topography is perhaps most suitable if for no other reason than that there is so much of it.

The image of Alaska held by most people who have never been there—a white land lifting upward through forests of spruce and birch to a crescent of ice-clad mountains—typifies only the central, or interior, section. Bigger than the state of Texas, this rolling plateau runs some 1,000 miles from the Canadian border westward to the Bering Sea. Two great rivers, the glacier-born Kuskokwim and the mighty Yukon, the latter rising in Canada yet flowing more than 1,500 miles through Alaska, combine with their tributaries to drain the area. Two great mountain ranges wall it off from the rest of the state. The Brooks Range—which is so big that it is often considered a separate section of the state—is an all but impenetrable barrier. A hundred and fifty miles deep, it runs some 600 miles from east to west and forms the Central Plateau's northern limit. To the south, this interior section of the state is contained by the Alaska Range, impassable even to pack animals for hundreds of miles. Mount McKinley, tallest peak on the North American continent, rises so high that the setting sun keeps its summit alight long after the plateau beneath it has been engulfed in darkness.

This enormous tract is rendered even more resistant to settlement by permafrost: subsoil frozen solid for depths of 1,000 feet or more by eons of cold. Deep digging is impossible save by artificially thawing the earth. But what makes permafrost even more of a problem is that it is by no means as permanent as its name implies. Temperature swings on the Central Plateau are spectacular— Fort Yukon has recorded minus 75 degrees in winter and plus 100 degrees in summer—and the summer heat melts the top several feet of ground, often turning it into a gooey sludge, while earth deeper down remains frozen hard. Walls crack, floors heave, and pipes and cisterns burst as the ground alternately freezes and thaws with the changing seasons. Ingenious remedies have been tried, including putting refrigerated jackets around the foundation pilings of buildings to keep the nearby soil frozen during warm weather, but nothing seems to work very well. The problem is not limited to the Central Plateau; permafrost underlies at least half of all Alaska.

North and south of the Central Plateau lie the

state's two other major geographical sections. The Pacific Mountain Area begins with the Aleutian Range and the steaming volcanoes of the Valley of Ten Thousand Smokes, then arches southward along the coast in a long line of sharp, prism-shaped peaks and tortuous glaciers. It includes the Chugach Mountains, a barrier 300 miles in length and 80 miles deep that effectively denies easy access to the Central Plateau, and the St. Elias Range, undoubtedly North America's most spectacular strip of mountains. These angular giants, towering over ice fields and turbulent glacier-fed streams, continue along the Gulf of Alaska for 250 miles before giving way to the Coast Mountains in the Alaskan Panhandle. The waters off the coast contain the remnants of ancient mountains, which were partially submerged at the end of the ice age. They give the narrow Alaskan Panhandle section (width: 125 miles) its essential character: mountaintops have been transformed into a labyrinth of islands; flooded valleys have become fiords and channels where the great glaciers and the great forests now come steeply down to salt water.

The third and last of Alaska's major areas—the Arctic Slope—lies to the north of the Central Plateau, walled off from it by the Brooks Range, which sweeps completely across the state above the Arctic Circle. Some 750 miles long and 250 miles wide, the Arctic Slope begins as a plateau close to the mountains. There sparse fringes of willows, stunted to the height of a man, mark the movement of watercourses through an otherwise treeless land. But even the willows vanish when the rolling tundra country evolves into the Arctic Coastal Plain. Wildly beautiful in its summer illumination of flowers, in winter the mile on mile of absolutely flat and featureless land becomes a white monotony.

The charm of the entire state—the "Great Land," as Alaskans sometimes call it—is its seeming immutability. Particularly today when smog hangs heavy over cities in the Lower 48, when the bulldozer blade spares neither hill, forest nor valley, when the white water of many rivers is only a froth of detergents sliding seaward, the sight of an unchanged wilderness brings a special kind of joy. The feeling is that of being brought face to face with an ultimate in nature, something permanent and unchangeable. Alaska's glaciers appear poised —frozen in time as well as substance; the green forests of pine, hemlock, spruce and cedar have an eternal look about them; the hundreds of miles of tundra, emerging flowered every year from the deadly arctic cold, imply indestructibility; the range on range of mountains look as if they had

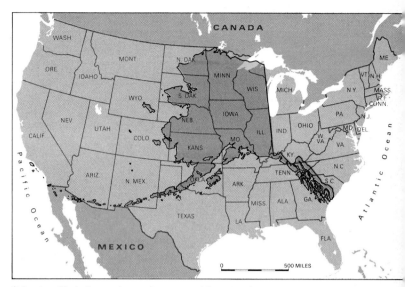

Only when Alaska is superimposed on a map of the coterminous United States *(above)* do the 49th state's mammoth dimensions become apparent. The bulk of Alaska's 586,400 square miles —nearly one fifth the area of the entire Lower 48—would almost entirely blanket five Midwestern states as well as large portions of four others. Its northernmost boundaries would graze Canada's border, its Panhandle would thrust to South Carolina's Atlantic coast, and its Aleutian chain would swing through the Southwest, nudging into Mexico, before spilling into the Pacific Ocean.

been untouched since the world began and would remain that way to its end.

Yet Alaska's immutability is more apparent than real. Its glaciers are the galloping kind; now and then their rate of movement unaccountably increases 10 times, or even 100 times, above normal, occasionally moving them seaward at the fantastic speed of nearly 50 feet a day. Its mountains along the Gulf of Alaska are rooted in a major earthquake area, while a volcanic zone, scene of one of history's most violent eruptions (Mount Katmai, 1912), extends a full 550 miles along the Alaska Peninsula, the rocky base from which the Aleutian Islands thrust out into the Bering Sea. As for the seeming durability of forest and tundra, once the chain saw has opened a little path among the stands of Alaska's shallow-rooted timber, the wind topples the remaining trees like tenpins. And just running a swamp buggy over the summer tundra alters that most tender of environments. The simple pressure of the vehicle's tires kills the vegetation; the denuded earth, exposed to the sun, then begins to thaw and new watercourses flow, changing the whole complexion of the land.

But whatever confusion there may be about appearances, the practical effect of Alaska's terrain is only too explicit. Given the ubiquitous glaciers, no roads connect the capital, Juneau (1963 population: 9,000), and the other Panhandle cities—Ketchikan (7,000), Sitka (3,200) and Petersburg (1,800)—with one another or with the urban centers to the north, nor are they likely to. The coastal plain itself is so narrow there that even the Panhandle cities, after building in the widest portions, are stretched out like strings between sea and mountain. Above the Arctic Circle the cost of crossing tundra, the boggy terrain called muskeg and innumerable waterways has foreclosed land linkage between Nome (2,300 people), Kotzebue (1,300) and Barrow (also 1,300). In the central area only a short-line railroad and a narrow highway connect the two biggest population centers, the Fairbanks area (32,000) and Anchorage's area (100,000).

Even though something akin to a transportation revolution has taken place in Alaska in the 1960s—jet service for passengers and freight, ships and barges capable of carrying strings of railroad cars, a first-rate ferry system, automated cargo-handling equipment—the pace of Alaskan development has been hobbled not only by the terrain but also by the state's sheer size. Ketchikan is 225 miles from Juneau as the crow flies, Juneau 600 from Anchorage, Anchorage 260 from Fairbanks and Fairbanks 500 from Barrow. In between them lie Alaska's glaciers, barrier ranges and quaking tundra.

It has been impossible to treat so vast an area as one economic unit. Its unemployment—the highest in the U.S.—resists cure since Alaska is so huge that workers find it hard to move from a city where work is scarce to another where jobs are available. It has also been impossible to exploit much of the area's wealth save along the coast or adjacent to a few navigable rivers. Something less than 1 per cent of Alaska's land mass has been adequately explored for minerals. The state may indeed, as the U.S. Department of the Interior asserts, have all save diamonds and bauxite from among the 33 "critical minerals," and in sizable quantities, but the big question is where. Overall, we know more about the surface of the moon than we do about some of the remote areas of Alaska, as the department noted in 1966.

The second determinative influence on the state's development—its climate—is a sore point with some Alaskans. They chafe over the image of their state as a frozen wilderness, particularly since tourist dollars continue to show an unshakable preference for "following the sun." Winter temperatures, they point out, are roughly the same in Ketchikan as in Washington, D.C., while Juneau's approximate those in New York City. Anchorage is actually warmer than cities in northern New England, Wisconsin, Minnesota, the Dakotas, Wyoming and Montana. All very true. Unfortunately there is more to Alaska's icebox reputation—and its inhibitive climate—than the winter temperatures in a few hand-picked cities would indicate.

In the Panhandle, an area of mild winters and cool summers, the burden is not the cold. It is rain, rain, rain. Little Port Walter, located on the same island as Sitka, has achieved the soggy distinction of receiving more rainfall than any other spot in Alaska—an annual average of more than 18 feet. Quite a few other Panhandle localities average 100 inches of rainfall. In short, the climate for this part of Alaska is "maritime": frequent fogs, frequent winds of 70 to 90 miles per hour during the winter at exposed points among the islands, general cloudiness and rain. Juneau, deluged with some 56 inches of rain and 92 inches of snow or sleet, has only 45 clear days in a typical year. Yet the climate is well within the philosophical capabilities of the inhabitants. They know the abundance of rainfall has given their area practically all of Alaska's merchantable timber and that it feeds the streams that help make fishing the state's biggest industry. Rain is something to be taken in stride. As a lifelong resident of Ketchikan cheerfully remarked, "I was born wet and haven't got dry in fifty-five years."

Going northwest from the Panhandle, the climate undergoes a gradual change for the worse. To be sure, the Japan Current still manages to preserve some of the pleasanter aspects of a maritime climate along the seaboard. Summers in Anchorage are often warmer than those in Juneau; the temperature of a typical July day ranges comfortably between a low of 49 and a high of 65. And in the nearby Matanuska Valley, celebrated for its fertility, cabbages have attained bushel-basket size under the prolonged sunlight. But the growing season, the period between killing frosts, is far shorter than in even the coldest parts of the Lower 48. This, plus the shallow and acidic nature of much of Alaska's soil, helps explain why this immense state produces less of its food supply than any other state in the Union (roughly 10 per cent). And when winter comes to Anchorage and the surrounding countryside, it comes hard. Over a typical five-month winter period (mid-November to mid-April), Anchorage has 35 days of temperatures of zero or below. Snow then covers the ground virtually without interruption. So deep does it get in seaboard towns like Valdez that houses are completely enveloped. Fifty feet of snow falls at nearby Thompson Pass, and it falls during a relatively short period

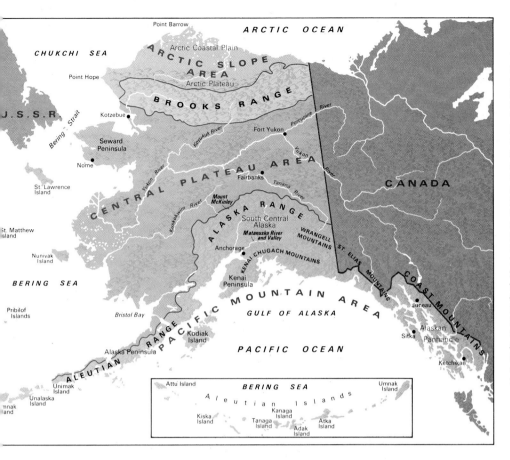

Topographically, Alaska consists of three distinct tiers of land divided by two mountain ranges, one of which, the Brooks Range, is so massive that it is virtually a separate area in itself. The southernmost tier, the Pacific Mountain Area, includes the Panhandle, South Central Alaska, part of the Alaska Peninsula and the Aleutian Islands. Though, as its name indicates, this section is mountainous, many of its valleys and coastal areas have a damp but moderate climate that is suitable for settlement, and here live most of Alaska's residents. Dividing this southern tier from the Central Plateau is the Alaska Range. The Central Plateau consists mostly of tablelands and lowlands; its long, cold winters make human habitation difficult, but, as the people of Fairbanks can attest, life here is not impossible. Still farther north the Brooks Range effectively isolates Alaska's third major area, the Arctic Slope. This northernmost section, mostly a wilderness of ice and snow, is sparsely inhabited.

each winter, creating vast, impassable snowbanks. The Alaskan record, set there in 1952-1953: 975 inches, the height of an eight-story building.

Where the Alaskan climate becomes prohibitive, however, the trouble is only partly connected with snow. As a matter of fact, the fall at Barrow, on the Arctic Ocean, Alaska's northernmost city, averages only 26 inches a year; moreover, snow actually performs the useful function of filling in the muddy interstices between the hummocks of tundra, opening up this and other areas to the dog team, the ski plane and the tractor train. The insupportable aspects of an Alaskan winter arise rather from the long continuance of very low temperatures, often accompanied by very high winds.

Contrary to popular supposition, these characteristics do not attain their most objectionable levels in the arctic area. The coldest part of Alaska is not the Arctic but the Central Plateau. In the Arctic only two of the five government weather stations have experienced record lows of minus 50 degrees or more; in the interior, nine out of 10 have. The prolonged hours of summer daylight—the sun never sets in some interior localities for a solid month—are followed by equally prolonged periods of winter darkness. The result is some astonishing temperatures at both ends of the scale.

As noted earlier, Fort Yukon has gone from 100 in the summer shade to 75 below zero in winter, a swing of 175 degrees. Extreme lows of minus 70 or more have occurred at points well distributed over the plateau while lows of 40 or 50 below zero are a day-after-day commonplace in Fairbanks, Alaska's second-largest city.

Winter temperatures in the arctic area, on the other hand, are only milder by contrast. They range between eight and 13 degrees below zero, with 45 to 60 below zero at the extremes. But strong winds are prevalent here, not uncommonly roaring along the coast at 50 to 60 miles per hour. The combination of temperature and wind, often expressed in a mathematical index called the "chill factor," makes winter lethal in this arctic area. On one of its milder days, when the temperature might be 10 degrees, a wind driving at 20 miles an hour can increase the chill factor so much that conditions are equivalent to 30 below.

Nature has effectively equipped certain animals to survive in such an environment. Arctic creatures seem to have evolved along the lines of an evolutionary principle known as Allen's rule after its formulator. According to this conception, animals in cold climates conserve body heat by evolving rounder bodies and much smaller appendages, such as ears, noses, tails, legs and muzzles. The arctic fox, for example, has a round face and short ears in marked contrast to its cousin, the desert fox. The latter's large ears and pointed face function to dissipate heat, not conserve it.

Many physiologists believe they can see similar physical adaptations to cold in the Eskimo, who is generally chunky, with short arms and legs. His psychological adaptation to his severe environment is obviously complete. After centuries of coming to terms with the Alaskan cold, he is at home with it. He has learned that to work too strenuously outdoors means sweat, and sweat will soon become a coating of ice next to his skin, bringing death. He knows that with prolonged exposure the corneas of his eyes will freeze, leaving him blind on the trail or at sea. Bred in him is an indifference to cold, even a relish for it, which is only this side of immunity. "The high-Arctic Eskimos," observed the celebrated explorer Peter Freuchen, "take a peculiar delight in sleeping while half-freezing. It is said to be pleasant, as it provides the best dreams."

The effect of very low temperatures on the white man, of course, is something else again. More often than not, the arctic winter is a time of travail for him, both physically and mentally. Even in a modern city like Fairbanks, there is an unmistakable feeling of depression when the cold really settles in. Winter sports become impossible and the children cannot play outdoors. Ice fog, a greasy ocean of ice crystals, with many of the characteristics of heavy smog, envelops the city as the thermometer drops into the minus 20s. People working indoors seldom see the sun, for by the last week in December, dawn is at 10 a.m., sunset at 1:30 p.m. Toilets freeze, electric heaters must be installed on automobile engines to keep the oil from solidifying, cars clump around on "square" tires (a portion of the tread having frozen flat during a period of immobility). The alcoholic intake increases, yet no one is bounced from the bars because heaving a stupefied man out into 40 below would be tantamount to homicide.

Under the circumstances it is idle to claim—as some Alaskans do—that winter deep in the interior or the arctic area or even Fairbanks is no worse than that of North Dakota since the minimum temperatures are comparable. What makes the difference is the length of the Alaskan winter. As month follows month of oppressive cold, one becomes an easy prey to "cabin fever." Then Alaskans often feel, as one observer put it, that "the darkness and cold outside is a sort of living being reaching in through the keyholes." The Alaskan climate, in sum, has always been a force to be reckoned with. Ignoring it, warns the U.S. Weather Bureau, "may be to invite disaster."

The third formative influence on Alaska's development, its history, is somewhat surprising in that there is precious little to show for so many years of it. Almost exactly a century and a quarter was spent under Russian dominion, yet aside from a handful of place names—Baranof, Shumagin, Wrangell—and a scattering of Russian Orthodox churches, the impress is minuscule. Sitka may once have been worthy of description as "the most brilliant capital in the new world," aglitter with the uniforms of Russian officers, its streets crowded with the gay and the adventurous from halfway around the world; today all that is left of those imperial days are a few crumbling structures.

By the same token, ephemerality marked the 92-year period between 1867, when the U.S. bought Alaska from Russia for $7.2 million, and 1959, when the territory finally won statehood. A feeling of impermanence and insecurity overhung Alaskan affairs during that whole period, with progress coming little and late—or sometimes not at all. One year the little town of Nome would be bulging with the Gold Rush of 1899-1900: fifteen thousand "stampeders," enduring short rations, little water and no sanitary facilities, living in tents or out in the cold sea winds, to scrabble for gold along the beach; three years later, with the abruptness of someone striking a tent, almost all of them would have pulled up stakes and gone, and the only thing left to show they had ever been there was a litter of rusted machinery in the surf.

The reasons for this state of affairs are simple: (1) exploitation, not colonization, has always been the controlling consideration in Alaska, and (2) Alaska has always been under the thumb of national policy, local needs running a poor second to the desires of the absentee owners in St. Petersburg or Washington. Under the Russians, dominion over Alaska began with its "discovery" in 1741 by Vitus Bering, a Dane sailing in the service of Czar Peter the Great. Russian fur traders moved into the Aleutians with a greed and impetuosity matched only by gold-struck Americans a century and a half later. "With God high in His heaven and the Czar far away," the sword, the knout and the flintlock soon subjugated the Aleuts, and when even these docile, Eskimoid people revolted at rape, pillage and enslavement, they were all but exterminated; 3,000 were economically murdered, blown up in groups or tied back to back and shot with a single musket ball.

After the fur resources of the Aleutians had been exhausted—just the *recorded* shipments of sea-otter skins ran to 186,754 over a period of 56 years—the Russians no longer had any reason to stay on the far-flung islands and moved their headquarters to Sitka. By then (1804) St. Petersburg had given the exclusive rights for the exploitation of Alaska to a commercial enterprise, the Russian American Company, and made a Siberian dry-goods salesman, Alexander Baranof, lord over all its domain. Tough, shrewd and competent, Baranof used his Aleut slaves to help make war on the fierce and intractable Tlingits, the Indians who were battling the Russians for control of Sitka, but he also lived up to the requirements of the new and more humanitarian charter of 1799. Under it Baranof built schools and churches and fostered agriculture, although trade and exploitation were still his overriding responsibility.

The Russian holdings eventually extended as far south as Bodega Bay in California, where Fort Ross was established, and as far north as the Arctic Ocean. Baranof himself schemed to establish Russian domination over Hawaii, as a base for control of the Pacific sea lanes to China, the greatest market for furs, and as part of a grand plan to put the entire northern Pacific under Russian hegemony.

Baranof's master strategy was upset in 1863, however, when St. Petersburg decided that leaving its sole maritime province in the hands of a commercial enterprise was unwise and refused to renew the charter on its original terms. The end of an era for Imperial Russia, and for the Russian American Company as well, followed within four years.

A primary reason for this change, which culminated in the sale of Alaska to the United States, was the Russians' realization during the Crimean War that their naval power was completely outclassed by that of the British. They saw that they would not be able, in the event of a showdown, to control the sea lanes in the North Pacific. The strains imposed by the Crimean War had also shown St. Petersburg the nation's desperate need for political and economic reforms. A major turning point in policy resulted, the Czar and his advisers deciding to disencumber themselves of their Alaskan outposts, which they feared they would not be able to hold in the long run anyway. As Senator Charles Sumner put the case in urging purchase on the U.S. Senate, Russia "wished to strip herself of all outlying possessions, as Napoleon had stripped himself of Louisiana, in order to gather her strength for her struggle with England for the control of Asia."

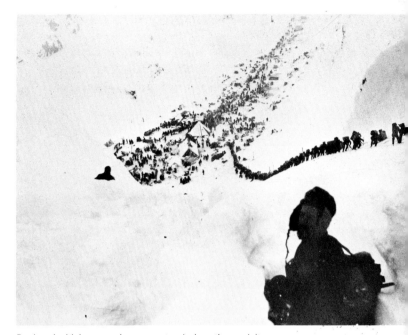

Burdened with heavy packs, prospectors inch up the precipitous Chilkoot Pass on their way to the Klondike gold fields of the Canadian Yukon during the winter of 1898. Traffic along this tortuous trail was heavy because it was the shortest route to the Klondike from seaports. Such treks through the Alaskan Panhandle helped make Americans aware of their vast northern territory.

Under the Americans the pattern of life in Alaska continued much as before. People did not come there to stay; they came to make their stake and get out. In general, they traveled light, bringing only what they could carry on their backs. They built what served the exigencies of the moment and, when they departed, left nothing that was valuable or memorable behind them. Whether they were trappers after fur, lumbermen after timber, prospectors hunting gold or canners in search of salmon, the gold-rush psychology was always paramount. The brotherhood of exploitation left few monuments to culture or civilization, only that which was worn out, burdensome or valueless.

This state of affairs was fostered by Washington's vague and often contradictory policies. The axiom voiced by Frederic L. Paxson in his *History of the American Frontier*—"No American ever made a reputation founded upon his knowledge of territorial affairs, and his success in administering them"—fitted Alaska perfectly. From 1867 to 1897 it was a place burdened by legal aberrations and bizarre behavior. As geologist and explorer William Healy Dall wrote, Alaska was "a country where no man could make a legal will, own a homestead . . . or so much as cut wood for his fire without defying a Congressional prohibition; where polygamy and slavery and the lynching of witches prevailed, with no legal authority to stay or punish criminals."

The Gold Rush of 1899-1900 briefly captured the attention of the government in Washington, and so did some succeeding attempts to make Alaska "the prize package of the great corporations." These aroused the conservationists, who began to beat the drums for protecting Alaska's resources. Federal protective measures resulted, safeguards that were quite in keeping with the idea that federal stewardship of Alaska had been established to preserve its resources for posterity, i.e., the future state. But as with all stewardships too long continued, the end was lost sight of in perpetuation of the means. Indeed, in many cases the provision for posterity seemed simply to be job opportunities for as yet unborn generations of Washington officials. Conservation for eventual use, which was the thesis of the era's great conservationist, Pennsylvania Governor Gifford Pinchot, was largely supplanted by conservation for its own sake. And since the territory, long derided as an "icebox," had turned out to be packed with goodies, the government seemed intent on putting them all into an official deep freeze or, at the very least, making Alaska a national park of subcontinental dimensions.

Tremendous areas of Alaska were reserved for some special federal purpose, and there they sat, awaiting the will of Washington. In 1923 the Navy and Interior Departments put the whole Arctic Slope—roughly a twelfth of Alaska's 375-million-acre area—into their Petroleum Reserve Number 4. Potentially one of the most valuable parts of the territory, Pet 4 was closed to private exploitation; and though Navy geologists believed a very large oil field was there, the Navy itself engaged in only the most nominal sort of exploratory work.

Elsewhere in the territory determined bureaucrats had established reserves for any of a hundred reasons: national parks or national monuments, sanctuaries for the moose, the reindeer or the brown bear, bombing ranges, military reservations, water-conservation districts, mineral withdrawals, road rights of way, ad infinitum.

In the main, official frivolity continued until the air age and until World War II emphasized the territory's strategic importance. Yet even in the mid-1950s the history of Alaska was marked by the magnitude of Washington's power over its affairs and the federal government's diffidence about resolving the state's problems. From the bureaucrat's point of view, Alaska was clearly the last best hope in North America. Nowhere else under the flag had the federal government such a grip on the lives of U.S. citizens. Cut a tree, build a house, harness a stream, shoot a bear or net a salmon on 99 per cent of the land and a bureaucrat would be on hand to say you Yea or Nay; pass a territorial law and a Washington-appointed governor could veto it; enter the transportation or construction business and the government could make your fortune or double your competition; go mad in Alaska and a bureaucrat would arrange for your commitment in an Oregon asylum.

In the days since statehood, Washington's grip on Alaska has little abated, if at all. Major decisions affecting the state's well-being are still more likely to be made in Washington than in Juneau and probably will be for many years. Bureaucracy dies hard at best, and with Alaska so greatly dependent on federal largess there will be much to keep it alive.

One example of the tenacity of federal control is the fact that the U.S. government still owns two thirds of the Alaskan land—and is ceding to the new state only bits and pieces of the other third, which was guaranteed it on statehood. (Alaska has asked for only 17 million acres, a minuscule part of its total 103-million-acre allotment; it succeeded in prying loose only 5.2 million between 1959 and 1967.) The Bureau of Indian Affairs, the agency with overriding responsibility for Alaska's Indians, Eskimos and Aleuts, retains its suffocating grip on the native population. The Fish and Wildlife Service very nearly hamstrung oil development on the Kenai Peninsula, which has since meant the difference between black and red ink in the state budget. The source of official obstructionism in this case was concern among the service's conservationists for the moose in the area. Putting in new roads between drilling sites would, they maintained, upset the animals' pattern of life, eventually destroying them. Quite the reverse occurred. The moose took to the roads happily, galloping up and down them, their search for forage and mates much facilitated. As a result, the moose population in the area has virtually doubled.

Inasmuch as Alaskan history, topography and climate have combined to produce so unusual a state, it should be no surprise that the Alaskans themselves are quite an extraordinary group of people. The typical Alaskan is likely to be a young man, for the average age of the population is 23, lowest of any state in the nation excepting New Mexico, and men outnumber women by a ratio of 132 to 100. (The balance swings the other way for the nation as a whole, women outnumbering men 100 to 97.) What women there are, on the other hand, appear to be both uncommonly cherished and uncommonly influential: Mrs. Sylvia Ringstad served as mayor of Fairbanks, retiring only at the age of 80; Edith Bullock heads a half-million-dollar barge line in the arctic town of Kotzebue; Mrs. Brideen Crawford is board chairman of one of Alaska's largest banks. Other women boss airports, captain shrimp boats or, if Eskimo, Aleut or Indian, run family affairs with the free hand taken for granted in those matriarchal societies.

It might be supposed that Alaskans possess the heterogeneity of other U.S. citizens, since the bulk of them came up from the Lower 48 only a short time ago, and from a variety of states at that. But the reasons behind their coming to Alaska are so uniform that the state contains a high concentration of people with common characteristics. They have come to Alaska, in the main, because its needs for skills of all descriptions are so great that almost anybody can go farther and faster there than anywhere else in the Union. Good teachers at the University of Alaska become deans in short order (the university has almost as many deans as Wisconsin, although the student body of 2,600 is less than a 15th as big); good reporters become editors 10 years ahead of time. Young lawyers reach the top of the heap in a single step: state jobs at $18,000 in Juneau have gone begging because attorneys could drag down $50,000 to $70,000 a year in private practice in Anchorage.

On the "iron islands"—the oil-drilling platforms that stand stiff-legged in the icy waters of Cook Inlet—an electrician willing to work 12 hours a day can have $5,000 at the end of a month; divers who maintain underwater gear average $4,000 per month for making some 20 dives in the tide-swept inlet, staying on the bottom no longer than 30 to 35 minutes at a time. Fishermen who own nothing more than their oilskins have been known to tot up their share of the catch in figures that would make a baseball player blush: in 1966, the most successful season since 1949, five months of work netted one crewman $16,643. Three others who worked eight months took home $18,947, $20,305 and $34,751, while one king crab fisherman pocketed $95,509 for a full 12 months of labor.

Aside from being a place where a stake can be quickly accumulated and success achieved in short order, Alaska also attracts people who prefer the impersonal rigors of a tough natural environment —the Great Land—to the social pressures of the Lower 48. Many Alaskans describe themselves as "small town"; they dislike a highly structured society and want the freedom of individual action

that Alaska affords. Since the pond is so small, everybody in it is a big frog; this puts the average citizen on a first-name basis with virtually anyone of power and importance—business leaders, judges, mayors, the governor, the two U.S. senators and the state's lone congressman.

On the lighter side, Alaskans cherish the tall story (in part because of the credulity of the *cheechako*—the "newcomer"—about everything Alaskan, in part because nothing is so preposterous it could not have happened in their extraordinary state). They also have a love for the out-of-doors and a passion for flying and for cashing checks. Man for man they cash more checks proportionate to total bank deposits than any other group of Americans, while their enthusiasm for taking to the air ranks the state No. 1 in number of passengers, tonnage of freight, quantity of aircraft and number of pilots.

Unhappily, Alaskans also have the highest accidental death rate in the world, almost three times that of the rest of the U.S., and a disquietingly high incidence of alcoholism and suicide. Alcoholism was probably latent in its victims to begin with and not actually caused by living in Alaska, but there can be little doubt that cabin fever and the trauma of "arctic imprisonment," with its cold and isolation, have helped push the Alaskan's historic fondness for the bottle out of control. As for the suicides, some came to Alaska as the end of the trail and lacked the strength to press on elsewhere; others doubtless concluded that if they could not make it in Alaska they could not make it anywhere, and that was that.

Not surprisingly, the typical Alaskan exhibits as many contradictions and incongruities as does the state he lives in. Chauvinism never seems to lie far below the surface and can be quickly aroused by any belittling of such sacred cows as "frontier farming" (it would be cheaper to create synthetic food than to depend on local agriculture to feed Alaska). Yet in the next breath Alaskans will declare that the state's problems are so formidable they see no way out. By the same token, they reveal a genuine love for the beauties of the Great Land, yet are willing to let pollution gain a foothold on their rivers and ignore such defacement of the landscape as the 30-odd miles of junk, jerry-built structures and litter along the Anchorage-Seward highway. They are money-conscious to a marked degree and yet have a sort of easy come, easy go attitude toward Alaska's high prices, far and away the steepest in the U.S. It is almost as if they were afraid to move against prices—which fluctuate between 25 and

50 per cent above Seattle's—for fear of imperiling the equally high wage structure.

Many Alaskans subscribe to the notion of Social Darwinism, the economic survival of the fittest, yet hate competition with the ardor of the monopolist. They denounce "government interference"—and think nothing of increasing their dependence on Washington the next moment with a plea for more money. They move from the Lower 48 to Alaska with singular frequency—the last census revealed that some 46 per cent of the population had lived in the state no longer than five years—yet their mobility from one Alaskan area to another is so slight as to create serious sectional misunderstandings and jealousies. Warm and friendly on the trail or in the bigger cities, they tend to become ingrown and antisocial under the "garrison life" of smaller communities. A pleasant, perfectly acceptable young couple, for example, will live 14 months in Nome (population: 500 whites and 1,800 natives) and never see the inside of an old resident's home. Similarly, the whites at Kotzebue, although hardly more than a handful in this predominantly Eskimo town of 1,300, hold themselves aloof from one another: the Bureau of Indian Affairs teachers do not mix with the Civil Aviation people, nor the CA group with the doctors and nurses of the Public Health Service hospital, while the local Air Force staff sticks to its compound on the hill. Many Alaskans, it seems, just do not want a lot of people around. If the state should ever start filling up, then, as a clerk at the Fairbanks Chamber of Commerce remarked, "That's when I leave."

Two additional characteristics of the Alaskan are worthy of note. He lives in a society that makes almost no social distinctions. Virtually any kind of honest work with the hands is as respectable today as it was when the state's founders were felling the forests, catching fish or mining gold. Yet it is a curiously truncated society. There is almost no upper class. As a result, the middle class exercises a disproportionate amount of power. One reason for this unusual state of affairs is that older people, who would normally comprise an upper class, are rarely able to stand the climate. The rigors of the Alaskan winter induce them to depart from the scene just at a time of life when their counterparts in other states are beginning to lend balance, luster and affluence to the social structure. Whatever this upper-class drain does in providing an abundance of room at the top, it is a handicap of major proportions. Think, if you will, of Texas or California or New York being compelled to develop without the money and the experience of its older

bankers, lawyers, merchants and other civic leaders.

Finally, the Alaskan dislikes change. He generally wants to keep things the way they were. But for all this, the nature of his society and its economy has compelled him to accept change as a way of life. He has had to inure himself to the pronounced seasonal swings of Alaska's major industries, such as fishing and timber. He also knows that about an eighth of Alaska's population—32,000 servicemen—will be continually moving in or out on a two- or three-year tour of duty. Beyond that, new concepts in military strategy and new weaponry can—and do—alter defense outlays for Alaska almost overnight; expansion or contraction of federal employment can bring bloom or blight, for in Alaska 56 people out of every 100 in the labor force work for the state or federal government (the national average: 16).

There is another reason for the prominence of change in the Alaskan scheme of things. The state's main attraction is as a treasure house of natural resources—fish, timber, minerals, oil—but the hostility of nature and the high cost of development prevent orderly exploitation. It goes by fits and starts. Some technological advance, a rich find or a scarcity-fed boost in raw-material prices will ameliorate the problems of cost and weather, and there will be a burst of activity. Among such recent, isolated developments has been the construction by the Japanese of a $66 million pulp mill at Sitka that has transformed the economy of the town. The estimated $600 million oil development on Cook Inlet and the Kenai Peninsula, south of Anchorage, will have an even more pervasive, and jolting, effect on the state. Kennecott Copper's project in the desolate, poverty-ridden area by the Kobuk River could transform that entire part of the state if the copper lode lives up to expectations; nearby Eskimo villages are already denuded of men who have gone to work in the mine. The combination of big stakes, giant companies and the most advanced technology available makes for an unusual kind of "leapfrogging" development. There is no growth of small companies into bigger ones; they must come big to begin with or they cannot afford the price of admission. And whether the giants are coming or going, their movement is bound to perpetuate change as a way of life on the "Last Frontier." George W. Rogers, a Professor of Economics at the University of Alaska and long an eminent economic historian of the state, put the situation succinctly when he wrote in 1959: "Alaska is not something that is or has been; it is a promising potential of something that can be."

High in the Alaska Range a deep recess cradles a pocket of
snow. In such clefts, glaciers are born. Each year the
accumulation of snow exceeds the amount that melts until, in
time, the weighty mass begins to grind down the mountain.

The grandeur of an endless wilderness

In the cold, remote, largely uninhabited
vastness that is Alaska, the rough edges of
creation still show. Along the 1,400-mile sweep
of the Aleutian arc, at least 27 volcanoes
threaten the land with fire and ash. Throughout
the state, countless barren, ice-encrusted peaks
—many of them unnamed—are embraced by the
howling winds. From under innumerable
glaciers, streams run milky with the dust of rock
that has been ground down by the rough passage
of billions of tons of ice. Beyond the northern
slope of the arctic Brooks Range, the flat tundra
stretches cold and forbidding to the horizon—and
beyond. The aerial photographs on the following
pages reveal the incredible topographical
variations found within Alaska. Here is a
glimpse into the untamed beauty of a primeval
world that is America's great northern frontier.

Photographed by William Garnett

A mountain fastness
in an encircling sea

The dark, cindery cone *(foreground)* of Mount
Edgecumbe stands in sharp contrast to the
dazzling patches of snow on the slopes beneath
its lip. Behind the cone, to the north, a cloud
rests in an older crater as if filling a cup with
some evanescent brew. Though now quiescent,
Mount Edgecumbe erupted recently enough so
that stories of its power and fury still form part
of the lore of local Indian tribes. As the short
summer progresses in Alaska's southern
Panhandle region, snow on the mountain's
summit retreats into the shadows of the deep
gullies that water erosion has gouged from the
slopes. By July the corrugated flanks of the
mountain appear festooned with ragged white
ribbons of snow *(next page)*.

   Viewed from the city of Sitka, 16 miles away
and out of the picture, Mount Edgecumbe
presents the clean lines of a classic volcano,
and many argue that its beauty rivals that of
Japan's Mount Fuji. Certainly Edgecumbe's
statuesque dignity is enhanced by its setting.
Separated from the mainland by Sitka Sound
and rising on an island that it helped form, the
mountain faces the cold, steel-blue waters of
the Pacific. From its summit, land and clouds
and ocean all seem to intermingle, and as the
eye reaches toward the horizon, it becomes
difficult to distinguish one from another.

On Edgecumbe's slope, ribbons of summer snow are protected from the sun's slanting rays in deeply shadowed gullies.

The birth and death of glaciers

A glacier is fed from snow that collects in high, sloping valleys. As the snow accumulates to great depths, the lower layers are compacted into a mass of ice. In time this mass grows so heavy that it begins to shift, ever so slowly and ponderously, downhill. In the picture above, many small glaciers are converging to form a single gigantic ice flow. As they inch their way downhill, during a lifetime that may last thousands of years, these rivers of ice gouge great valleys out of mountainsides. For a glacier, journey's end comes when its forward motion is halted by the sun's melting rays. Such a terminus is reached by the Mendenhall Glacier *(left)* just 12 miles north of Juneau, where a 115-foot-high wall of ice abuts a lake made of its own meltwater.

A towering peak
in a wall of stone

Jagged crests, numberless and unnamed, stretch away to a horizon dominated by Mount McKinley, its massive, snow-clad form jutting above a layer of clouds. To McKinley's left stands Mount Foraker, and in the far right foreground, between rocky ridges, run the icy ribbons of a glacier. This is the Alaska Range as seen from an airplane. From a satellite it would appear as a wide, curving mountain wall, some 600 miles long from west to east. South of it lies a region of lesser mountains, valleys and lowlands that slope down to the Gulf of Alaska; to the north stretch the state's vast interior plains and plateaus. Though the Alaska Range cuts off the coastal region from the Central Plateau, it is not a particularly high chain, the average altitude of its crests being about 8,000 feet. Yet it boasts a few real giants, chief among which is Mount McKinley, at 20,320 feet North America's tallest peak. As such, McKinley presents a powerful challenge to mountain climbers, so much so that it was not until 1913 that a party succeeded in conquering it.

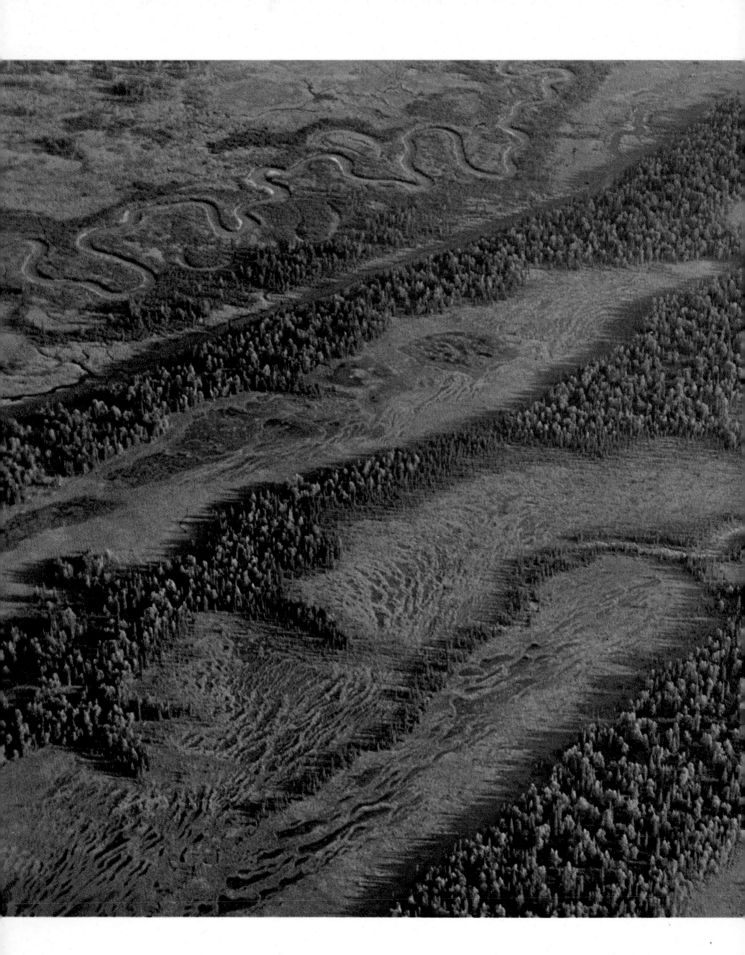

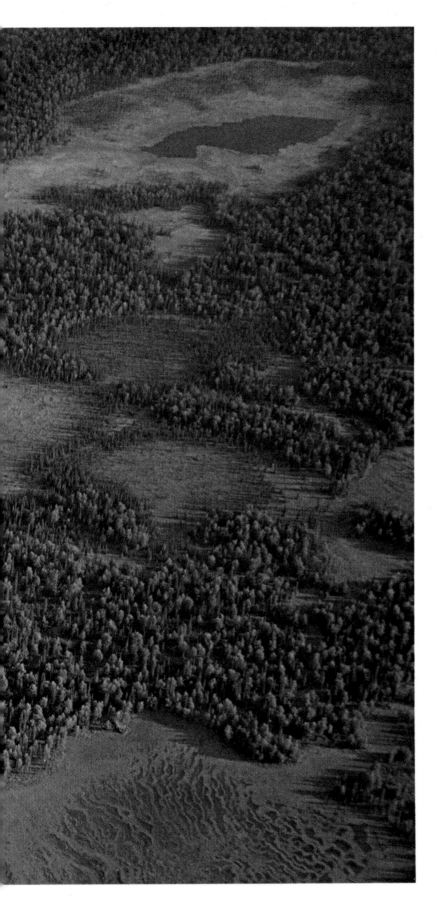

A soggy wasteland of earth and water

From a height of a few thousand feet the flat Susitna Valley of South Central Alaska takes on the aspect of an irregularly worn green carpet. Sluggishly moving water *(upper left)* cuts stream beds that loop and twist like slithering snakes across the nearly gradeless plain. Shallow lakes and ponds, peat bogs and grassy swamps are interlaced with patches of bare gravel and broad swatches of slightly higher ground that is thickly forested with spindly pines. From high in the Alaska Range to the north and west and from the Talkeetna Mountains to the east, melting snow and ice pour down into the Susitna Valley by the billions of gallons along such routes as the Kahiltna, Yentna and Susitna Rivers before emptying into Cook Inlet near Anchorage. These and many smaller rivers follow a great maze of channels that carve out islands with features that change with every spring flood. Across the width of the valley floor the water table lies only a few feet beneath the surface. Geologists call this formation a flood plain. During the great ice age 10,000 to 15,000 years ago, the entire valley was covered with one enormous glacier that reached far down into Cook Inlet. As the glacier retreated, it left behind a continuous blanket of stony soil, creating an area that is geologically similar to a river delta but much stranger and more varied.

Islands beset
by fire, fog and gale

A thin line of white water marks the cutting edge where a cold, rushing ocean breaks against low cliffs of an Aleutian island. Laid down as lava in ages past, the damp grass- and moss-covered land rolls backward a mile or two before subsiding into the sea again. In the distance, outlined against a narrow band of sky, volcanic peaks jut above the surface of the Pacific. And over all hangs a leaden layer of moisture-filled clouds. The Aleutians—14 major islands, some 40 lesser ones, and countless islets and rocks strung in a pendant chain between Alaska and Siberia—boast some of the world's most intense volcanic activity and some of its worst weather. As if to complement the explosive terrestrial turmoil manifest in its active volcanoes, fierce gales lash the islands with monotonous regularity, making it nearly impossible for trees to grow. But lush grass, moss and shrubs proliferate, the result of the relatively mild temperatures and the heavy rains and fog that cushion the islands. Not more than 25 clear days can be expected in a whole year.

2

The Crisis of the Alaskan Native

It should occasion no surprise that, with change having become a way of life for the white Alaskan, the companion impact of change on the state's native population—the Aleuts, Eskimos and Indians —has been little short of revolutionary. Within a single generation, jet aircraft have come to people whose lives had been conditioned by the speed and range of a dog team or reindeer herd; the nuclear age has burst over cultures rooted in the Stone Age; the cash economy has dealt a mortal blow to the subsistence economy and the old ways of living off the land. The result: the Alaskan native is now enmeshed in social, political and economic problems of such severity as to jeopardize his own future and even that of the state. In 1966 a report to the President of the United States by the Federal Field Committee for Development Planning in Alaska declared: "We find the native population surviving on a mixture of subsistence economy supplemented by a few jobs but principally by relief checks. Housing standards are deplorable and clearly the worst in the nation."

Under the fascinated gaze of her grandson, an Eskimo woman at Kotzebue brings a fish through a hole in the ice to add to her already large catch. In this isolated town north of the Arctic Circle, fish caught in this manner help supplement winter diets.

Such a state of affairs might have been borne submissively, if resentfully, by the Alaskan native only a few short years ago. But not today. He has taken the offensive in his own behalf and has done so in a way that has focused attention on him and his problems. The same year the Federal Field Committee made its report, an aroused native population filed claim to more than half of Alaska on the basis of aboriginal rights. This brought to a halt the state's acquisition of much of the federal land granted it by Washington with statehood. A dark cloud was cast over Alaska's oil and mineral development, for until the matter of aboriginal land claims was resolved, no one could know with certainty who had the right to collect money due for leases and royalties.

Alaska's native peoples—it has the largest percentage of aboriginals of any state in the Union— now number roughly 50,000, or between a fifth and a sixth of the total population. They are not a homogeneous group; indeed they have little in common save being administratively classified as "Indian." Indians, in fact, make up only a third of the Alaskan natives; the remainder are Eskimos and their cousins, the Aleuts. Among the Indians there are four linguistic groups. Three of them—the Haidas, Tsimshians and Tlingits—are sea hunters

The story of Raven and Petrel

Indian fables, primarily entertaining, were also meant to impart the folk wisdom of a tribe. This modern woodcut *(above)* depicts the climax of an old Tlingit tale *(below)* that explains how the rivers, lakes, glaciers and streams were formed.

In all the world there was no fresh water save for a single spring that belonged to Petrel the seabird, who watched it carefully, building his house over the water so that he could guard it even while he slept. One day, Raven [a major protagonist in many Tlingit legends] thought, "How fine it would be if there were fresh water all over the earth. Then people could drink, and salmon would have a place to swim to." So Raven preened his feathers, which were then snow white, and set off to visit Petrel and steal his fresh water. But Petrel was wary and would not leave Raven alone by the spring for even a moment, try as Raven might to lure his host away. Finally, while Petrel slept, Raven took some mud and covered his host with it. Then he cried out: "Oh, poor friend, you are covered with dirt." Petrel awoke and saw that this was true and rushed outside to clean himself. Left alone, Raven jumped to the spring and began gulping the fresh water. It was nearly gone when Petrel returned. Now Raven, to make his escape, flew toward the smoke-hole, and Petrel in anger cried out to his smoke-hole spirits, "Grab him, hold him!" The smoke-hole spirits did so, but Raven wriggled free, though not before the bird's white feathers were covered with black soot. While flying, Raven tried to clean his feathers, but his beak was filled with the water he had stolen, and each time he opened it some liquid spilled to earth. From these splashes came the rivers, lakes and glaciers. As for Raven, he never could get clean and remains sooty-black to this very day.

and fishermen who live in southeastern Alaska, predominantly on the islands of the Panhandle. The fourth group—the Athabascans, historically nomadic hunters—is concentrated on the Central Plateau. The Haidas and the Tsimshians are relatively few in number, the bulk of their tribes living in Canada, and are notable mainly for their skill as fishermen, the beauty of the Haida totem poles and slate carvings, and the Tsimshians' model village of Metlakatla, a shining exception to the usual Indian standard of living. The Tlingits, who like the others originally came from Canada for the fish and game of the Alaskan coast, are both the most numerous and most interesting of Alaska's Indians.

The Tlingits' history is one of talent in the crafts and resourcefulness in business. Highly skilled in the carving of wood and the weaving of ceremonial blankets from cedar bark and goat hair, they were also hard traders and formidable warriors. The first Russian settlement at Sitka was wiped out by them, and their armed truce with the Russians never removed the possibility that they might again overwhelm this biggest of the Russian bases. After the Americans took over in 1867, soap replaced urine for washing to an encouraging extent, but there was little change in the nature of Tlingit society or the characteristics of its members. They continued to be a people who lived largely in the present, with little thought for the future. Conspicuous consumption was embraced to a degree that would have astonished even Diamond Jim Brady. Great festivals, or "potlatches," were held by clans to honor deceased nobles and validate the heir's right to his dead relative's titles, property and prerogatives. The central point of the ceremony was to achieve status in the eyes of other clans by giving away the wealth of the village or actually destroying it in the presence of the guests. On occasion a Tlingit chief would have some of his slaves killed to impress a rival chieftain, who would then feel obliged to kill off a greater number of his own. This could go on until no slaves were left.

The holding of potlatches naturally required the generation of additional wealth. Fortunately, salmon could always be had in abundance and the Tlingits made the most of other opportunities. Full compensation was demanded, and if necessary exacted by force, for any infringement of their hunting or trading rights or any damage to their goods or property. As for actual trading, the very first Europeans found the Tlingits more than a match in bargaining over the rich furs of the area, and time did nothing to dull their acumen. The Tlingits not only sold furs in hard bargains, one pelt at a time, but were prone to repudiate any bargain if on second thought it seemed a bad deal.

The Tlingits also acted as middlemen in the fur trade, and they guarded their position jealously, keeping Athabascans *in* central Alaska and whites *out*, while reaping the benefits for themselves as mediators between the two. So effective were the Tlingits in buying Athabascan furs on the cheap and selling them high that American trading companies operating in Alaska were never able to equal the profits of the Hudson's Bay Company in Canada. At the same time, the Tlingits were imprisoned in a cage of their own making; powerful taboos limited their freedom of action and cultural development. As the German geographer Aurel Krause observed, after living among them in the 1880s, "Any departure from custom or anything extraordinary was called 'chlakass' and considered as the cause for any mishap, like bad weather, illness, or misfortune in hunting or war."

The Athabascans of the interior were similarly inhibited by their beliefs. Originally one of the hardiest of northern Indians, they had flourished as nomadic hunters in the Alaskan forests for 600 years or more—until the arrival of the Russians around Cook Inlet in 1787. Thereupon tuberculosis, measles, smallpox and venereal disease—all ailments against which the Indians had no immunity—wrought havoc among them; so did the Russian demand for large quantities of furs. The number of Athabascans declined by more than half in a relatively short span of time. This resulted in fewer hunters to meet the Russians' mounting demand for skins and in turn compelled entire families to join the hunt under the harshest conditions of the Alaskan winter. Misfortune in the forests produced paralyzing fears that malevolent beings, against whom they had no defense, were bent on their destruction. There were so many accidents and disappearances in the woods that children from an early age were overwhelmed by the tribal response of hopeless anxiety.

The lot of the Athabascans under American rule was hardly an improvement, save during the three decades between the end of Russian dominion and the beginning of the Gold Rush when hardly a white man was to be found in the Alaskan interior. The coming of the prospectors disrupted the Indians' economy and their way of life once and for all. The high pay in the gold fields lasted only long enough to arouse their interest in a cash income and give them a taste for whiskey (which neither they nor any other Alaskan natives have had the mores to control). Subsequent employment as

woodcutters for the Yukon River steamers was more durable, but that ended after 20 years, upon completion of the Alaska Railroad. When the Indians eventually returned to their homes, they found that the herds of caribou, their traditional source of sustenance, had thinned out or moved elsewhere. Moreover, there was little money to be made from their old stand-by, trapping. Fur prices were low and the scarcity of game required longer trap lines set farther and farther afield. In short, the natural resources of the land gradually became insufficient to support them. And there was not even a minor place for them in the new order of things. Their situation stood in marked contrast to that of the Tlingits, who were valued by white cannery owners because of their skill as fishermen; or the Eskimos, whose mastery of how to live in the Arctic made them valuable to the white man. Fatalism, demoralization, listlessness and chronic unemployment came to typify many Athabascans.

The Aleuts and Eskimos also had a difficult time with the white man and the changing environment, if in varying degrees. The near-extermination of the Aleuts by the Russians has already been mentioned—a disaster from which these inhabitants of the stormbound Aleutians have never fully recovered. Although the Aleutian winters do not possess the lethal cold of those in the interior, and food in the form of fish, shellfish and sea mammals could be had, epidemics, dislocation and demoralization had made the Aleuts' situation so desperate by the early 1950s that a government report declared them to be "a dying race."

The Eskimos themselves experienced a somewhat less difficult development, in part because of their isolation, in part because the Russians decided their continued independence and freedom of movement was best for the fur trade. But in 1848 American whaling ships began coming into arctic waters, and it was not long before the white crewmen's ways began to infect and destroy the Eskimo culture and economy. The "Boston Men," as the New England mariners were called, forced Eskimo men and women to labor on the ships, prostitution sprang up in the coastal villages, and gunpowder and whiskey were introduced. Tuberculosis gained a foothold, then became endemic. The walrus and the caribou diminished. In 1866 a Western Union Telegraph expedition penetrated the Eskimos' part of Alaska in a fruitless attempt to bring off one of the miracles of the modern world—a cable connection with Europe via Siberia—and left the Eskimos with the wonders of syphilis.

What prevented a disintegration such as befell

Tlingit Indian dancers attending an unusual tribal ceremony called a potlatch pose in full regalia at Sitka around 1900. Tlingit art was revealed in these ornate costumes worn for the potlatch. Elaborate headdresses and intricately woven robes portrayed venerated animal spirits, and the long wands were stylized weapons. The potlatch itself was a ritualistic orgy of conspicuous consumption, but it played an important role in the social life of the Tlingits. It gave the hosts a chance to display their wealth—by squandering it —and thus win status in the eyes of their peers. During the ceremony the host distributed valuable crockery, lavishly burned oil, wasted quantities of food and even killed some of his slaves—all to the accompaniment of frenzied music and dances. Often a number of gorgeous blankets, each representing months of work, were cut up and distributed to the guests as souvenirs of the evening's destructive festivities.

the Aleuts and the Athabascans was the Eskimos' highly specialized capacity for survival. Centuries of struggle in the Arctic had taught them how to use every available material, how to think like an animal in order to kill the animals that were their main sustenance, when to fish and when to hunt, when to keep to their subterranean sod houses, and how to turn the cold to good account, even down to using frozen hides for the runners of their sleds. The cruelty of the Eskimos' environment seems to have weeded out the dull-witted, thereby leaving a generally alert and intelligent population. The Eskimos, like their cousins, the Aleuts, possessed a genius for cartography and astonishing inventiveness. They also recognized the importance of sharing food with others and the therapy of laughter.

Nevertheless, their cheerful self-reliance and uncomplaining attitude were often maintained at the price of inner tension. The Eskimos had a high incidence of mental illness, as they still do. They have also been subject to hysterical outbursts. "Sometimes," wrote Merle Colby in his memorable book, *Alaska*, "an Eskimo, overwhelmed by the vastness of the land in which he lives, weighed down with the immensity of the struggle for existence, his nerves on edge with long vigils during the bright summer night at the hunting lodge, is

turned by a trifling incident, quite crazy for a few moments. He will break everything within reach, shouting meaningless sentences. The fit lasts only a short time, and he is soon quite calm, rather the better for his attack of 'arctic hysteria.'"

Unfortunately for the Eskimos, the intensive specialization that enabled them to cope with their environment, and even to survive initial contact with whites, had the weakness of its perfection. Eventually, the Eskimos came to exemplify the aphorism that in evolution nothing *fails* like success. They had achieved what they achieved, observed Arnold Toynbee in *A Study of History* (1934), "by discarding as far as possible the infinite variety of human nature and assuming an inflexible animal nature instead. Thereby they have set their feet on the path of retrogression. Biologists tell us that animal species which have adapted themselves too nicely to highly specialized environments are at a dead end. . . . That is exactly the fate of the arrested civilization."

This is not to say that the Eskimos are doomed to extinction—the government is not going to stand by while they starve—but rather that their reluctance to change their specialized way of life is a crippling handicap. Their unwillingness to move, for example, from villages too small for adequate schooling, medical care, sanitation, water supply systems, even sustenance, has put them under an enormous disadvantage. In their present capacity for accommodating to the white man's civilization, balancing its benefits against its destructiveness, the Eskimos lag behind Alaska's other native groups. Although precise comparisons are difficult to make, the Tlingits are considered by some Alaskans to have adapted best to modern ways, the Athabascans next, the Eskimos last. Contact with whites has had much to do with this. The Tlingits also have had the advantage of possessing a culture more easily adjusted to that of the whites: their tradition of economic competition on a barter basis was not very far removed from economic competition on a cash basis. Moreover, they were not burdened by what must be considered today a psychological infirmity common to the Eskimos: a reluctance to excel, to stand out from the crowd. An account from the writings of Charles K. Ray, Dean of Education at the University of Alaska, illustrates this Eskimo attitude:

The owner of a salmon cannery in the Bering Sea village of Alakanuk decided to try to increase efficiency and to reward a particularly productive worker by publicly announcing that he was to be paid 50 cents an hour more than the others. Far from causing the other Eskimos to work harder in the expectation of a similar reward, the raise evoked a storm of protest. The manager was obliged to rescind it. Later on, however, its reinstitution on the quiet was allowed, since the increase was no longer an open affront to the Eskimo tradition of egalitarianism. Similarly, the qualities of drive and leadership that had earned the Eskimo foreman of this particular cannery his job were those most resented by his fellow Eskimos. As one of them put the case to Dean Ray, "A man is proud when he thinks he is above all the others. He looks high over the people and likes to be a boss over people. . . . I hear in the old days they used to make medicine about a man like that, and he would get sick. Even now I always tell my kids, when lots of people are talking, not to talk first or give an answer first. Why? Because maybe they will say something that gets someone else angry. It's better they wait and see what other people do first. . . . Sometimes I don't like to answer things because others will say that 'he thinks he knows everything' and they will think that I am proud."

The notion of doom for the Eskimo, glimpsed by Toynbee in 1934, took on apocalyptic reality for all Alaskan natives only 20 years later with the publication of the so-called Parran Report in 1954. A survey commissioned by the U.S. Department of the Interior, it found that a fifth of Alaska's population, through no fault of its own, was economically depressed, culturally unstable, socially insecure and riddled with disease. The tuberculosis mortality for natives over 45 was 20 times that of the same age group in the Lower 48. For those under 14, it was 100 times the stateside rate.

"White Alaska," the report declared, "with a relatively young, vigorous, generally urbanized population, shows a record of life-expectancy as favorable as that in the majority of the states. . . . In tragic contrast, the indigenous peoples of Native Alaska are the victims of sickness, crippling conditions and premature death to a degree exceeded in very few parts of the world. Among them, health problems are nearly out of hand. If other Americans could see for themselves the large numbers of the tuberculous, the crippled, the blind, the deaf, the malnourished and the desperately ill among a relatively small population, private generosity would dispatch shiploads of food and clothing for Alaska alongside the cargoes setting out for Korea; doctors and nurses would be mobilized and equipped with the urgency of the great hospital units in wartime; the Alaskan missions would not need to beg for support. Flood victims in Europe and famine victims in India are the prompt beneficiaries of generous U.S. government assistance, but our own year-in-year-out victims of hunger, disease and exposure are unpublicized and still 'far away.'"

Change could no longer be postponed. In 1955 responsibility for the health of the native peoples was transferred from the Bureau of Indian Affairs to the U.S. Public Health Service. A decade later the Surgeon General could report 39 per cent decline in infant mortality, a reduction of 84 per cent in deaths from tuberculosis and 78 per cent decline in the incidence of new tuberculosis cases. Yet ironically this indisputable change for the better tended to compound the natives' problems, at least over the short term. Better health meant an increased population, and there were no resources to support these additional people. Some small villages could no longer sustain their populations and had to be abandoned, family life was disrupted, and adults were forced to depend more and more on the money economy (and relief checks) instead of procuring their own subsistence.

In 1950 the native population had had a very high birth rate (40.6 per 1,000 people each year) and a death rate of nearly 17, which combined to produce a rate of natural increase of 23.7. Ten years later, intensive health programs by the federal and

This six-story-high copy of a Haida Indian totem pole was erected in Sitka in 1940. To the Indians who carved the prototype more than a century ago, the pole was undoubtedly evocative of several familiar legends, but today which myths it recalls is a subject of dispute among experts. Some authorities believe that one tale is the story of Peesunt *(large figure at top)*, a fair Indian maiden who was forced by a grizzly bear *(bottom figure)* to marry him. Peesunt bore her husband twin sons who combined the characteristics of bears and humans. Wise in the ways of bears, the youngsters grew into expert hunters. They helped Peesunt's brothers kill many grizzlies, thus bringing great wealth in furs to their human relations.

state governments had caused a tremendous drop in the death rate (to 9.4) and a significant rise in the birth rate (to 47.8), the two combining to produce a yearly rate of increase of 38.4 people per 1,000. In the opinion of economists such as George W. Rogers and Richard A. Cooley, the growth was explosive: if continued, it would result in a doubling of the native population in less than 20 years.

The implications of this rapid growth were sweeping, to say the least. Huge areas of Alaska in the northwest and southwest, main abodes of the Eskimo, were already overpopulated in terms of the available food supply. Now the 38.4 rate of increase of the Alaskan native created population pressures even greater than those in such underdeveloped countries as Colombia and Mexico, where they had become a matter of grave concern. If the Eskimo stayed put and continued to multiply, wholesale relief would be needed to prevent starvation.

Reading the writing on the wall, some Alaskans concluded that the best way of resolving the situation was to move the natives out of their villages and into the mainstream of the economy. Certainly the logic was impressive. The native culture was breaking down rapidly and would doubtless disappear anyway in the normal course of attrition. Family life, once a powerful cohesive influence, was increasingly ineffectual. One reason: the larger and larger numbers of surviving children put caring for them beyond the capability of many mothers, and children were farmed out to relatives for months, sometimes for years. To get even an elementary education, many children had to be sent away to school, for it was obviously uneconomical to set up a local school for a handful of students. There was no employment beyond fishing and trapping, and even in the larger villages there were only a few paying jobs—as postmaster, custodian of a school, Civil Aeronautics Authority worker on the landing strip, manager of the community store. The relief rolls, already jammed with native claimants, were bound to grow longer as the age-old native tradition of sharing with relatives and neighbors continued its fall into disuse.

In a medical emergency the best an Eskimo in one of the smaller communities could do was to try to get to some village big enough to have a native medical aide and there have her radio the symptoms to a distant Public Health Service doctor, and then receive back the treatment instructions during the afternoon "agony hour." Water supply systems and sewers were far beyond the financial reach of the small villages, yet there was no longer the natural protection against pollution, the moving on of a nomadic people when the accumulation of human and animal waste became unbearable.

As a matter of fact, small village life was at the root of many alarming features of existence in northwestern Alaska (nearly 80 per cent native) and southwestern Alaska (almost 70 per cent). The 1960 census revealed that in the northwest only 4 per cent of the houses were sound and equipped with the usual plumbing fixtures; for southwestern Alaska the figure was 22 per cent, compared to 57.5 per cent for all Alaskan housing units and 73 per cent for the U.S. as a whole. The percentage of people over 25 with no formal education whatever stood at 11.2 in the northwest and 22.2 in the southwest, a significant departure from the state's low overall percentage of 3.5. In northwestern Alaska more than 35 per cent of the employable population had not worked at all in the year before the census, another 20 per cent had worked less than 13 weeks, while the percentage of those in southwestern Alaska doing no work was 32. Yet the dire need for jobs was apparent in the fact that for every 100 people of employable age there were 70 dependents in the southwestern section and nearly 90 in the northwest.

It would be pleasant to record that in the years since the census of 1960 the problems of native Alaskans have substantially lessened. Indeed, some progress has been made. The Radio Corporation of America trained 80 Eskimos to man some stations in its "White Alice" arctic communications system, for the Eskimos have an instinctive way with modern machinery. Kennecott Copper has employed local Eskimos to work a copper mine in a remote area bordering the Kobuk River. The largest native settlements—Barrow, Kotzebue and Bethel—have been growing bigger, hence more viable, though less from any forced consolidation of nearby villages than from the pull of jobs, relief checks, schools and better living facilities. The establishment of a health and education complex at Barrow, together with new job opportunities and the availability of natural gas, which is now piped in to produce heat and turboelectricity for the community, has attracted an increasing number of families since 1965. Public Health Service doctors have been quietly, and unofficially, fitting native women with free contraceptive devices. Lee Salisbury, director of the drama department at the University of Alaska, has helped to bridge the communications gap with his "Theater to the Bush"; remote villages are offered programs that emphasize the commonality of men, rather than their differences, through a medium that is part of native culture: the acting out of stories and legends to teach a moral.

Native education is also being improved, partly through the help of a $500,000 grant from the Ford Foundation. The first phase of that program provides for recruiting the sort of people who enroll in the Peace Corps, teachers whose orientation will allow them to avoid the error, common in the past, of trying to impose middle-class values on primitive peoples whose schools sometimes smell overpoweringly of urine and whose methods of hunting, trapping and skinning game can horrify the squeamish. Phase two—preschool and summer education with particular attention to language problems—should help upgrade education generally. It should also lessen sad situations like that of the valedictorian of a native high school in southeastern Alaska. Put through a special test after she had gotten all F's in her first semester at the university, she was found to be at the fourth-grade educational level. High-school education has been expanded under the Bureau of Indian Affairs' able new U.S. Commissioner, Robert L. Bennett. Enrollment at Sitka's Mount Edgecumbe, until 1966 the only high school solely for natives, is being increased from 700 to 1,000; a new school has been established in Nome, and construction of two nonboarding high schools at Barrow and Kotzebue has been completed. Facilities for 1,000 additional high-school students are expected to be available by 1972.

There have also been instances of natives showing they could effectively handle very large amounts of money. The Tyonek Indians, a group of Athabascans so impoverished that they had to be saved from starvation in the mid-1950s by airlifts of food, suddenly found themselves in 1964 the beneficiaries of $12 million from the sale of oil exploration rights on village-owned lands. For a time the Bureau of Indian Affairs, because of its status as guardian, was able to maintain a death grip on the money, but once this grip had been legally broken by the tribe's friend and adviser, Anchorage attorney Stanley McCutcheon, things began to move.

First, the Tyonek council authorized an initial payment of $5,000 to everyone on the tribal rolls, both the 200 who lived in the moldering village and the 100 who had abandoned it, stipulating only that the bulk of each allotment had to go for houses or education. The tribe's business manager was sent to New Mexico for a course in tribal business administration offered by the state university; a firm of accountants was hired. Then the Tyoneks began rebuilding their village. Sixty houses went up at an average cost of $25,000 each. A modern

$830,000 schoolhouse was built (the Tyoneks chipping in $145,000 for it, with the government putting up the rest), plus a power plant, a fire station and a store. Moving on to wider horizons, the Tyoneks bought into the Anchorage construction firm that had built their homes and made plans to put up a one-million-dollar office building in Anchorage as a communal investment. Here they were blocked by the Anchorage city council—until they took the provocative step of shopping outside Alaska for $1.5 million worth of house furnishings. Local merchants then put pressure on the authorities to give the Tyoneks a building permit.

As erection of the office building proceeded, so did the education of the Tyoneks in the building trades, for all of their construction contracts stipulated that as many villagers be hired as needed jobs. If, in the future, an oil strike should take place on their lands—a big one could bring them $50 million in annual royalties—the Tyoneks intend to be ready. Three of their number are studying oil-rig techniques in California, and another has completed a course in diesel engineering in Chicago. Significantly, the intent of the Tyoneks is not to keep a future bonanza solely for themselves: they would use it to establish an education fund for all of Alaska's natives and to help every native family build homes like theirs. They would thereby hopefully loosen the hold of the Bureau of Indian Affairs on the rest of the native population.

Substantive change for the Alaskan native, however, must necessarily be long in coming. This is partly because of his own limitations and partly because of the magnitude of the transformation confronting him. The average native is unaccustomed to steady work, for example, because his age-old way of life had been built around periods of strenuous activity, when fish were running or trap lines had to be tended, followed by days of doing little or nothing. And this, of course, often makes him an unsatisfactory 9-to-5 employee. His general attitude toward education is passive. He permits his children to go to school if they want to, but not if classes interfere with family responsibilities or the tradition of seasonally pulling up stakes and moving on; 60 per cent of Alaska's native students drop out before they reach the eighth grade, 50 per cent of the remainder drop out of high school, and only 2 per cent of those who get to college stay to graduate.

Furthermore, the native's problem of communicating with the white world—and the white world with him—is awesome and not to be resolved just through learning English by rote; radically differ-

ent viewpoints and attitudes are involved. Self-effacement and silence, as we have seen, are pillars of the Eskimo culture. Any aggressive behavior, whether verbal or physical, is to be controlled. There is little open conflict of ideas. Questions are regarded as pushy, and one hears of members of the same family keeping silent for an entire week, in perfect amiability, "because there was nothing to say." The effect of this taciturnity on a white visitor to a native village is often destructive of the rapport he had hoped to establish. His custom in "polite society" is to fill in silence with talk, but to the Eskimo this automatically puts the visitor in the alienating role of authority and leadership.

There is in addition the difficulty of making plain to natives who live in small villages the sights, sounds and smells of modern Western society, in which they may someday have to make their way, when books are their only means of comprehending the brute power of a locomotive, the relative height of a skyscraper or the pressures of urban life. Yet inducing the natives to move to larger villages, both as an initial step toward their incorporation in modern society and as a means of interesting them in better jobs or better education, has been a difficult and disappointing business. The native villages are highly individualistic. Each has its own chief and he is unlikely to want to consolidate his village with another where he would have to share power. Many of the people agree with their chiefs —they like their villages and feel very ill at ease when they move, or are forced to move by the Bureau of Indian Affairs, to larger settlements.

Some natives, unable to stand their new environment, have in fact tried to move back to the bush. The King Islanders, who relocated in Nome when the Bureau of Indian Affairs closed down their school, have been clamoring to leave the squalor and alcoholism of their new location for a remote coastal village, opposite their old island home. A group of Athabascans who had drifted into Fort Yukon not long ago left to establish their own village back in the bush after finding that town life was turning their men into drunkards and their women into prostitutes.

One recent development might bring about a more rapid improvement in the lot of the Alaskan natives than the foregoing suggests: their newly acquired political power. Before Alaska became a state, only the Tlingits and Haidas of the southeast carried any weight politically; they had organized the Alaskan Native Brotherhood back in 1913 and had made it an effective instrument both in winning local elections and in getting federal work projects for their area. The northern Indians and the Eskimos, on the other hand, were politically impotent. They had neither native associations nor community of interest.

With statehood, however, it became obvious to a few native leaders and to the Association on American Indian Affairs (AAIA), the nationwide organization that has long promoted Indian welfare, that a potent unifying force was present in the 102 million acres of land the U.S. government had agreed to give Alaska on its becoming a state. They contended that much of this acreage was not the federal government's to give—it belonged to the natives of Alaska who had lived on it "from time immemorial." The AAIA was instrumental in helping both Eskimos and Athabascans to form associations of their own to safeguard native rights. As additional native associations came into being, the Northwest Alaska Native Association was established. All the while this was going on, the AAIA was making sure that the natives understood what was endangering their lands and what action they could take to prevent "expropriation." When the state government actually began to make selections of parcels from the 102-million-acre statehood grant, the AAIA kept the natives abreast of the published notices and helped them draft protests. Later on, as the number of selections increased, the AAIA persuaded the Interior Department to be responsible for notifying the scattered villages and, in the event of a protest, for sending a Bureau of Indian Affairs representative there to draw up an assertion of their aboriginal rights to the land.

Then in 1962 the movement was given enormous momentum by the establishment of a weekly newspaper, the *Tundra Times*. "Owned, controlled, and edited by the Eskimo, Indian, Aleut Publishing Company, a corporation of Alaska natives," it took up the cudgels on behalf of aboriginal land claims—and everything else its Eskimo editor, Howard Rock, considered important to the native peoples.

Inevitably, as the number of claims mounted and the number of native political aspirants kept pace with them, tension appeared between white and native Alaskans. Oldtimers began to murmur that if the Eskimos ever got hold of the land, the whites would have to move out, for whenever in the past the Eskimo had had the upper hand he had shown himself to be very hard to deal with. Other whites reacted resentfully to young opportunists like Willie Hensley, executive secretary of the Northwest Alaska Native Association until his 1966 election to the state legislature. To their way of thinking, if he had been born a Negro instead

Three Eskimo masks

Alaskan Eskimo masks were carved to gain the good will of the deities and spirits the tribesmen venerated. The masks were thought to represent the deities whose powers might be transferred to the wearer during ritual dances. Their design was based on the visions of tribal priests.

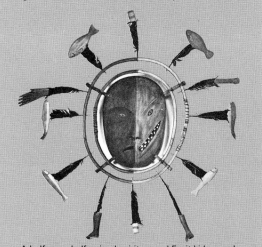

A half-man, half-animal spirit named Excit kidnapped humans but then gave them good fortune in hunting.

Clutching a fish in its beak, a bird with a human face on its back represents a spirit of hunting and fishing.

The traits of a wolf—its quickness and hunting skills—might be acquired by wearing this ominous mask.

of an Eskimo he would be a "Black Power" advocate. Indeed, during the 1966 campaign, it was difficult to leave a conversation with Hensley without the feeling that he really did not want a settlement of the controversy, either by cash payment or an assignment of acreage, but preferred to keep the matter, and his own political career, at a boil.

Yet there was none of the raw hatred sometimes shown by Negroes or Puerto Ricans toward whites elsewhere in the U.S., and no suggestion of violence. In fact, the Eskimos rejected an offer by Alaskan Negroes, of whom there are some 5,500, to make common cause with them on civil rights because, as Howard Rock pointed out, "to natives, discrimination is not really a big problem. We are more concerned with education, sanitation, and political action." The most likely course for "Brown Power" in Alaska would seem to be one of consolidating a fragmented people, identifying a few unifying issues and exercising the vote to move politicians into line—in short, adopting ethnic politics of the sort practiced by the Italians in Connecticut or the Irish in Massachusetts. The 1966 formation of the Alaska Federation of Natives seemed a further step in this direction.

But regardless of the nonviolent nature of native protests, the whole land-selecting program did come to a violent halt. The federal government, which still controlled some 90 per cent of Alaska, was importuned to put all royalties into escrow until the ownership question was settled, and to permit no future land leases. The federal agency concerned, the U.S. Bureau of Land Management, promptly obliged. It refused to release any lands involved in the claims. This decision put the entire state in a quandary. The "frozen" land was rich in oil and minerals. Those who wanted to develop it were clamoring to have the ban lifted as quickly as possible. The natives insisted that their claims had to be settled first and received support in their contention from the federal Land Law Review Commission. In September 1966 a spokesman for that agency announced that there could be no solution to the public-land problem in the new state until the aboriginal claims were settled and that only Congress could determine the extent of native land rights. Meanwhile, the unsettled claims have continued to cast a shadow on the validity of the oil leases the state intends to entertain bids on. Oil, of course, has kept Alaska from drowning in red ink since 1962. Eighteen million dollars from oil went into the Alaskan treasury in 1966 alone.

By mid-April of 1967 native claims, some overlapping, had reached the astronomical total of 372,097,206 acres, about two thirds of Alaska's entire area. Included was the whole Arctic Slope, containing the Navy's petroleum reserve, and the potentially rich mineral area around Kobuk, where Kennecott Copper had spent upward of $7.5 million on exploratory mining. So epidemic did the indemnity fever become that some Bristol Bay natives maintained they should be compensated for the destruction of the local salmon fishery through maladministration during the pre-statehood years by the U.S. Bureau of Commercial Fisheries.

At present, effort is being concentrated on temporary solutions that will allow land selection to proceed while Congress addresses itself to the protracted process of resolving the claims. The outlook is depressing. In a thorough study of the situation released in January 1967, Anchorage attorney W. C. Arnold concluded that unless the "disputes over Indian title can be considerably modified, Alaska's phenomenal economic expansion will falter and the adult men and women, both native and white, who now [chart] its course, will have gone to their graves before the controversy is settled. There will be few winners and many losers. The natives will bear the principal burden. They can advance and develop only with Alaska. Unlike most of the whites, they cannot go back to their former homes. They are already there."

They are indisputably "there." And they will remain "there" far longer than the time it takes the courts or Congress to settle the controversy. But it should be noted that they are now "there" with a difference. The galvanic effect of the land fight has produced a shift in the balance of political power, away from the whites and toward the natives.

The natives had always had one thing going for them: they were stable. The white body politic, on the other hand, had always been, as it still is, in a state of flux, its highly mobile members being more sojourners than residents. Hence the natives have the potential of being a political force of greater power than their numbers might indicate. The 1960 census revealed that they had an additional advantage: their rate of increase was higher than that of the whites by 13.3 people per 1,000 and had risen nearly 40 per cent since 1950—in comparison to a nonnative increase of only about 30 per cent. Barring a sizable in-migration of whites, it seemed inevitable that the natives' percentage of Alaska's total population would also increase, giving them proportionally greater weight at the polls. Now the beginnings of native unity and the emergence of a native leadership meant they could turn their special advantages to better account.

An Eskimo woman carries her child along a rocky path on Little Diomede. Beyond the sign—a whimsical souvenir from the mainland—rise the dark cliffs of Russian-owned Big Diomede, three miles across the water.

Eskimo life on a bleak island

A 30-mile stretch of rough sea, virtually impassable from October to April, separates the mainland of Alaska from the tiny island of Little Diomede in the Bering Strait. This body of water has been a blessing for the approximately 90 Eskimos who live on the island, for it has shielded them from most of the pressures of Western civilization. Life on Little Diomede still depends on hunting and fishing, and unlike most of Alaska's Eskimos, the islanders have been able to retain the life pattern of their ancestors. True, the harpoon, the seal-oil lamp and the paddle have been largely replaced by the rifle, the gasoline lamp and the outboard motor. But, as in centuries past, the migrations of seals, walrus and birds that funnel through the strait determine the daily round of activities on Little Diomede and provide the natives with all the basic necessities of life.

Photographed by Lee Friedlander

A rock-bound village by an icy sea

Few places on earth appear more hostile to man than the island of Little Diomede, a mere speck of crumbling rock three miles long by a mile and a half wide. Almost from the very edge of the sea, high, boulder-strewn walls of rock vault upward to be joined at 1,300 feet by a flat wasteland. Upon the barren hillside there are the graves of generations of Eskimos. Only along the narrow, rocky beach can life exist. Here lies the village of Ignaluk *(below)*—21 weather-beaten dwellings, a general store and a school.

Despite its unprepossessing appearance, Ignaluk serves its citizens well. Its buildings, made largely of driftwood, are reinforced with sod and boulders for increased protection against the howling winds. To conserve heat, all the houses are small, many containing only one room. But all have storm entryways; the older dwellings, in fact, can be entered only through a tunnel and trap door.

For food the islanders look to the sea, where seal and walrus are plentiful. Eastward lies Alaska, a door to the world, where many Diomeders spend their summers, visiting relatives and working at temporary jobs before the hunting season takes them back to their island home. Only three miles to the west lies Big Diomede (glimpsed again in the background at right). Once the two islands were linked by ties of blood and commerce, but today Big Diomede is a Soviet military base, closed to visitors. Between Little and Big Diomede runs the international date line; when it is Sunday on the smaller island it is Monday on the larger.

Home to Little Diomede's Eskimos is this village set on a boulder-strewn beach.

Villagers gather to greet visitors arriving from the Alaskan mainland.

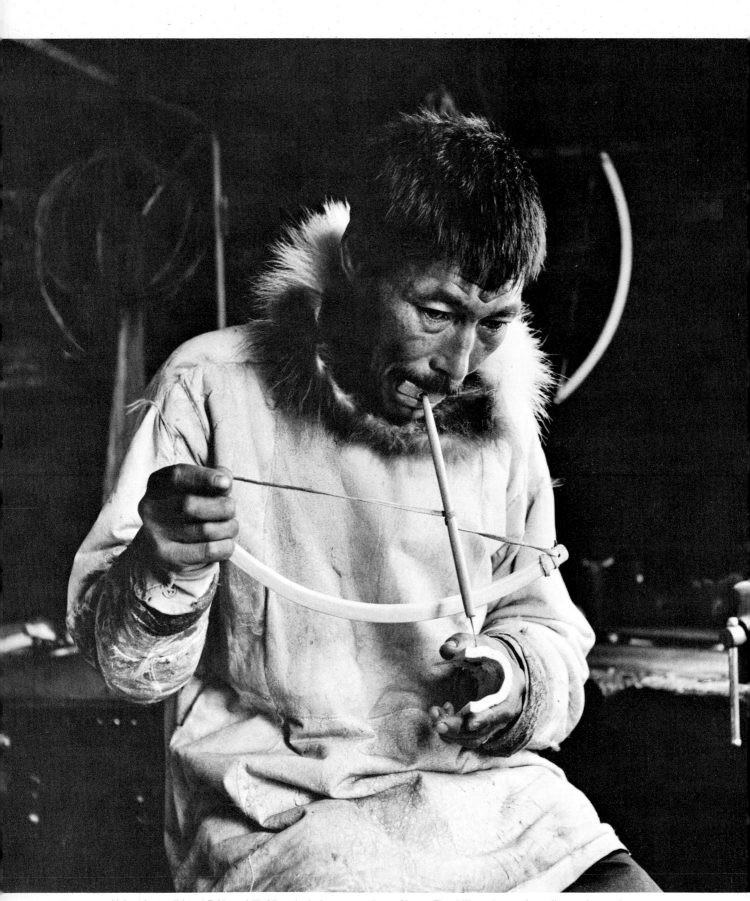

Using the traditional Eskimo drill, Albert Iyahuk carves a piece of ivory. The drill revolves as he pulls on a bowstring.

Maintaining the traditional arts and crafts

Three finely wrought examples of the ivory-carver's craft.

Annie Iyahuk crimps the sealskin sole of a boot with her teeth.

The art of ivory carving, at which the islanders excel, began with the sculpting of small talismans. The early natives believed that these charms had magical properties that would protect them from the dangers of the hunt and increase their kill. If magic no longer sustains the ancient craft, profit does. It is estimated that walrus-tusk figurines —like the fox, rabbit and walrus at left—bring in a cash income of about $16,000 yearly to Little Diomede. Although all of the island's males are reared in the tradition of the craft, some, like Albert Iyahuk *(left),* are true artists. So successful has Iyahuk been that he is one of the few islanders who find a private studio necessary.

Just as ivory carving is man's work, sewing is woman's labor. On Little Diomede, store-bought clothes are generally worn only during the summer: in winter, when the temperature is often 30 degrees below zero, the islanders wear the time-tested and immensely practical homemade Eskimo garb of skins and furs. Thus it is that women, like Albert Iyahuk's wife, Annie *(above),* are kept busy working skins, chewing hides to make them supple and stitching pelts with the finesse of a professional furrier.

Islanders repair an oomiak frame before covering it with walrus hides.

Wet skins are measured on the frame before cutting and sewing.

Making an oomiak seaworthy

Skin-covered boats called oomiaks are as essential to the natives of Little Diomede as the automobile is to most other Americans. Oomiaks are used for any activity that takes the islanders to sea—hunting seals and walrus, trips to the mainland. Oomiaks often are 25 feet long and can carry a dozen people as well as hundreds of pounds of cargo. Although an oomiak is normally owned by one man, its construction and upkeep depend on many helping hands, and all involved are entitled to share in its use. The men who help build and maintain the boat often act as its crew during the hunting season.

Aside from the addition of an outboard motor and the substitution of wood for whalebone in the construction of the frame, the skin boat's general design has changed little over the centuries. With proper care a frame may last for a decade or more; the skin covering loses its elasticity after three years, however, and must be replaced. This tedious job requires many walrus hides, which are sliced to half their thickness and then cured. Soaked in sea water to make them pliable, the skins are measured on the frame and then quickly sewed together and attached to the hull, where they dry and shrink into a tough, close-fitting shell.

Women stitch skins that will dry and shrink on the oomiak frame.

On the steep, boulder-studded hillside high above the village, Pat Omiak nets an aukle

A bounty in birds
for the taking

Live birds are strung up as decoys.

Live birds are strung up as decoys.

Each June vast flocks of sea birds—auklets, murres and dovkies—descend on Little Diomede in search of breeding grounds. The arrival of the auklets is the signal for the islanders to take their nets up the steep slope behind the village and engage in a bird-capturing spree. Concealing themselves behind blinds built from rocks, the hunters snare their quarry as it flies by. The first catch is generally the hardest, for the islanders must rely entirely on luck to bring a bird within reach of their nets. But one catch generally leads to another with each succeeding triumph becoming easier than the last, for the captive birds become unwitting accomplices of their executioners. Each captive is strung through the beak and hung between two upright sticks, as in the top picture on the right. The more birds on the string the more effective the decoy, for their frantic flappings attract other birds, which are quickly netted by the skillful hunters. In this way a lone hunter is often able to take as many as 100 auklets in a single day.

The islanders are also enthusiastic murre hunters, but these, being bigger birds, are taken with shotguns. Once murres were valued for their skins, for in the days before store-bought underwear was available, the Eskimos would fashion the skins, feathers and all, into warm vests. Today, the birds are used only for meat, and when preserved in seal oil, they provide the islanders with a welcome relief from their normal winter diet of walrus and seal meat.

A highly esteemed delicacy is the meat of the dovkie. These too are sometimes netted in great numbers, and when about 700 have been collected they are stuffed into a whole sealskin. The sealskin bag is then buried beneath rocks to be dug up during the winter. The blubber inside the sealskin both preserves the birds and imparts to their flesh a flavor that the Eskimos cherish.

Helpless, an auklet lies entangled in a net.

A lucky find
for ivory hunters

Walrus are mostly seen off Little Diomede during the early spring, when they migrate northward through the nearby ice floes. Occasionally, however, one shows up close to shore at a different time of the year, and when that happens the islanders are quick to make the most of their opportunity. The young bull shown at right was sighted in July, swimming so close to shore that the islanders were able to shoot the animal from the beach and then go out in their boat to harpoon it. By custom both the tusks and the best cut of the meat are awarded to the man who fired the first successful shot, but in this case the Eskimos already had more walrus meat than they needed, and so the ivory was the only prize.

Walrus meat, in fact, is usually in surplus on the island, for every spring the hunters kill some 300 of the animals and the average carcass weighs about a ton. The meat that is not immediately consumed is stored in communal caches. From these reserves villagers may take all they want. In time, the meat becomes rancid, but the bitter taste of the aged walrus flesh only increases the islanders' appetites.

It might be thought that such uncontrolled killing of walrus would eventually lead to the extinction of the breed. But if this happens it will not be due to the efforts of the islanders. Only if walrus begin to be threatened by highly efficient commercial fleets will their survival be in doubt. Certainly, any attempt to limit the hunting rights of Little Diomeders would meet with outraged protests from these Eskimos, for whom the walrus means food, boat coverings and cash in hand—in other words, life itself. With walrus to hunt, the islanders have remained essentially self-sufficient and therefore remarkably immune to the social decay that has beset other Eskimo peoples.

The walrus is dragged to a place where it can be beached.

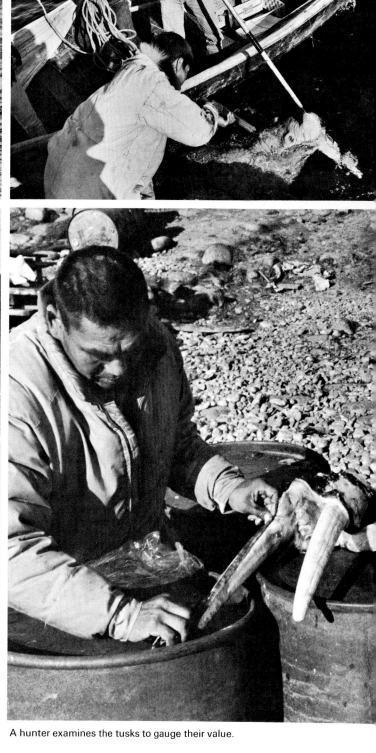

On shore the men begin the skinning and butchering.

A hunter examines the tusks to gauge their value.

53

The rugged peaks of the Chugach Mountains reflect the last rays of the sun as Anchorage, already in shadow, turns on its evening lights. By far the largest city in Alaska, Anchorage lies on a coastal plain between the mountains and Cook Inlet.

3

The Battle
of the Cities

One of the most important keys to an understanding of Alaska is something that was fomented in war, exacerbated by peace and consolidated through earthquake. It is the emergence of Anchorage as the state's biggest, richest, most powerful city. The full significance of Anchorage's rise is still to be comprehended, even on the "Last Frontier," for its consequences are so multifarious they will be borne in upon Alaskans only with the passage of time. But judging by what has already ensued, the total impact is bound to be epochal. The rise of the city has shifted the whole axis of power, economic as well as political, away from the Panhandle cities, its historic home, and northward into Anchorage's own section.

Anchorage, or to be more precise the city and the adjacent communities that make up the Greater Anchorage area, now possesses about a third of Alaska's population and 40 to 50 per cent of its employed workers and improved property. Nearly half of the state's retail sales originate there, more than half of the wholesaling. Some 40 per cent of all Alaskan income is earned in Anchorage, and the city's banks, the source of formidable economic power in a capital-short state, contain more than 60 per cent of Alaska's total banking assets. It is the state's oil capital, being the supply center for the rich fields in Cook Inlet and on the Kenai Peninsula. It is headquarters for the Alaska Railroad, that vital link to the interior. Its international airport is by far the biggest in the state, a stopping point for five foreign carriers and nearly a dozen

American ones that fly a busy great-circle route to Japan and the Orient as well as a transpolar route to Europe. Its seaport now handles more tonnage than any other in Alaska. In the course of all this, Anchorage has become less and less distinguishable from a small city in the Middle West, and the state itself has undergone a related change, for as Anchorage has absorbed more and more of Alaska's total population, some of Alaska's special flavor and distinctiveness has been lost.

Curiously, Anchorage's development was such that as late as 1940 its most fervent boosters would have been hard put to defend a prediction of future eminence. The city did not even exist in 1910, when the census showed that Nome had a population of 2,600, Fairbanks possessed 3,541 people (albeit mainly the flotsam and jetsam of an evanescent gold rush), and the established towns of the Panhandle—Juneau, Ketchikan and Sitka—could claim more than 1,000 people each.

Anchorage got its start in 1914 as Ship Creek Landing at the head of Cook Inlet, a construction camp for building an eastward extension of the federally owned Alaska Railroad. Initially a dockside tent town where water sold for five cents a bucket, where garbage was dumped on the outgoing tide every 24 hours and where the streets were two feet deep in dust, it was moved from the crowded waterfront to an adjacent site in 1915 as men and material for building the railroad began to pour in. The workmen, mostly single and mostly recruited in Southern Europe, were put at a safe remove from the town itself in a reserve district known as "Bohunk Village." A second reserve district—"South Anchorage"—was also set up, this one by the government. It was for the prostitutes. By 1916 "Greater Anchorage"—i.e., the tent town, Bohunk Village and South Anchorage (not necessarily in order of population)—could claim to be Alaska's biggest city. Six thousand inhabitants had at their disposal three churches, two movie theaters, a bank, two hotels, a hospital and a $30,000 Labor Temple, monument to an early and successful strike for higher wages.

Unfortunately for Anchorage, its boom was a case of easy come, easy go. American involvement in World War I braked progress on the Alaska Railroad, and by 1920 Anchorage had shrunk to 1,856 people, ranking only third among Alaskan cities. Moreover, the federal policy that had resulted in building a railroad to open up Alaska's natural resources was soon followed by the antithetical policy of conserving those resources for use in some distant future: immense federal land reservations

Ship Creek Landing—the forerunner of Anchorage—was a turbulent, dust-choked outpost that vanished several weeks after this picture was taken on July 5, 1915. The town had a flimsy air; a hotel, the Crist House *(large structure at far right),* was merely a tent, and

left a development railroad with nothing to be developed. Anchorage languished. In 1940 it was still a long way from the size so briefly attained in 1916. With 4,230 people, the city was smaller than Ketchikan, much smaller than Juneau. The difference was that this time another World War was about to restore to Anchorage all that the first one had taken away, and a lot more besides.

Alaska had once been described by that prophet of air power, Brigadier General Billy Mitchell, during his evangelical campaigns to get the Army out of the swivel chair and into the cockpit, as "the most central place in the world of aircraft, and that is true either of Europe, Asia, or North America, for whoever holds Alaska will hold the world." Subsequently Alexander de Seversky (author of many provocative articles on the future importance of air power) had laid great stress on Alaska's strategic importance in the air wars of the future. The War Department had also taken up the cudgels for an Alaskan air base, pressing it upon Congress from the mid-1930s onward. The decisive arguments, however, remained to be made by the German Luftwaffe rather than American military experts. In the spring of 1940, with Hitler's forces occupying Alaska's transpolar neighbor, Norway, Congress at long last appropriated $12.8

gambling dens and gin mills were housed in equally ephemeral "buildings." Most of the community's 3,000 residents were laborers on the Alaska Railroad, but prostitutes, gamblers and reputable tradesmen helped swell the population. Already the town was bursting at the seams and the decision had been made to found a more permanent settlement nearby. Lots in the new site were auctioned, and by mid-August, 1915, Ship Creek Landing was no more, its tents having been shifted to the new town of Anchorage.

million to build Elmendorf Field just outside Anchorage. After that, the city simply took off.

Construction workers, military personnel and federal money poured in. A huge Army installation, Fort Richardson, was built near the new air base. All told, the government spent $53 million in the city's environs on wartime construction, while the number of military personnel stationed there reached a 1942 peak of 15,584 men. Anchorage was the eager recipient of money from both.

Government spending, though it waxed and waned, continued on after war's end. By 1950 the population of the city itself had soared to 11,250 and that of Greater Anchorage to 32,000, an increase of more than 750 per cent in just 10 years' time. In the process of again becoming Alaska's biggest—and this time richest—city, Anchorage reverted to many of the characteristics of the booming, knuckle-busting tent town on Ship Creek. Visiting journalists took to describing it, with equal amounts of accuracy and sensationalism, as possessing three basic industries: liquor, vice and the military. One reporter noted that Anchorage "generates so much lust, sin, and violence, on a 24-hour-day basis, every day of the week, that it must be rated the bawdiest community in North America and could be referred to as 'bawdy, brawling Anchorage, vice capital of the Far North.'" Another writer saw the city as "coated with dust, drenched with whiskey and plagued with overcrowded quarters and a high cost of living."

Some local businessmen even decided to exploit what they could not prevent. In a newspaper advertisement one trucking firm advanced the notion that violence was actually a virtue in disguise: "Some people think that Anchorage is a disconnected, brawling, hard-drinking town. They are given this impression by the ubiquitous display of those engaged in the 'spirits' industry, and by the not-infrequent, flashy headlines of stabbings and other violence. What they do not see is the peculiar meaning behind all this. Simply, Alaskans are energetic, vigorous people with heavy appetites for activity. This fact, in turn, is one of the main reasons Alaskans are so prosperous. The displays of violence are merely manifestations of frustrations due to lack of vigorous activity and we [the trucking firm] are here to provide that vigorous activity."

Time, growth and continued prosperity, however, were soon to bring an end to the image of Anchorage as a fire-breathing frontier town. The influence of the oldtimers was diluted by the influx of newcomers, most of them both better heeled and better educated than their predecessors were. A new conservatism took over. Anchorage began to look—and act—like any other American city of comparable size. Its streets were cleaned up, its new buildings were built in conformance with the "international style" of architecture that has given such glossy sameness to so many U.S. cities, and its braggadocio went underground to be replaced by subtler, if no less intensive, efforts toward self-aggrandizement. New and glittering horizons appeared in 1957 when the Swanson River Oil Field opened up only 50 miles from the city (its production by 1966: more than 50 million barrels). Indeed, the new Anchorage seemed to be fortune's favorite child right down to 5:36 p.m., March 27, 1964. Then, in the short space of five minutes, about the time it takes to smoke a cigarette, the city sustained $200 million worth of damage.

The earthquake that worked this havoc upon Anchorage, as well as other cities in the area (Seward, Valdez, Kodiak), was rated at 8.4 on the Richter Magnitude Scale. It was the most severe ever experienced on the North American continent, the second strongest recorded anywhere in the world. The needles on seismographs thousands of miles away jumped clear off the machines. Streets and their buildings dropped 20 feet in Anchorage's downtown district; cars piled up on top of one another in the undulations; 77 homes in one suburb slid into Cook Inlet. Ninety-five per cent of the city's high-rise apartments were subsequently condemned as unsafe; roughly three quarters of its total developed worth suffered damage in some degree. Almost miraculously, death claimed only nine in Anchorage, but the question that arose from the ruin was whether the city could bank on having such a miraculously small number of casualties should another earthquake strike. Did it make sense to rebuild and repair the city at all?

For the 1964 earthquake was not an isolated event. Anchorage had had an average of six noticeable seismic shocks every year between 1936 and 1954; Alaska as a whole had experienced three major earthquakes during the 20th Century; and the borders of the Pacific Ocean had long been recognized as an active earthquake zone, some 80 per cent of the world's seismic energy being released there. Moreover, much of Anchorage was underlaid by an unstable stratum known as "Bootlegger clay." This clay had compounded the earthquake damage by causing disastrous landslides. The U.S. Geological Survey, in a report on the potential dangers of the stratum made five years earlier, cited a number of places along the bluffs of Anchorage where the clay, named for Bootlegger Cove, once

a rendezvous for rumrunners, had absorbed water, turned into a slippery soup and plunged its overburden into the sea. At that time, the geologists had gotten nothing for their pains except hostility and the intimation that they were "Catastrophists," adherents to the theory that periodic cataclysms, eliminating all life on earth, were part of the divine scheme of things. But now, was it wise to rebuild on Bootlegger clay—and right in the middle of a major earthquake zone to boot?

The leaders of Anchorage may have thought hard about this question, but they did not think long. With $280 million in government aid, and with money from their own pokes (earthquake insurance at the time of the disaster had totaled only $55,000), they immediately turned to and rebuilt the city bigger and glossier than ever. As University of Alaska Dean Leo M. Loll Jr. observed at the conclusion of a 1965 economic study: "A city's place in the world depends on its dynamism, and Anchorage is a dynamic, growing community. The greatest tribute to Anchorage's recovery from the earthquake is after all that less than two years after such a destructive experience, it has been possible to write an article about the Anchorage economic community with only passing reference to the earthquake's economic impact."

Prior to the earthquake, this same dynamism —which less charitable observers saw as an incorrigible grabbiness—had produced an informal anti-Anchorage coalition among Alaska's other major towns and cities. In the years following the phoenix-like emergence of an even more powerful and aggressive Anchorage, the alliance has been stiffened by the reopening of old scores and the addition of new ones.

One such old grievance is harbored by Valdez, a small community about 120 miles due east of Anchorage. Valdez is still smarting over its loss of the Third District Court, resident in this coastal town from 1909 until 1942. When the courthouse burned to the ground during that wartime year, Anchorage had offered to provide "temporary" quarters for the court until Valdez could build a replacement at war's end. But somehow Anchorage managed to turn the temporary quarters into permanent ones. Since then, Valdez has been hard-pressed. It was never able to make up the loss of the business it once got from jurors, witnesses, lawyers, court officers *et al.*

Seward had bitterly resented its loss to Anchorage of the headquarters of the Alaska Railroad in 1919, and then had had salt rubbed in its wounds when the Anchorage *Times* demanded that the

Alaska Road Commission stop building roads to Seward because the town would never amount to anything anyway. The unforgivable injury, however, came hard on the heels of the 1964 earthquake. The quake and its attendant tidal waves smashed the port of Seward, destroying its oil-storage depot and flattening the four-million-dollar docks of the Alaska Railroad terminus. The quake, on the other hand, had left Anchorage's own port substantially operational.

Up until then Anchorage, the self-styled "Seattle of Cook Inlet," had had a much smaller facility and had handled only 382,000 tons of cargo the year before the disaster, about half as much as Seward. As a matter of fact, it was operating at a substantial deficit, in part because of pressure exerted by the Alaska Railroad, which could not afford to lose the freight revenues generated by the longer haul to Seward, and in part because of the skittishness of some ship captains. They were apprehensive, groundlessly as later experience was to prove, about negotiating Cook Inlet's ice fields and tides, at 33 feet the second highest in the world (after those in Nova Scotia's Bay of Fundy). But with its chief rival out of commission, Anchorage turned handsprings rebuilding—and expanding—its own port. So rapidly did it move that by the end of 1964 a total of 748,802 tons of cargo had come across its docks, an increase of 196 per cent over the previous year's total. Although Seward made a partial recovery in 1965, it could not stop Anchorage. The latter's port kept reaching out for more and more tonnage until it had supplanted Seward as Alaska's most important harbor facility.

Fairbanks' antipathy for Anchorage springs as much from its own competitive limitations as from encroachments by the "Diamond on the Buckle of the Rail Belt" (as some unabashed Anchorage boosters like to call their city). Fairbanks has long had a reputation for high prices (in 1965 the cost of living stood 32 per cent above that in Seattle, compared to 23 per cent above for Anchorage and Juneau). Its merchants tend to look on their customers as a captive market, and indeed have sometimes blandly stated as much from the rostrum at welcoming dinners given new University of Alaska faculty members. From a civic point of view, Fairbanks leaves much to be desired. Too many of its streets are unpaved or in disrepair; its housing too frequently consists of slum shacks, packed with poverty-stricken natives. There is no community-wide cohesive force or spirit at work within the city. Moreover, the property situation —numerous small parcels of land in the hands of

die-hard locals or absentee owners who will not sell —complicates slum clearance and civic planning.

On top of these shortcomings, there are Fairbanks' rugged winters and the even more rugged individualism of its inhabitants. When the cold wears on, patience wears out; "cabin fever" shows up in the proliferation of domestic brawls, virtually nonexistent in the summer, that crowd the police blotter. By February the number of letters to the editor in the *Daily News Miner*—mostly letters *against* something or someone—are running triple that of the summer months even though the population has shrunk by half. As for rugged individualism, one local school of thought holds that this is just general cussedness, a defense mechanism set in motion by the continual realization that only accident (a gold strike on nearby creeks) got the city built so far from the coast, in such an inhospitable environment, and that only federal policy now keeps it from becoming a ghost town. The typical Fairbanks citizen, as one of them explained recently, "feels like the prospector out in the desert: it's tough but it goes against his grain to pack up and move out."

In any event, he insists on going his own sweet way as long as he is there. Politicians who take him for granted do so at their peril, for his independence leads him to vote with studied unpredictability. Fairbanks, in general, is hostile to growth and change. Its orientation is toward the past, when society was "freer." Preservation of the Old Alaska —the values, attitudes, license and pragmatism of the gold-rush era—is as much Fairbanks' stock in trade as the pursuit of modernity is Anchorage's.

All this might have been very well, or at least venial, if Fairbanks' economic base were robust. To be sure, it benefits from the University of Alaska's enrollment (2,600 as of 1968-1969) and the university's many state and federally financed programs such as those at the Arctic Research Laboratory, the Geophysical Institute and the Institute of Arctic Biology. And the military at nearby Fort Wainright still constitutes a mainstay of the economy, although not one likely to grow much. But Fairbanks now has virtually no industry. The gold-mining dredges have shut down, the federally fixed price of gold being too low to justify continuance, and the furnaces have long since grown cold at the U.S. Smelting and Refining Company. Significantly, more than half a million tons of railroad freight rolls into the city in a typical year while only some 25,000 tons move out. As for population, Fairbanks' election district had a net *out*-migration of 5,190 persons between April 1960 and July 1965, a period when Anchorage's district experienced a net *in*-migration of 5,141.

On top of this, a catastrophe equal to Anchorage's earthquake was visited upon Fairbanks in August of 1967. After record rains the rampaging Chena River inundated most of the city. All highways were cut, communications knocked out and hundreds of homes rendered unlivable since not enough time was left to dry them out before the Alaskan winter froze their water-soaked insulation solid. "The Golden Heart of Alaska," as Fairbanks likes to call itself, had been beating, although slowly, before the $200 million calamity; now it had ample cause to beat more slowly still.

Where the city's fondest hopes lie are in the prospect of continuing to be the trading center for the vast area to the north. And therein can be found the tangible reasons for Fairbanks' chronic hostility toward Anchorage. Fairbanks is losing ground to Anchorage as a trading post. Not only has the latter been expanding its own commercial operations to the north, but businesses are quitting Fairbanks because they can transship more cheaply to the north direct from Anchorage's seaport.

Fairbanks has further cause for concern. As late as 1967 it had won state endorsement—and even that of Anchorage—for its attempt to make the city a junction point on a Pan American World Airways route to the Orient. But when 10 other airlines filed for a route to the Orient via Anchorage, the latter decided it wanted them all, Pan American included, and undertook a Washington lobbying campaign that amazed even hardened veterans of Capitol Hill. Then Anchorage's leaders marched on the state government, brandishing figures that showed jet fuel was 4.1 cents a gallon cheaper in Anchorage than in Fairbanks. (This works out to a saving of $410 on the 10,000 gallons customarily taken aboard by a jet liner for the Anchorage-Tokyo leg of the trip.) Anchorage also purred that while its good fortune was to be located in Alaska's balmy "banana belt," Fairbanks' even higher summer temperatures would place drastic restrictions on jet take-off weights: the warmer the air the less the lifting power. On the other hand, Fairbanks' winter ice fog would severely hamper flight.

When the matter came to a preliminary hearing in 1967 before a Civil Aeronautics Board examiner, Fairbanks' state support withered away. Instead, the state government intoned that it would endorse any airline providing the same service on any similar route—in other words, via Anchorage *or* Fairbanks—just so long as it was economically sound. The Anchorage delegation at the hearings then proclaimed that the full support of the State of Alaska had been thrown behind its city's case.

Like that of Fairbanks, Juneau's resentment of Anchorage is caused by an admixture of the general and the specific. The state capital, in common with Ketchikan, Sitka and the other Panhandle cities, is locked in the peculiar sectionalism that breeds so much prejudice and misunderstanding within Alaska. So fundamental is this sectionalism that as far back as 1903 a distinguished citizen of Juneau believed that the only logical solution was to split the Panhandle and its cities off from the rest of the territory. "Nature has divided the district of Alaska at Mount St. Elias by impassable glaciers," Federal Judge James Wickersham told a Congressional committee. "That point ought to be the division between the future commonwealths. The needs and wants of these districts are so dissimilar that they have no relation one with another at all."

Nor, the good judge might have added, did they want any. Even after statehood, Alaska remained a loose confederation of diverse natural and economic sections rather than a cohesive entity. What is needed, perhaps, is some middle level of government that, in huge Alaska, would perform some of the functions of state governments in the Lower 48, calming rivalries between the far-flung cities and finding solutions to sectional problems.

Juneau's early attitude toward the northern area's "upstart" cities of Anchorage and Fairbanks, however, was mainly that they were to be ignored. It had no sense of being challenged by them, certainly none of having been put on the defensive. After all, had not Joe Juneau's gold strike in 1879 established the city a full generation before Fairbanks emerged from the diggings of Felix Pedro, and was Juneau not made the Territorial Capital in 1900, 14 years before even a tent went up at Anchorage? Juneau was the epicenter of Alaskan political power and economic power as well; the timber, fish and metals that then comprised the bulk of Alaska's wealth were at its very door. Let the Johnny-come-latelies go north. Juneau sat there beside the green waters of Gastineau Channel, established, content, cooling its back with the white cataracts that plunged from the forested mountains rising abruptly behind it. The roar of float planes lifting off the channel's mirror-smooth surface, the deep horns of the ships at its docks, the incessant cries of the wheeling gulls all seemed to combine in saying Juneau was unassailable.

The trouble was that Anchorage, in the short space of the 10 years from 1940 to 1950, changed

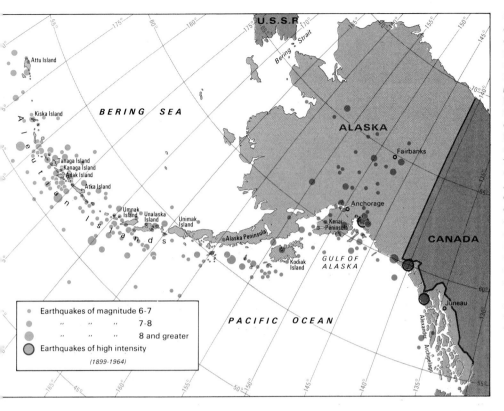

Six of every 100 major earthquakes originating near the earth's surface occur in Alaska, one of the world's most earthquake-prone areas. The map locates the sites of the 298 high-magnitude seismic disturbances *(green dots)* that struck Alaska between 1899 and 1964. Magnitude is a scientific measurement of an earthquake's physical severity. The highest-magnitude tremor ever recorded reached a peak of 8.9 on the Richter Scale. During the 65-year period covered by the map, Alaska suffered eight earthquakes of or above magnitude 8, including one of 8.4. The map also pinpoints seismic disturbances of high intensity *(dots circled in purple)*. Intensity is a measure of the damage caused by a quake. Because few Alaskan earthquakes have affected built-up areas, most have been of low intensity, but the 1964 tremor, which centered east of Anchorage and wrecked much of the city, was one of the most destructive in recent history.

from having 2,000 fewer people than Juneau to being a city with twice the population of the state capital. On the spur of this shift in relative importance, Anchorage set about doing two things that were to turn Juneau's disdain into active enmity. The first, undertaken in concert with Fairbanks, was a redoubling of efforts to achieve statehood. For its part, Juneau remained a leader of the opposition, on the grounds that statehood would disrupt the status quo, result in heavier taxation and deprive the Panhandle of its political power. That all these apprehensions quickly turned out to be valid once Alaska became a state did nothing to lessen Juneau's hostility to Anchorage. But worse was still to come. Anchorage launched a determined drive to have itself made the capital instead of Juneau. Here it went down to defeat, although not without having kept Juneau in a quandary until two referendums settled the matter.

Anchorage's campaign in a sense backfired, for it activated the anti-Anchorage coalition. Sensing a common adversary, Fairbanks and Nome joined Juneau and Ketchikan in trying to contain the ambitions of the "Outlet on the Inlet." Even so, the feeling in Juneau over thwarting Anchorage was that only a battle had been won, not the war. When Walter J. Hickel became Alaska's governor

in 1967, he felt he had to calm Juneau's fears by declaring in his Admission Day speech that "it is time we stopped talking about moving the capital and started thinking about getting the capital moving."

Yet the presentiment could not be downed that Anchorage would try to achieve by subterfuge what it had failed to accomplish through frontal assault. Substantial portions of such departments as highways, health, education and welfare, and the Alaskan National Guard could (and might) be gradually and quietly shifted to Anchorage. In that case, as Robert De Armond, a native-born chronicler of the Alaskan scene, put it, "We in Juneau would wind up with all the chiefs, while most of the hired help, who support the town, would be elsewhere. After reaching that point, it would be much easier for Anchorage to campaign for moving the chiefs, too, to create greater efficiency."

Important as Anchorage has already become, it now seems to have entered a new and accelerated stage of development. By 1965 nearly half of all Alaskans already lived within 25 miles of the city. This may not seem an unduly large percentage—New York City contains more than 44 per cent of all the people in the Empire State—but Alaska is different. The 50 per cent not clustered around

Anchorage is scattered generally, if not uniformly, over an area one seventh the size of the Lower 48. When one city attains such concentration in a vast and otherwise sparsely settled state, its power and influence increase by geometric progression. Dynamic absorption begins to take place. The big-city advantages Anchorage alone can offer exert a preemptive influence on newcomers to the state who might otherwise have chosen other cities. And since Alaskans tend to stay put in whatever city they initially adopt (cost, distance and weather deny them the mobility that is taken for granted in the rest of the U.S.), Anchorage keeps them.

In essence, Anchorage has attained such proportions vis à vis competing Alaskan cities that they are progressively outclassed. Where Juneau has eight hotels and motels, Anchorage has 52. Where the jewel in Fairbanks' crown is the University of Alaska, Anchorage has two colleges, Alaska Methodist University and Anchorage Community College. The latter, a branch of the University of Alaska, has grown so rapidly that its enrollment is now larger than that of its parent, although few of its students are full-time. The economies of large-scale operation are working to give Anchorage a greater variety of life's amenities—and at lower cost. Price competition is virtually unknown in such cities as Nome, Sitka, Ketchikan and Juneau, since they are too small to sustain chain-store branches. In consequence, the customer has no choice but submission to local merchants—or accepting the delays of the mail-order catalogue. Anchorage, on the other hand, is a sizable enough market to attract the chains, and the competition they have provided has had a salutary effect on prices.

So much power would seem to be in prospect for Anchorage that some of its more thoughtful citizens are seriously worried lest the city come to dominate the whole state legislature. Under the reapportionment that followed the 1960 census, Anchorage got seven of the 20 state senators and 14 of the 40 representatives. But the city has been growing so much faster than the rest of Alaska that House Majority Leader Ted Stevens, an Anchorage Republican, predicted in 1967 that more than half the members of both Senate and House would come from Anchorage within five years—put there after the census of 1970 had confirmed the population surge and forced another reapportionment. His proposal for avoiding "total Anchorage influence": the state's Senate and House should be replaced by a unicameral legislature made up of 55 senators from as many districts, the expectation being that geographic factors might then help counterbalance

Anchorage's disproportionately large population.

In the final analysis, the possibility of Alaska's becoming a one-city state, as some fear and others hope, will depend on how much countervailing power can be brought to bear. If the population and employment projections of George W. Rogers and Richard A. Cooley in *Alaska's Population and Economy* are realized, then the Panhandle will experience some counterbalancing economic growth, founded, in the main, upon expansion of the distributive industries, natural-resource extraction and manufacturing (forest products, fish, minerals), and tourism. Concomitantly, the section would increase in population, boosting its proportion of the state total from the 15 per cent of 1960 to possibly 26 per cent in 1980. At the same time, the Rogers-Cooley projections envision a slight decline in the relative position of South Central Alaska, Anchorage's area. From possessing 44 per cent of Alaska's 1960 population, it would have only 40 per cent by 1980. These statistics argue for some check in the runaway development of South Central Alaska versus that of the Panhandle.

The salient question, however, is what relative degree of *urban* concentration there will be within each of these two sections of Alaska in 1980. Barring a natural catastrophe, Anchorage would seem destined to become even more of a concentration point for Alaska's population, power and wealth. Whether the cities of the Panhandle will be able to attract enough of their section's population increase to provide them with some of the advantages of size now enjoyed by Anchorage is less certain. Their geographical situation—they occupy a narrow littoral between mountains and the sea—would seem likely to put limits on their physical expansion, at the very least. But for all of that, the Battle of the Cities is certain to continue. So is an expansion and consolidation of the anti-Anchorage coalition. It is worth remembering that small as were the city-states of ancient Greece in comparison with mighty Athens—the biggest of them being less than a sixth Athens' size—they successfully preserved their own identities. Even when they banded together into a league for mutual defense against Persia at Athens' urging, the resulting "Athenian Empire" never really coalesced into an actual kingdom or empire. Each city-state retained its own government and a degree of independence that made its citizens act like foreigners to the rest. Greece's geography—it is a land cut up into islands and valleys by mountains and the sea, much like Alaska—made it impossible for one city to keep another in thrall for very long.

Woodsman Ken Clark, a trapper by trade, also presides over the profitable hunting lodge and cabins that he has hewn from the wilderness with his own hands. His ingeniously decorated lodge attracts hunters from all over the nation.

A refuge for individualists

For most of its residents, Alaska is merely a way station on the road to riches. After a spell of drawing the high wages that skilled personnel command there, they retreat to the relative comforts of the Lower 48 to enjoy—or invest —their gains. But for some, Alaska's inhospitable climate and isolation are made to order. Dynamite would not blast them loose. For in the 49th state, a man can enjoy the exhilaration of challenging nature at its meanest while delighting in a primeval landscape as yet untrammeled by tourists and unsullied by billboards, trailer camps and other adjuncts of civilization. Given the state's small population those who succeed there and remain—like Ken Clark *(above)*—soon stand out. Such contented Alaskans are points of stability around which a still-forming and highly individualistic society is taking shape.

Photographed by Lee Friedlander

Prospectors

The Englehorn brothers, standing in front of their cabin on Cache Creek, have been prospecting for Alaskan gold since the early 1920s. Theirs is a lonely and difficult life, for the nearest hamlet, Talkeetna, is 50 miles away and with each advancing year their dream of really striking it rich grows ever dimmer. But their needs are simple and the freedom of being their own bosses helps sustain the brothers as they pan through the mud for precious gold dust. What they collect goes first into a pickle jar and then into Anchorage for appraisal, and while they no longer think in terms of millions, the Englehorns still hope to find a vein that will fill their glass jar a little faster.

Big-game guide

In his snug house in Kotzebue, above the Arctic Circle, Nelson Walker talks animatedly about hunting. Walker—who settled in Alaska after World War II, married an Eskimo girl and now has eight children—does his guiding by small plane. "I like hunting wild sheep and caribou," he says. "Polar bear are okay, but it takes two and a half hours' flying time just to reach them. When we track one from the air we know what we've got before we find him. A big, heavy bear will leave tracks in the snow you can see from four hundred feet up." Recently, Walker tracked down the largest polar bear ever taken. Eleven feet long and 1,400 pounds, its pelt dwarfed even the enormous trophy tacked on Walker's wall *(below)*.

Village magistrate

When first elected magistrate in 1960, Sadie Neakok *(left)* held court in her kitchen because Barrow, Alaska's most northerly community, had no courthouse. It still has none, but today Mrs. Neakok presides in a room in the firehouse. The couple before her at the right, involved in a family quarrel, got off with an hour-long lecture. Mrs. Neakok is the daughter of Barrow's first white settler, Charles Brower, who arrived in 1884, married and started a trading post so profitable that he became known as King of the Arctic. Mrs. Neakok was born in Barrow and knows most of its 2,000 inhabitants by name. In a muddy street *(below)* she stops to chat with two residents. As a young woman she taught school and did welfare work —while raising 12 children of her own. Of her present duties she says, "Maybe I should be more strict, but these are my people, and I guess I'm still a welfare worker at heart."

Bush pilot

Jim Magoffin and his wife, Dottie, race an outboard across their private lake, 110 miles northeast of Fairbanks. In 1946 they arrived in Alaska with one two-seater plane and founded Interior Airways, Inc. They had come to the right place at the right time with the right idea. For in Alaska, where the distances are great and the roads few and primitive, aircraft are essential for travel. The Magoffins now own 23 planes, serving most of the state. They live on a 167-acre ranch near Fairbanks. "We lived in town for nineteen years," says Magoffin, "but the traffic got too heavy so we moved to the country." When even their country place seems too close to civilization, they load a dozen friends into a plane and fly up to the lake to hunt and fish.

Riverboat captain

Captain Jim Binkley handles a mooring line as his 90-foot tour boat *Discovery* docks near Fairbanks. A true native son of Alaska, Binkley has held a riverboat pilot's license since he was 18. He grew up in Alaska at a time when everything moved by water and the Alaskan river valleys echoed to the blasts of steamboat whistles. Today, *Discovery* is the state's last stern-wheeler. For the tourists who ride its deck, the boat is a reminder of a lustier age, and Captain Binkley's running commentary heightens the illusion. Once a homesteader on shore, angered by the boat's piercing whistle, fired a shotgun across its bow. So skillfully did Binkley weave the incident into his talk that his passengers thought it part of the show.

Arctic ecologist

Professor John Teal casts a benevolent smile over the massive heads of two of his 41 domesticated musk oxen at the Institute of Northern Agricultural Research near Fairbanks. Musk oxen, shaggy relations of the sheep and goat, long ago roamed the Arctic tundra in vast herds, but centuries of unrestricted hunting brought them to the edge of extinction before conservation laws were passed. A man with a mission, Teal envisions re-creating these herds, which he believes can form the basis of a new industry and help bolster the fragile Arctic economy. Though the musk ox is valuable for its meat, its incredibly fine underwool, called qiviut, is what holds the greatest promise for profit. More precious than cashmere, it brings $50 a pound. It is Professor Teal's ambition to establish a string of stations where Eskimos can be taught not only how to capture, herd and breed the musk ox but also how to spin and weave its wool.

Official greeter

In clothes that bespeak an antique gentility, Mrs. Eva McGown sits in her Fairbanks office, a good Samaritan to hundreds of newcomers. With a kind smile and a touch of Irish humor, she goes to work, finding a room for the homeless, a job for the jobless. Mrs. McGown was a young bride when she arrived in Alaska from Ireland in 1914. Spurred by memories of her own difficult adjustment, she decided to smooth the road for others. Since 1963 she has been the official hostess for the state, but she still recalls how she felt during her early days in the Far North. "If anyone had told me," she says, "that I would spend more than fifty years enjoying Alaska, I would have told him to go boil his head."

White Indian

Dressed in the robes of the once-ferocious Chilkat Indians, Carl Heinmiller leads a spirited tribal dance. When Heinmiller settled in Alaska's Panhandle in the 1940s, he found himself among Indians whose culture had been all but destroyed through contact with the white man. Primitive arts happened to be his hobby, and almost singlehandedly he revived the natives' interest in their own heritage. This eventually led to the founding of Alaskan Indian Arts, Inc., a nonprofit corporation that manages the Chilkat Dancers, who have performed in many parts of the world. Now, under Heinmiller's urging, a new generation of Chilkats is passionately pursuing the arts and crafts of a colorful past.

4

A New Kind
of "Empire"

When explorer Vilhjalmur Stefansson's provocative book *The Northward Course of Empire* first appeared back in 1922, the most perplexing question about Alaska—what the future held for the Great Land—seemed to have been answered once and for all: Alaska would inevitably undergo an economic and cultural flowering such as had occurred long ago in the sun-kissed lands bordering the Mediterranean Sea.

Stefansson based this rather astonishing prediction on the theory that through the ages mankind had been building cities and civilizations in colder and colder localities. Ancient Sumeria, which had a mean annual temperature of 76 degrees according to Stefansson's calculations, had been followed by Phoenicia (70 degrees) and Phoenicia by Rome (65 degrees), while among modern cities, Berlin's average temperature was 49 degrees, Chicago's 47 and Moscow's 39. This northward drift was both clear and irreversible, and it would soon lead man to populate the great northern land masses—Alaska, Canada, Greenland, the upper reaches of

A passenger vessel sails through Alaska's "Inside Passage," a route that snakes between the many islands of the Panhandle. This area's cities, located on islands or the narrow coastal plain, cannot be linked by roads and must be reached by ship or airplane.

Scandinavia, the far-northern areas of European Russia, Siberia—and convert the sea they bordered, the Arctic Ocean, into a new Mediterranean.

It did not matter that these lands seemed forbiddingly cold. In their northerly progress, men had always tended to view the area immediately to the north as uninhabitable—until they had moved into it. Stefansson cited the Canadian province of Manitoba, established in an area once declared uninhabitable by a commission of experts. Furthermore, the airplane would make it easy to cross the once impassable Arctic Ocean, and transpolar air routes would provide the shortest connecting links between the established centers of world population. Therefore Alaska and the rest of the northland would soon come into their own, the general northward thrust ending only when, after the fashion of the East running upon the West in an earlier meeting of civilizations, North met North at the Pole.

Unhappily for Alaska, time has proved Stefansson a better explorer than a prophet. To be sure, the coming of jet flights over the North Pole has been cited as proof of his prescience, although the total transpolar air traffic by 1968 was only a fraction of that flying on other intercontinental routes. And some have said that the population growth in Russia's northern areas substantiates Stefansson's thesis. Since the Soviet need for raw materials and additional farmland prompted them to develop their northlands, five cities above the 60th parallel have grown to possess more than 100,000 people each. On the other hand, Canada has done little to develop its huge Northwest Territories—a mere 29,000 people live there—and it is becoming increasingly plain that, as far as the U.S. and Alaska are concerned, a number of new factors have combined to neutralize any Northward Course of Empire.

Russia's changing policies in Siberia throw new light on a few of these factors and on what may reasonably be expected to happen in Alaska in the future. The Soviets have recently abandoned their drive to settle a large population in Siberia—a holdover from the 19th Century military doctrine that the only way to hold land was to fill it up with people—for that has proved too costly and inefficient. The Russians' object is no longer to colonize on a broad base, but rather to concentrate population in key centers. As a 1966 international conference on the "Middle North" revealed, some of these centers will be permanent while others are expected to be temporary, intended to last only until the raw materials being exploited nearby are exhausted. But all of them will be essentially operational bases from which the resources of the surrounding terrain can be developed, sparing the workers the hardship of actually going out to live in the surrounding wilderness.

Alaska has been moving tentatively in this direction for some time. Oil crews, trappers and many commercial fishermen now fly out of central cities for several weeks of work and then fly back again, much as the suitcase farmers of the U.S. South live in town and drive out to their fields of a morning. Improvements in transportation and communication facilities have made it increasingly unnecessary for people to stick it out in remote, isolated communities: Alaska's Arctic already has radio relay stations and outposts containing scientific equipment that require not residents but circuit riders who drop in at intervals to check up on things. Moreover, the growing native population has now outstripped the food supply in Alaska's wilderness areas; as want sharpens, necessity can be expected to force many natives off the land and into the cities or larger villages.

Thus the likelihood is strong that Alaska will not follow the classic colonization pattern of the American West. No waves of people will roll out from the towns to establish permanent settlements in the hinterland, with these in turn becoming the bases for further outward thrusts until the frontier has been swallowed up by towns and farms. Alaska seems destined to go in the opposite direction. Its cities can be expected to keep pulling people in from the wilderness until the state becomes a handful of urban centers exploiting an essentially empty ocean of land. Such people as do appear upon the land will do so transitorily, like ships moving across the sea. They will function as task forces, going out to do a specific job and, when it is done, returning to their city-base—or to the Lower 48. Future Alaskans appear likely to reject any permanent settlement on the frontier in favor of "garrison life" in a large town or city with its amenities and air-age mobility.

Another factor certain to impede the Northward Course of Empire in the way that Stefansson foresaw it is something that was not apparent when he was working out his formulation. The main stream of American migration is not toward the North, but away from it. The trend, however it may fluctuate from one year to the next depending on regional circumstances, is unmistakably a movement into the South and West at the expense of the Northeast and the Great Plains. Except for the metropolitan areas, the whole northern tier of states is losing population while Florida, Arizona and Southern California are gaining substantially. By the same token, northern Canadians are quitting rural areas for the metropolitan centers in the southern sections of their country.

If the pull of a warm climate and the pleasures of coastal living were unaccompanied by challenging economic activity, then Alaska would stand a better chance of luring people north to exploit its natural resources. But Americans who "follow the sun" find that the warm areas offer the same challenges and the same competitive incentives that typify the nation's most advanced states. The difference is that the residents do not have to contend with a harsh climate while meeting them. Accordingly, it seems safe to hazard that the population explosion in the Lower 48 will do little spilling over into Alaska. William A. Spurr, Professor of Business Statistics at Stanford's Graduate School of Business, would go further than that. "There is more likely to be a net out-migration from Alaska," he wrote in a 1965 forecast of the state's growth in industry and population, "than an in-migration during the next 20 years, even with a continuing high level of government expenditures." The Census Bureau's own projections for the Alaskan population in 1985—432,000 people—hardly suggested a teeming northland when they were first made in

1965. The following year the bureau decided even that total was too optimistic and cut it to 396,000.

But if Alaska seems unlikely to turn into an "empire" in the foreseeable future, what is its probable course of evolution? That depends first and foremost on government policy. New concepts in military strategy and new weapons can alter defense outlays for Alaska almost overnight, as they have in the past. But more important is the whole U.S. attitude toward Alaska. The nation clearly does not want to follow the Russian pattern of pouring money into its far-northern areas in an effort to become self-sufficient in all vital raw materials. Instead, the U.S. has long been embarked on an antithetical program of promoting trade with other nations by importing raw materials from them. The effect of this on Alaska, as Chairman Joseph H. FitzGerald of the Federal Field Committee for Development Planning in Alaska views it, is pervasive: "The state, being in a resource development stage, is singularly dependent on national policy to see whether something is going to be developed here." The exploitation of Alaskan copper, for example, is now considered to be in the national interest—the metal was in short supply in 1965-1966 —so exploratory mining is being done by Kennecott Copper at Bornite near the Kobuk River. At the same time, Washington has made it very clear that the aim of government policy is not to make the U.S. self-sufficient in copper, for that would conflict with another policy: to buy the metal from a friendly South American nation, Chile.

There is also the question of whether Alaska will continue to benefit from large federal expenditures for civil as well as for military purposes. In the past, Alaska has been the beneficiary of the largest per capita outlays of public money of any state in the nation. Economists have pointed out that in 1960 seven eighths of the workers in Alaska's labor force owed their employment directly or indirectly to public expenditures (federal, state or municipal); only one eighth were supported by the private sector in such activities as the forest-products industry, oil and gas production, commercial fishing and mining. The trouble is, from an Alaskan point of view, that Congress has shown an increasing reluctance to honor the state's mounting demands on the federal treasury. After the substantial outpouring of government money to speed recovery from the disastrous earthquake of 1964, the feeling on Capitol Hill was that this marked the end of special consideration for Alaska for some time to come. Yet Alaska is going to need special consideration, and plenty of it.

In the first place, if the state is ever to exploit its mineral wealth, that wealth must be pinpointed. A new method of surveying the mineral resources of the state by satellite with remote-sensing equipment obviously requires federal help to be brought to fruition. Satellite charting, moreover, would have to be followed by a more selective cataloguing of Alaska's all-important minerals—less than 1 per cent of the state's land mass has been adequately explored for them—and this, in turn, would require even more massive government outlays. Once the minerals are discovered, federal subsidies or inducements will be needed to attain a meaningful level of exploitation. (Ottawa's assistance has already had exemplary results on mining development in the wilderness areas of Canada.) Washington will also have to help Alaska overcome its unique geographical problems with unique financial support if the state is to have anything more than a totally inadequate road system. Merely meeting the requirements of the U.S. highway program (the state must match federal outlays with funds of its own) has left Alaska with virtually no money for building other essential roads. All this argues for Washington's rejection of grandiose projects like Rampart Dam—a $2 billion to $2.5 billion hydroelectric installation that has been touted for the Yukon River—in favor of expanding various kinds of federal assistance that will make Alaska more self-supporting.

The state's predictably slow transition from a military-governmental economy to one based on natural-resource exploitation may be considerably accelerated, however, depending on the future impact of two new influences. The first of these is the oil industry.

The discovery of oil on the Kenai Peninsula south of Anchorage on January 19, 1957, has been set down by the University of Alaska's *Monthly Review* as "perhaps the most important date in all of Alaska's colorful history." Within five years of the time the Richfield Oil Company brought in that first significant well, natural-gas and petroleum production accounted for 77 per cent of the money coming in annually from the sale of Alaska's major minerals. At $33.5 million, it was worth nearly seven million dollars more than the gold mined during Alaska's best year (1940) for that historic metal. Within a decade of Richfield's first big commercial well, Alaska possessed five oil fields— four of them giants with reserves in excess of 100 million barrels. Three major gas fields had been found. Oil production stood at 40,000 barrels per day in 1966 and was expected to reach anywhere from 100,000 to 400,000 barrels a day by 1971. Then, in July 1968, came an even more significant discovery as a mammoth oil field with an estimated yield of five to 10 billion barrels was opened up at Prudhoe Bay on the Arctic Slope—potentially the richest field in North America.

To date the discoveries have brought more promise than profit to the companies involved. Besides the high cost of doing any sort of business in Alaska, there were many other obstacles: Cook Inlet's 30-foot tides, severe weather conditions on the Arctic Slope (where winter temperatures hover endlessly around 30° to 40° below zero), treacherous terrain over which roads must be built, and vociferous opposition from conservationists objecting to the proposed construction of an 800-mile pipeline from the Arctic Slope all the way across the state to the warm-water port of Valdez, near Anchorage.

But even if the oil companies are still in the red, there is little doubt about their staying in Alaska. Even before the Prudhoe Bay strike, *The Oil and Gas Journal*, the industry's leading publication, had predicted that Alaska would soon rank with Texas and Louisiana as a top oil producer; the Arctic Slope discovery put it indisputably in the lead. All during the late 1960s prospecting crews were busy in Bristol Bay and the Gulf of Alaska, probing new areas of Alaska's coastline for future drilling sites. New pipelines were being laid at Cook Inlet and elsewhere. A boom was already under way as men and materials began moving to the site. Hotels at Fairbanks, the major transit point, were jammed, property values were soaring and plans were being made to expand and modernize the city.

As for the importance of the oil industry to the future of Alaska, Juneau jubilantly predicted that by 1970 the state's income simply from production taxes in the Cook Inlet area would amount to $30 million a year, and this would be substantially increased by leases and rentals there and elsewhere.

The second important new influence on Alaska's future is, surprisingly enough, Japan. Many Alaskans believe their state's economy in the years ahead will be more closely connected to the Western Pacific and the Japanese than to the Lower 48. The sea distance between Anchorage and Yokohama, 3,900 miles, is 1,300 miles shorter than the route from San Francisco to Yokohama. Moreover, as the westward-looking Alaskans point out, Japan —which economists predict will shortly become the world's fourth-largest industrial power—will be in great and increasing need of raw materials if that nation is to approximate its current rate of economic growth. Roughly 90 per cent of the raw materials needed by Japan's industrial machine must be imported, but eight are of particular urgency: petroleum and related products, wood pulp and lumber, iron ore, cotton, wool, wheat, nonferrous metals and nonferrous ores. Of these, the Alaskans consider their state a source of supply for all but cotton and wheat. What is more important, the Japanese are coming to agree with them.

A Japanese company, Alaska Lumber and Pulp, built a $66 million installation at Sitka in 1958. By 1966 the mill's annual output—$25 million in wood products—was accounting for more than two thirds of Alaska's exports to foreign nations. Expansion of Japanese investment in Alaskan forest products seems assured; by 1975 Japan's total imports of wood chips, the raw material for pulp, are expected to soar from the 182 million board feet of 1965 to 4.6 billion. The Japanese are also involved in the Alaskan fishing industry. Pacific Alaska Fisheries, Incorporated, a three-million-dollar joint venture with an American firm, operates two salmon canneries in western Alaska. Another joint venture was inaugurated in November 1966, the Japanese and Americans investing some two million dollars in the Orca-Pacific Packing Company's fish cannery near Cordova.

In addition to wood and fish, Alaska's coal and iron are of interest to the Japanese despite certain drawbacks. The state's present coal fields do not contain the sort of bituminous usually employed in making coke for steel production; thus Australia and the Lower 48 have remained Japan's major sources of supply. But since Japan has no coal reserves, the Alaskan fields may be exploited in the future. As for Alaska's abundant iron ore, it is both low in grade (requiring concentration) and high in titanium (adding to the cost of processing). Nevertheless, Japanese steelmakers have followed the exploration of deposits near Haines and Juneau with recent investigations of iron-ore bodies on Cook Inlet's west shore. It has remained for oil and gas, however, to provide an almost overnight enlargement of Japanese investment in Alaska.

Japan possesses almost no petroleum or natural-gas reserves and is virtually dependent on imports for its supply of other fuels as well. By 1985 imports will have to make up almost 90 per cent of Japan's energy requirements. Small wonder that with the discovery of oil in the Cook Inlet area, Japanese interest in Alaska became galvanic. The Tokyo Gas Company and the Tokyo Electric Power Company contracted to buy some $30 million worth of liquefied methane gas per year over a period of 15 years. The gas, to be liquefied in an estimated $50 million plant built by Phillips Petroleum for that purpose, will be shipped to Yokohama in the Marathon Oil Company's specially designed refrigerated tankers. An additional use of Alaskan gas will be for the manufacture of urea and ammonia. In 1966 the Japan Gas-Chemical Company announced plans for a joint venture with a subsidiary of Union Oil—construction of a 365,000-ton-per-year urea plant (the biggest in the world) and a 530,000-ton ammonia plant, a giant by any standards. This was followed by the creation of the $44 million Alaska Petroleum Development Company, Limited, backed by Japan's biggest banks and manufacturing companies, to carry on exploration and exploitation in the 49th state. As an American oilman put it, "The Orient is the great future petroleum market for Alaska." Then he added, "The Japanese are sharp businessmen; they'll want a piece of the action."

Undoubtedly they will, but how much of a piece depends on the attitudes of both parties, the Alaskans and the Japanese. For the latter, Alaska has the advantages of political stability and, of course, abundant raw materials. Its disadvantages range from the sparsity of roads, harbors, low-cost power and fresh water to the simple lack of information on geologic structure, land titles and mineral claims. But the prime limiting factor is one that bedevils the Japanese as it has perplexed the oilmen and indeed every other investor in Alaska: costs. "High costs," declared Dr. Arlon R. Tussing, Professor of Economics at the University of Alaska, "are a reflection of the remoteness of much of Alaska, of the winter cold and of permafrost, of managerial inefficiency, and above all of the small size and fragmentation of Alaska's markets. The growth of Alaska's resource exports is assured, and Japan will undoubtedly be a major market, but the speed of this growth depends on Alaska's success in coping with high prices and high costs generally."

For the Alaskans' part, many of them remember too well the strangle hold Seattle once had on the territorial economy to look with perfect equanimity on a new set of absentee owners, and foreigners to boot. There is, moreover, the unsettling fact that the Japanese companies in Alaska are essentially chosen instruments of the Japanese government; the companies' commercial interests, and certainly the interests of Alaska, are subordinate to policy established in Tokyo.

The Alaskans have already had dramatic proof that the Japanese government has a decisive say-so in Japanese commercial matters. Not long ago Alaskan state officials conducted some preliminary negotiations with a Japanese firm that wanted to establish a pulp and lumber business in southeastern Alaska, only to have the Japanese government kill the deal. The prospective investor was simply warned off on grounds that the area had been reserved for the initial Japanese enterprise, Alaska Lumber and Pulp. Intervention along the same lines occurred in oil. While a number of Japanese companies received their government's authorization to get into the Cook Inlet oil play, only one—Japan Gas-Chemical—was permitted to join Union Oil in making ammonia and urea from the natural gas. The implications for price control and monopoly in the future are obvious, given a higher level of Japanese economic penetration.

Another cause for worry is Japanese business practice. In Japan, if the conditions under which a contract is signed should change, then a businessman feels no hesitation about renegotiating or even canceling it, legal stipulations notwithstanding. A shiver of apprehension ran through Alaska's business community in 1967, for example, when word was received that some Japanese financiers had declared their contract with the Tokyo Hilton null and void and had seized the hotel. Such considerations, however, should not be allowed to obscure Alaska's manifest advantage in trading with Japan: it opens a golden door leading to independence from federal handouts.

Whether the Japanese are increasingly engaged there or not, it seems clear that Alaska will inevitably become even more of a big-company state than it is today. The inflation from which it suffers is an open invitation to a take-over by giants. These alone can absorb the high costs of an Alaskan operation, spreading initial losses over divisions of the firm in the Lower 48 until the Alaskan venture gets in the black. Conversely, where Alaska has enough people, as in Anchorage and Fairbanks, the prevailing high price level is an 18-carat opportunity for the giant chain stores. J. C. Penney, for one, was able to come in, undercut the prices of the local merchants enough to get a good chunk of their business and still turn in what is undoubtedly the best profit showing in the entire chain.

Among the other opportunities Alaska offers the enterprising is one that has been all too frequently overlooked—the riches of the ocean. It would not be surprising 20 years from now to find that Alaskan activities at sea have achieved parity with those on land. After all, the sea is scarcely any more hostile an environment than much of the state's terrain, and the technology for getting at the ocean's wealth of minerals is at hand. The Martin

Dredging company, although small, has already been digging in the surf off Nome on the correct assumption that the river that brought the gold down to the famous Gold Rush beaches carried some of it out to sea. Reynolds Metals also holds options on extensive underwater acreage off Nome and has asked for federal cooperation in its plans to mine the ocean floor at depths of up to 300 feet.

Other technological developments promise help in overcoming some of the special challenges Alaska offers. Large sections of the state's traditionally impassable terrain are now on the way to being conquered by Hovercraft, the British-invented vehicles that ride on a cushion of air. Though uneconomic for cargo carrying at present—only small passenger versions now operate in Cook Inlet—they are undergoing a rapid evolution in both speed and carrying capacity. In Alaska, where the roads and railroads needed for development are inordinately difficult and costly to build, Hovercraft would be a giant stride indeed. To them, tundra, water, ice and tidal flats are all readily traversable.

Someday technology may even tackle Alaska's greatest liability, cold, on a grand scale. In recent years a Russian scientist tentatively advanced a plan for damming the Bering Strait where Siberia and Alaska are only 46 miles apart, and then gradually pumping the Arctic Ocean's cold surface water into the Pacific so that the underlying warmer waters would release what heat they hold throughout the Arctic, moderating the climate. A more immediate possibility is that ways will be found to turn the cold of Alaskan winters into an asset. Kenneth M. Rae, Vice President for Research and Advanced Study at the University of Alaska, along with other scientists there, is excited about the possibilities of using Alaskan permafrost to freeze roads. Cold might also be used to make docks of ice, freeze mine pillars to insure their stability, purify sea water by freezing and in the process extract such minerals as magnesium from it.

Whether or not Alaskan cities will ever be covered by huge plastic domes—establishing a so-called controlled microclimate—is a moot question. The Russians have plans to insulate some of their far-northern towns. But the feeling at the University of Alaska is against isolating people from their environment, against such a capitulation to nature. The Alaskan of the future, in their book, will do better trying to turn the environment to good account. And what will that typical Alaskan be like 20 years down the road?

He will be younger. If the present trend continues, by 1977 more than half of all Alaskans will be under 18. He will also be smarter. The state's urgent need is for highly trained specialists, not common labor. He will be more mobile. The 95 per cent turnover of workers in some Russian mines is an indication of the difficulty, even in an authoritarian economy, of getting people to stay put in the Far North. He will probably be colder. Data collected by climatologists on Mendenhall Glacier near Juneau indicate that the North American continent is at the end of a 45-year warm spell; by 1975 Alaska may be more frigid still as the entire northern part of the U.S. experiences a return to deep snows and lower temperatures.

Change will shake him as it shakes present-day Alaskans. He will have to inure himself to the pronounced seasonal swings of some of Alaska's major industries—fishing and timbering, for example—which are also subject to unpredictable fluctuations from year to year. (The 1967 salmon catch, for example, was a disaster: the worst since 1899.) He will also have to accept the fact that nature's hostility and high costs will continue to prevent the orderly exploitation of the state's natural resources. It will always go by fits and starts. Most of the development will be done by giant companies since small ones will not have the resources to survive the high costs involved. And whether the giants are coming or going, their movement is bound to perpetuate change as a way of life in Alaska.

Overall, the Alaskan of the future will likely find upon arrival in the 49th state that he is just as unsympathetic to the "Stefansson Syndrome," a tendency to overstress the importance of the Far North, as to the animalism of Jack London's Alaska, the dog-eat-dog viewpoint that "on the savage frozen frontier the only warmth, food, and life existing outside one creature was another living thing." Yet he will hardly have unpacked before he is bound to feel caught up in these and other manifestations of the mystique of the North, for the Last Frontier will still be there. In contrast to the Winning of the West, there will be no sweeping victory over the wilderness of Alaska, no comparable degree of settlement. Geography, weather, climate, economics and human inclination will see to that. Rather the difference between the Alaska of today and the Alaska of the future is that the latter will increasingly become the beneficiary of the very latest technology the 20th Century has to offer. It will remain a frontier, but one with the fullest recourse to modern science—and a special appeal for all those in need of a faster route to the top, a refreshing respite from the clangor below or a chance to feel the authentic touch of the primeval.

Gingerly lifting a king crab from a storage tank, a crewman unloads his valuable cargo at Kodiak Island. Increasing demand for this shellfish has made king crab processing the fastest-growing sector of the entire U.S. fishing industry.

Thawing out Alaska's assets

When President Andrew Johnson and Secretary of State William Seward paid Russia $7.2 million for Alaska in 1867, many Americans were outraged. "Seward's icebox," "Johnson's polar bear garden" and "a dreary waste of glaciers, icebergs . . . and walruses" were just a few of the milder comments that greeted the purchase. Yet barely a century later the exploitation of Alaska's natural resources is grossing more than 40 times the original investment each year. From the waters of the Pacific, fishing fleets are harvesting a wealth of seafood. Along the southern coast, lumbermen are logging thick stands of timber and workers are plumbing the offshore depths for oil. While Alaska's rigorous climate and poor roads hamper development, great rewards may await those who can conquer this young and forbidding land.

Fisheries: tapping the ocean's wealth

For a few months every year the salmon boat above waits offshore in the waters near Juneau, casting its nets for Alaska's biggest money-making crop: salmon. After a day at sea, salmon boats return to port *(right)*, and if luck has been with them, they are bulging with fish. Commercial fishing is Alaska's most profitable industry; in 1966 fishery products were worth more than $195 million, and salmon accounted for two thirds of the bonanza. But despite this total, salmon fishing has been generally in decline. Increased competition from foreign fleets and decreased consumer demand have cut into profits. The seasonal nature of the work has also played a role in driving many boatowners into other branches of the industry. As a result more and more fishermen are turning to the king crab for their livelihood. The crabs can be caught during most of the year, and the demand for their succulent meat is skyrocketing. In 1960 king crab fisheries brought in only 5 per cent of the industry's income; by 1966 this had gone up to 20 per cent.

Timber:
a growing investment

Every summer Silver Bay in Alaska's Panhandle becomes a watery warehouse crowded with booms of huge logs *(right)*. Such timber, from millions of acres of virgin forest, constitutes Alaska's second most valuable product; the state's forest products were worth $68 million in 1966. Although a third of Alaska is woodland, the best stands are along the southern coast. These forests are close to the bays where processing plants, like the Japanese-owned Alaska Lumber and Pulp Company's Sitka mill *(above)*, can work the raw timber into pulp for immediate export. In recent years the Japanese have been investing heavily in Alaskan timber. The relatively low cost of shipping to the Orient from the Pacific Coast, combined with Japan's need for lumber and pulp, makes Alaska a logical recipient of Japanese capital. By 1966 shipments of forest products to Japan accounted for about three quarters of the value of Alaska's total foreign exports.

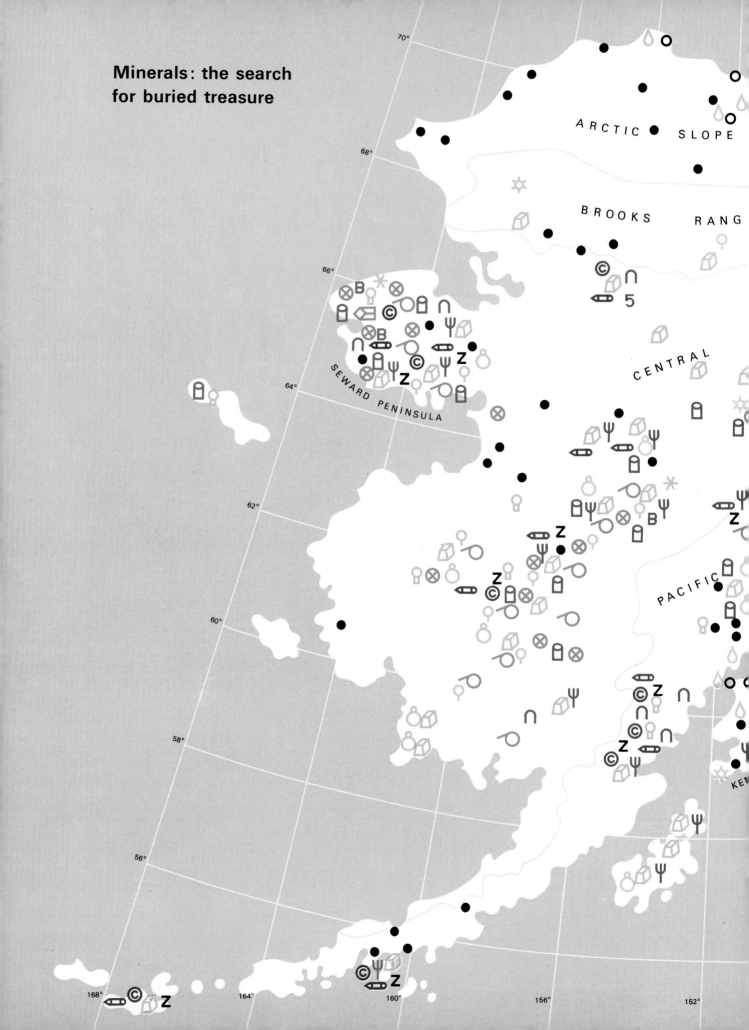

Minerals: the search for buried treasure

Minerals in abundance constitute one of Alaska's most important but least exploited resources. In 1966 fewer than 10 minerals (not counting oil and natural gas) accounted for the bulk of the state's mining income of some $35 million. There are still at least two dozen other types of minerals in unknown quantities just waiting to be dug out. This map shows the location of the state's known deposits. The areas richest in these mineral deposits are the Panhandle, the Pacific Mountain Area, the Kenai and Seward Peninsulas, and the Central Plateau.

Of all Alaska's underground resources, oil and natural gas are likely to be the most valuable in the future. But the leading money-makers today among the solid minerals are sand and gravel; because they are common throughout the state, they are not shown here as specific deposits. Next in importance is coal. The six million dollars' worth mined in 1966 was all used within the state, much of it going to heat Alaska's large military bases. Since the fabled gold strikes of the early 1900s, more than three quarters of a billion dollars in gold has been mined in Alaska. In recent years, however, rising production costs have made this a less profitable business, and the gold output in 1966 was the lowest since 1886. Mercury, platinum, copper, silver, uranium and tungsten all contribute to Alaska's mineral output, though to a much lesser degree.

The search for new mineral deposits continues, but successful exploration and development depend, in large measure, upon the availability of prospectors willing to risk large sums of capital and brave a forbidding climate.

PLATEAU

MOUNTAIN

AREA

PENINSULA

PANHANDLE

| 0 | 50 | 100 | 150 | 200 | 250 |

Miles

Symbol	Mineral	Symbol	Mineral	Symbol	Mineral
◊	GAS	🔲	LEAD	∩	IRON
O	OIL	Z	ZINC	✵	CHROMITE
●	COAL	目	TIN	5	NICKEL
GOLD		⊗	TUNGSTEN	⊙	COBALT
Ψ	SILVER	◁	BERYLLIUM	◠	MERCURY
©	COPPER	¤	MOLYBDENUM	⍦	ANTIMONY
8	PLATINUM	✳	URANIUM	B	BISMUTH

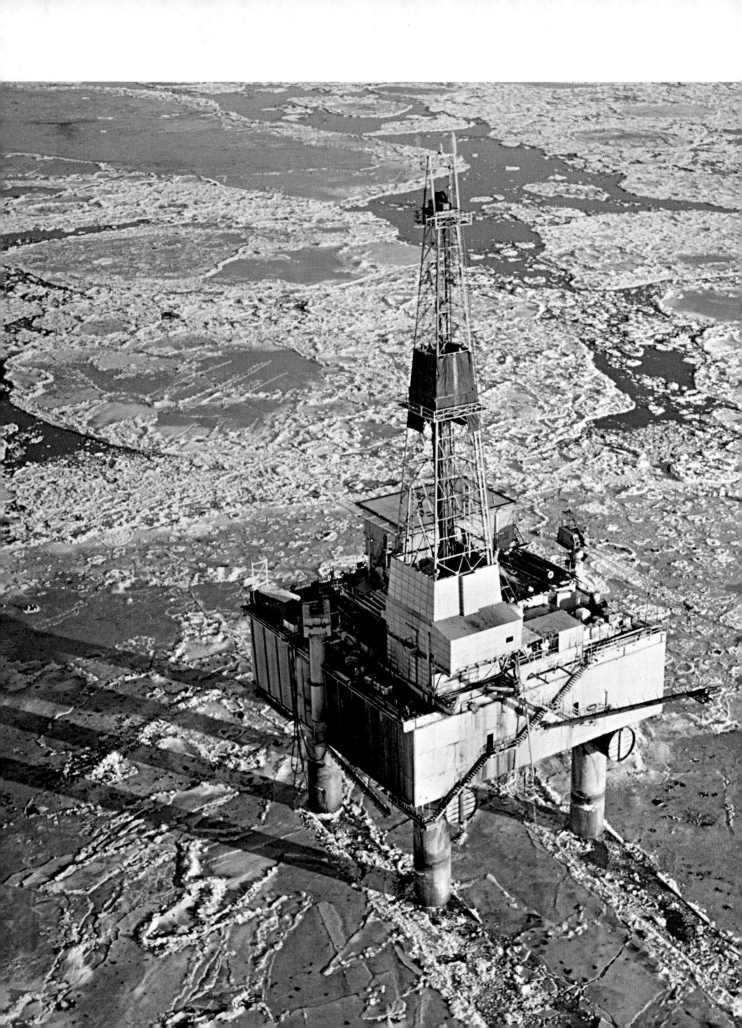

Petroleum: a bright future in black gold

More than 60 years ago prospectors dreaming of gold poured into Alaska in search of fortune. Today the rush is on again, but this time the prize is black gold—petroleum. The new prospectors are not grizzled miners with small grubstakes, but highly trained scientists and technicians employed by large corporations.

In the decade since the first commercially successful oil discovery was made on the Kenai Peninsula, some 30 oil companies have invested more than $600 million in exploration and development. The hazards and expenses they face are greater than those found by oilmen in most parts of the world. Four of the oil fields currently being worked lie under the icy waters of Cook Inlet, not far from the original 1957 strike. Offshore platforms, like the one at left operated by Shell Oil, must withstand 30-foot tides, strong currents and a battering by massive chunks of ice. High construction and labor costs add to the difficulties. Each of the four new platforms raised in 1966 cost about $10 million to build, and operating expenses per platform run to approximately $18,000 per day. But the oil companies expect their huge investments to pay handsome rewards. The discovery of a major new oil field in 1968 at Prudhoe Bay on Alaska's Arctic Slope intensified the zeal of the companies—though they realized that even greater expenses and difficulties would be involved in that remote area.

As often happens, the discovery of oil was followed by the tapping of natural-gas accumulations. Alaska's first major natural-gas field was discovered in 1959 in the Kenai area. By 1967 thirteen other fields—all but one in the same region—had been located. Even now technicians are probing for new oil and gas deposits in areas where few men have ever trod. The search will take decades, for there are still 100 million acres of potentially rich oil and gas lands to be explored, lands that hold out the promise of an economic boom of unlimited proportions.

5

HAWAII

Two Faces of Another Frontier

The designation of Hawaii as one of America's two Frontier States may seem incongruous at first glance, particularly in a pairing off with Alaska. Unlike its northern counterpart, the island group hardly appears to be burdened by an everlasting struggle with hostile nature. Quite the contrary. The elements that thwart and beleaguer men in the Far North seem benignly transformed once they reach Hawaii's shores. However icy the grip the Bering Sea may have on the Alaskan coast, its currents have a salubrious effect on distant Hawaii, keeping ocean temperatures there 10 degrees cooler than in other tropical areas in the same latitude. The Islands' summer, averaging 78 degrees, is but a heartier elaboration of springtime. Winter, with an average of 72 degrees, is little more than a figure of speech. What snow exists is of the pictorial variety, a crystalline adornment that never descends from the lofty summits of Mauna Loa and Mauna Kea. Hawaii's population density (116 people for each of its 6,435 square miles) and its wealth (per capita yearly income amounts to $3,143, compared with $2,940 for the U.S. as a whole) do not suggest a handful of settlements holding a vast wilderness at bay, but rather the comfortable circumstances of a stable New England state—Connecticut or Massachusetts, for instance.

Even metaphorically there would seem to be an obvious inconsonance between Alaska, the self-styled "Last Frontier," and Hawaii, the place Mark Twain once described as "the loveliest fleet of islands that lies anchored in any ocean." Yet all the same Hawaii can properly be called a frontier, and in two important senses of the word: sociological and geological.

As a sociological frontier the Islands constitute an advance area of ethnic cooperation—a significant pushing back of the too-familiar barriers to racial integration and a bringing together of many races of widely divergent cultures and viewpoints into an exemplary, if imperfect, partnership. They constitute the nation's first truly multiracial state. When the occasion has demanded, the state's citizens have shown a singular capacity for breaking the back of custom and stretching experience beyond old boundaries. The people of Hawaii have not had to adjust to new situations with the speed demanded of the Pilgrim Fathers when they first came to grips with the American wilderness

Rivulets of lava flow from fissures along the crater walls of Kilauea Iki on the island of Hawaii during a 1959 eruption. For more than a month the volcano spewed out gas and lava, killing nearby trees and covering the surrounding area with smoldering ashes.

Noble Hawaiian monarchs

Kamehameha I (pronounced ka MAY ah MAY ah), the most celebrated Hawaiian king, took the throne in 1795. A shrewd and dynamic ruler, he united the Islands and put an end to Hawaii's civil wars.

During the five-year reign of Kamehameha II—shown here *(front row, left)* while visiting England—the worship of idols was outlawed. This created a religious vacuum soon filled by Christianity. The King died in 1824.

in 1620, but in a mere two thirds of a century they have experienced a far greater change in their way of life. Some of the changes worked on the status quo at various times in Hawaiian history have been of such scope as to keep the entire social order "on the frontier."

The nature of these changes may be glimpsed in seven salient facts:

• The impact of Western civilization has virtually obliterated the Islands' original native inhabitants: 300,000-strong 190 years ago, there are only some 11,000 left by official count, and many of these are probably not of pure Hawaiian ancestry. The number of pure-blooded natives may be as low as 500.

• The rapidity of the change that has come to the Islands can be measured in the fact that within the space of only 66 years Hawaii was successively an independent monarchy, ruled by native Hawaiians; a republic, established by revolution and controlled by Caucasians; a territory of the U.S., run by a white oligarchy that exercised control over Hawaii's land, economy and politics; and a state of the Union in which the old Establishment finally came tumbling down, the two-party system became an actuality, and political policy could no longer be dictated by any one ethnic group.

• Between 1852 and 1930, 400,000 laborers were

brought to Hawaii, the bulk of them Orientals who soon vastly outnumbered the Islands' Caucasians. Today the population mix is 202,000 Caucasians, 203,000 people of Japanese extraction and 38,000 of Chinese, which makes Hawaii the U.S. state with the greatest proportion of Oriental citizens.

• Astonishingly, the descendants of these largely illiterate Japanese and Chinese laborers, imported to work the white man's plantations in the 19th Century, have outstripped him educationally in the 20th: 93 per cent of the 17-year-olds of Japanese extraction were attending school in 1950, as were nearly 92 per cent of the Chinese, while the percentage of the Caucasians was barely above 70.

• These same descendants of Oriental laborers have climbed a startlingly long way up Hawaii's economic ladder: on Oahu, the state's wealthiest and most populous island, the average family income in 1961 was $7,525 for the Chinese and $6,959 for the Japanese, but only $6,066 for the Caucasians.

• Mixed marriages have become such a commonplace that a large proportion of Hawaii's citizens are descended from two or more racial strains. The surname of the state's Chief Justice, William S. Richardson, for example, testifies to his English ancestry, but he also counts Irish, Chinese

Kamehameha III, who ascended the throne in 1825, granted his subjects religious freedom. His 30-year reign was the longest in Hawaiian history.

King David Kalakaua, a scholarly, well-traveled ruler, opened free trade between Hawaii and the U.S. During his reign—from 1874 to 1891 —Hawaii enjoyed unparalleled prosperity.

Queen Liliuokalani, Hawaii's last monarch, was a gracious but stubborn woman who tried to revoke the constitution of 1887. Her regime was overthrown in 1893, giving way to a republic.

and native Hawaiians among his forebears. In the period 1912-1916, inter-ethnic crossing took place in only 12 per cent of Hawaii's marriages; in 1956-1960, such crossings had increased more than three-fold, standing at 37 per cent of the total.

• When Hawaii became a U.S. territory in 1900, three fourths of its population was rural; in 1960 more than three fourths was urban and most of this was concentrated in metropolitan Honolulu.

As these dramatic instances of change demonstrate, Hawaii is and has long been a sociological frontier. The event that precipitated this chain reaction was the discovery of the islands in 1778 by Captain James Cook, who was looking for a route back to his native England. It was the original Hawaiians' first contact with an alien civilization and was to result, within the incredibly short time of three generations, in the complete alteration of the natives' religion and their whole economic and social order—even their natural environment. A Polynesian people, they had come to Hawaii from islands near Tahiti sometime between 600 and 1000 A.D., voyaging thousands of miles across the Pacific in open canoes. They continued to sail the ocean for centuries, but these incredible voyages exacted a formidable price both physically and psychologically. Eventually the Hawaiians found

the human costs of these voyages to be insupportable. When that occurred, the Hawaiian civilization went into a state of arrest.

"All these arrested civilizations," wrote Arnold Toynbee in discussing the kindred fate of the Eskimos and other peoples, "have been immobilized in consequence of having achieved a *tour de force*. They are responses to challenges of an order of severity on the very borderline between the degree that affords stimulus to further development and the degree that entails defeat. . . . The Polynesians, for instance, ventured upon the *tour de force* of audacious ocean voyaging. Their skill was to perform these stupendous voyages in frail open canoes. Their penalty was to remain, for an unknown but undoubtedly lengthy period of time, in exact equilibrium with the Pacific—just able to cross its vast empty spaces, but never able to cross them with any margin of security or ease—until the intolerable tension found its own relief by going slack, with the result that these former peers of the Minoans and the Vikings had degenerated into incarnations of the Lotus-eaters . . . losing their grip upon the ocean and resigning themselves to being marooned, each in his own insular paradise, until the Western mariner descended upon them."

The insular paradise, in the case of the native

93

Hawaiians, was characterized by Stone Age technology—for they had never extracted the iron so abundantly present in the Islands' rocks—but by considerably more than a Stone Age manner of living. At the time of the white man's first visit, there were several kingdoms in the Islands, all with highly developed aristocracies. A hereditary nobility held undisputed sway over a hereditary proletariat. The bloodlines of the former were protected to such an extent that brother and sister marriages were a common occurrence. So sacred were individuals with the longest bloodlines that no commoner dared touch them. When taken captive in war, they could only be dispatched by someone of equally high lineage. (No one could be found to execute one legendary chief of particularly noble descent, and his captors found themselves obliged to surround him at spear length until he starved to death.) A specially trusted retainer was even put in charge of a chief's excreta, carrying it off for burial lest it fall in the hands of some rival and thereby, according to superstition, cause the chief to lose his powers.

All land belonged to the head of each Hawaiian kingdom, and the gifts of land he made to his chiefs and they in turn to the commoners could be revoked at his pleasure. A tax system exacted contributions of labor and food for the maintenance of the aristocracy. A system of *kapus* (taboos) established what might or might not be done within the society; they regulated daily life and safeguarded caste, with death the common punishment for infraction. Wars occurred frequently but seldom lasted longer than a few days and safety was assured for those lucky enough to reach universally respected sanctuaries, the so-called "Cities of Refuge." Human sacrifices were demanded in the Polynesian religion, which was based on the worship of four main gods, chief among them being Ku, the war god; the victims were mainly captives taken in battle.

Two additional characteristics of Hawaii's indigenous civilization are worthy of mention for they made subsequent contacts with the Western world particularly disruptive. First, sexual intercourse was completely uninhibited among commoners; the average host thought no more of passing his wife to a guest than of passing him the ubiquitous Hawaiian food called poi. Second, the Hawaiians had achieved a delicate balance between their civilization and nature. The Islands were quite densely populated considering the fact that only a fraction of the total area was (and is) arable, but the natives were born conservationists. They subsisted on fish, carefully cultivated patches of sweet potatoes and taro root (the basis of poi), and kept their numbers down by infanticide and abortion. Famine generally seems to have been avoided.

The initial impact of white men on Hawaii might actually have been more catastrophic than it was had they come to conquer and subjugate. They did not. Captain Cook, Captain George Vancouver and the others who followed came there mainly to water and provision their ships. Nonetheless, the consequences of the contact, especially after the Islands in the 1780s became regular ports of call in the fur trade between the Pacific Northwest and China, were disastrous. The "Chinese disease," leprosy, became endemic; the sexual hospitality of Hawaiian women and the diseased condition of ships' crews spread syphilis far and wide. Tuberculosis and smallpox took their toll along with measles, which became a lethal malady among people without natural resistance. One outbreak of measles is supposed to have sent hundreds of Hawaiians dashing wildly into the surf in a vain attempt to escape their consuming fever. Cholera or bubonic plague—history does not record which—reportedly halved the population in 1804.

Even the cattle and goats, well-meant gifts from Captains Cook, Vancouver and others, seemed to work against the Hawaiians by upsetting the balance of nature. With a *kapu* protecting the former from slaughter and agility the latter, they consumed the local plants too rapidly for natural replenishment. With the vegetative cover nibbled away, the wind took over and blew the topsoil from arid localities; Kahoolawe, smallest of the eight main islands in the Hawaiian chain, eventually became an uninhabited "island of dust."

There were other changes, some to the good, some bad, but all making for a profound alteration in the old way of life.

The introduction of firearms in 1789 made it possible for one chief, Kamehameha I, to unite most of the Hawaiian Islands into a single kingdom with himself at its head. Maui, Oahu and the island of Hawaii itself were fashioned into an economic and political entity. The remaining major islands—Kauai, Niihau, Lanai, Molokai and Kahoolawe—were eventually brought under the monarchy.

As time passed, the Hawaiians abandoned their religion, with its *kapu* system, partly as a consequence of observing that foreigners had seemed able to flout the taboos without incurring the wrath of their gods. In 1779 Captain Cook's men had torn down the fence around a *heiau* (temple) for firewood; in 1819 the Hawaiians put the *heiaus* to the torch.

The substitution of a market economy for a subsistence economy took place—with disastrous consequences. A booming trade in sandalwood, the aromatic tree prized for incense in China, had developed in the early 19th Century and was followed later by a lucrative business in provisioning whalers. With money coming in from the sale of sandalwood, the local chiefs developed a voracious appetite for foreign goods; more and more commoners were sent into the forests to cut the logs. Some were literally worked to death, while here and there the neglect of their crops produced local famines. As the chiefs embraced conspicuous consumption, the hallmark of the new rich the world over, even greater exactions were demanded; the chiefs claimed rights to everything produced by the commoners, whether from the land or the sea. The advent of the whalers was hardly less disruptive. With some 10,000 seamen descending on the Islands in a typical year, they became what one observer called "a vast brothel."

In 1820 the first missionaries arrived: seven Congregationalists from New England. Those of other sects—Catholics and Mormons—were not long in following. The missionaries very quickly filled the void left by the native Hawaiians' destruction of their own ancient religion, moved into positions of considerable power as royal counselors and opened schools. Within 12 years of the arrival of the initial group, the missionaries were holding classes for 53,000 people; within 26 years (1846) 80 per cent of Hawaii's native people could read. At the same time, the very vigor of the missionaries' attack on paganism and illiteracy hastened the decline of the old Hawaiian way of life.

The contrast between the inflexible Calvinism of the Congregationalists and the anything-goes attitude of the natives suggested to even the most sanguine of these missionaries the width of the void between the two cultures. "The rigid fundamentalist," observed Professor Stanley Porteus (*A Century of Social Thinking in Hawaii*, 1962), "imbued with the spirit of New England morality, viewed the practices accepted by Hawaiians of high rank with loathing and horror," adding wryly, "yet could not avert their eyes."

Shocked the missionaries indubitably were, but not struck dumb by what they saw. "The great body of the people are in darkness and wedded to their lusts," complained the *Missionary Herald* in 1834. "Such a complication of darkness and stupidity broods over them, and so many degrading customs and habits prevail . . . that we should at times say that pure gospel light could never prevail here. . . . Pollution cleaves to the people." Three years later the mood of the *Missionary Herald* was still one of despair: "We need not tell you that a nation like this so sunk in indolence, ignorance, and mental imbecility cannot be elevated to enterprise, to intelligence and moral greatness in a day."

But if the missionaries were despairing, the feelings of the native Hawaiians must have been desperate beyond the power of words to capture. Their feudal society had smothered individualism at almost all levels, yet now individualism was at a premium; they were ravaged by disease and unequal to the demands of a mercantile economy; the chiefs who had once looked after their general well-being were now exploiting them. By the mid-1850s the native population had dwindled to 71,000, less than a fourth the number alive at the time of Captain Cook's arrival in 1778. Many of the men shipped off to sea aboard the whalers. Many of those who remained seemed caught in an overpowering lethargy, even a will to death, as some historians have concluded. Where the Hawaiians had been described as both intelligent and industrious by all who had contact with them beginning in 1778, they came to be derided as lazy, ailing and indifferent as early as the third decade of the 19th

Century. Certainly they were considered ill-adapted to laboring on plantations, and this in turn led to the next momentous change to rock the Islands: the importation of Oriental laborers, first for the sugar plantations, later on for pineapple plantations, on so vast a scale that the pure Hawaiians became a minority in their own land.

This importation had begun after 1848, when white foreigners engineered the passage of the Great Mahele, a land-reform measure. Dividing the Hawaiian land into thirds, one third for the king, one third for the government and a last third for the common people, this law allowed the ordinary native Hawaiian to own property for the first time. Two years later another legal milestone was passed. Foreigners—called *haoles* by native Hawaiians—had always been excluded from owning land, but now they were given the privilege of buying it outright. Because investment capital was now protected by landownership, the *haoles* began to displace Hawaii's feudalism with their own variety, the plantation system, in which they held sway over an imported citizenry. That citizenry was small to begin with: 293 Chinese were brought to Hawaii in 1852 as indentured laborers. But many more Chinese were soon to be imported, and they were followed by Japanese who came in such numbers that by 1900 Oriental migrants comprised nearly 75 per cent of Hawaii's population.

For the most part the Orientals were, as political scientist Norman Meller has described them, "illiterate laborers chosen not for brain but for brawn and tractability, peasants drawn from rural areas where one must be content with the station of life the gods have given and where an all-embracing family social system smothered individualism." As such they proved to be productive workers under the harsh, impersonal discipline of the plantations, and "King Sugar" prospered mightily. Within one short span of five years (1875-1880) the number of sugar plantations grew from 20 to 63.

The plantation-bred prosperity brought a further concentration of political and economic power among the *haoles*, who made up less than 10 per cent of Hawaii's population in that period. "In some ways," wrote Lawrence Fuchs, Professor of American Civilization at Brandeis University, "life in Hawaii soon resembled that of the post-Civil War South, with a small and powerful oligarchy in control of economic and social perquisites, and large masses of dark-skinned laborers whose direct contact with Caucasians was limited to working under *haole* overseers in the field."

The resulting situation must have appeared to be potentially explosive, even to newcomers. The economy was in a state of rapid evolution as the growing of sugar and pineapples superseded the provisioning of whalers as its mainstay. Political control still remained in the hands of the native Hawaiians and their *haole* advisers, but the sheer number of imported laborers constituted a threat that would one day have to be reckoned with.

What, then, eventually resolved the differences between the divergent groups? In part, marriage across racial lines, first of Orientals to native Hawaiians, then between Caucasians and Orientals. There was a long and respected tradition of interracial marriage in Hawaii, many Americans and British having risen to wealth and power through marriage into the native Hawaiian aristocracy. Drs. Newton E. Morton, Chin S. Chung and Ming-Pi Mi, authors of the *Genetics of Interracial Crosses in Hawaii*, believe that the part-Hawaiians have served "as a biological bridge between all the ethnic groups in the Islands."

A second reason for the harmony that developed among the groups was public-school education. This was carried out with determination by the *haole* oligarchy, despite the apprehensions of some of them that ultimately the process would not only put them at the economic and political mercy of the "Yellow Peril," but would also denude the plantations of workers. Third, mainland Caucasians moved to Hawaii in increasing numbers so that by 1910 the Islands had taken on their present-day character: a place where no single ethnic strain is in the majority. Finally, World War II brought hundreds of thousands of GIs flooding into the Islands—creating a new source of wealth and opening Hawaii to new ideas—and had a profound effect on the least assimilative group, the Japanese.

The Japanese had been accustomed to getting their brides from Japan or marrying local Japanese. But in the aftermath of Pearl Harbor, the Japanese community, feeling itself on trial, undertook a broad and deep severance of ties with the land of its ancestors. Japanese-language schools were abandoned, Shinto and Buddhist shrines and temples were temporarily closed, kimonos were laid away or discarded along with old-country keepsakes. By the 1950-1960 decade, as Irene B. Taeuber wrote in *Population Index*, there was significant intermarriage between the two groups whose mores were least likely to permit such mingling: Japanese men and Caucasian women. Indeed, Mrs. Taeuber observed, if the Islands were to be isolated, with movement of people in or out proscribed, the increasing rates of intermarriage would

Some early settlers

Hiram Bingham, leader of the first group of American missionaries in Hawaii, landed on the Islands with his wife, Sybil, in 1820. Bingham helped translate portions of the Bible into Hawaiian and established a mission in Honolulu that shortly became a powerful influence in the Islands' politics.

Charles Reed Bishop and his Hawaiian wife, Princess Bernice Pauahi Paki, were early exemplars of the Islands' tradition of racial tolerance. Bishop opened Hawaii's first bank in 1858 and later endowed a museum that has become the leading institution for the study of Hawaii's history and culture.

A medical missionary, Dr. Gerrit P. Judd arrived in Hawaii with his wife, Laura, in 1828. So taken was he with his new home that he resigned his missionary post and in 1842 became an adviser to the Hawaiian King. For the rest of his life Judd worked to create a strong constitutional regime in the Islands.

Sanford Ballard Dole, seen at right with his wife, Anna, was the son of a missionary and a distant cousin to James D. Dole, who built a fortune on pineapples. Sanford led the struggle to establish constitutional government on the Islands and after the monarchy fell in 1893 became Hawaii's President. In 1900 he was appointed Governor of the newly acquired U.S. territory.

eventually produce an ethnically integrated population. Looking at Hawaii in grand perspective, she concluded that it was unique among the islands and countries of the Pacific, as among the states of the Union, in the speed of ethnic assimilation.

The Hawaiian Islands, however, are more than a frontier in the sociological sense; they can lay claim to being one in the physical sense as well. Whether or not one would go so far as to say, as some do, that Hawaii is "a land half of which is built and the other half building," it is obviously very much in the process of being created. Dramatic geologic change is taking place right now. The reason for this is partly the encroachment of the sea and partly the volcanic structure of the whole archipelago.

The Hawaiian chain is the product of an enormous crack in the rocky floor of the Pacific Ocean, a crack that runs in a southeasterly direction along an almost straight line for some 1,600 miles. Through this crack, molten basalt—a dark, dense volcanic material—has flowed for millions of years, piling up thin layers of lava until a gigantic range of submarine mountains has taken shape. At the northwestern end of the chain the peaks of these mountains, though they rise thousands of feet from the floor of the Pacific, barely clear the ocean's surface, forming small islands, like Midway. Within the central section their black bulk is thrust somewhat higher above the ocean into pinnacles—La Pérouse rock and the Gardner Pinnacles—shards of once-great volcanic islands worn down by wind, rain and surf and diminished by a rise in the sea's surface.

It is only at the southeastern end that the mountains attain grandeur and the mass needed for habitation. There the eight main Hawaiian Islands tower above the blue ocean: luscious Kauai (1967 population: 26,000), well named the garden isle; tiny, dry Niihau, the private preserve of the Robinson family, with only 300 people; mountain-spined Oahu, center of the state's population (625,000), government and economic power; precipice-girded Molokai (5,700), a refuge for those of Hawaiian blood; the pineapple island, Lanai (3,000), its fields of fruit lying green in the dry embrace of red uplands; the valley isle, Maui (39,000), twin mountain peaks joined by a verdant isthmus; scorched Kahoolawe, an uninhabited place of burned black cliffs and blown red soil; Hawaii (61,000), the volcano island, bigger than Rhode Island and Delaware put together, indeed so big compared to the other islands that the entire chain bears its name.

Today the volcanic fires appear quenched on

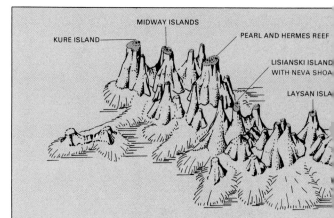

The Hawaiian chain

The state of Hawaii covers far more territory than just the familiar islands near Oahu. It extends from the giant island of Hawaii *(far right)* northwest across the Pacific some 1,600 miles to tiny Kure. Midway, though geologically part of the island chain, is controlled by the U.S. Navy and is not included within the state. The exaggerated scale and perspective of the above drawing show that the islands are the tops of underwater volcanic mountains. Known as the Hawaiian range, these mountains rise from a maximum depth of about 18,000 feet below the Pacific's surface. The highest peak, Mauna Kea, is about 32,000 feet above its base and 13,796 feet above sea level.

seven of the major Hawaiian Islands, and their growth from successive outpourings of lava has halted. For as the mountain chain was formed, each emergent island, in growing bigger and bigger through successive lava flows, in the end achieved such bulk as to seal the fiery crack immediately beneath it and force an eruption farther to the southeast along the fissure. In fact the relative ages of the Hawaiian volcanoes indicate this southeasterly progression in striking fashion: Kauai's volcanoes, the ones that created the great *caldera* of Mount Waialeale, an enormous pit 13 miles long by 11 wide, were the first to appear, 5.6 million to 3.8 million years ago. Those that merged to form Oahu, the adjacent island, were next in order of appearance and age (they are 3.4 to 2.7 million years old). And so it goes until Maui, the most eastward of the seven, is found to possess volcanoes thrown up a mere 800,000 years ago. About 1790 one of these actually produced a lava flow whose thrust into the sea created the beautiful blue bay of La Pérouse. But though the seven islands now possess no active volcanoes, and accordingly have ceased to grow, island building has continued to march inexorably southeastward.

Hawaii, the eighth and most southeasterly island of the main group, contains two volcanoes that are

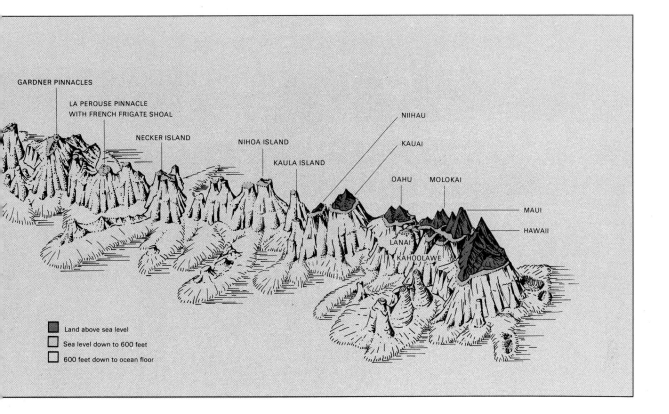

GARDNER PINNACLES

LA PEROUSE PINNACLE
WITH FRENCH FRIGATE SHOAL

NECKER ISLAND

NIHOA ISLAND

KAULA ISLAND

NIIHAU

KAUAI

OAHU   MOLOKAI

MAUI

HAWAII

LANAI

KAHOOLAWE

Land above sea level

Sea level down to 600 feet

600 feet down to ocean floor

still active: Mauna Loa and Kilauea. Mauna Loa, pushing its way upward through 18,000 feet of ocean and then rearing another 13,680 feet into the heavens, built itself into the biggest single mountain on earth and remains the world's most active volcano. Kilauea, 9,000 feet lower, on occasion becomes a caldron of incandescence beside which Vesuvius appears a mere teakettle. These two volcanoes have each emitted nearly a cubic mile of lava since 1823. Such massive outpourings have markedly, if gradually, altered the whole appearance and structure of the island of Hawaii. Its general height has increased on the one hand, and on the other the shore and reefline have been extended farther into the sea (500 acres of new land resulted from a single eruption in 1960, when lava cascaded into the ocean near Kapoho).

More than that, there is ample evidence that although Hawaii is the archipelago's latest example of the island-building process, it is unlikely to be the last. The thrust of volcanic activity has already moved away from the northern end of Hawaii. Giant Mauna Kea there, once a great circular crater possibly 100 miles in diameter and even now 13,796 feet above sea level, extinguished itself long ago by overbuilding; its lava then found another outlet, creating new cones elsewhere. Kilauea was

one of these. Then Mauna Loa burst out of a long spoon-shaped valley to the west of Kilauea and began covering a vast area with new lava.

In recent times, eruptions have taken place even farther to the south and east. These have occurred either on the flanks of Mauna Loa and Kilauea or from a chain of craters that has sprung up eastward over a fissure in the earth's crust called the east rift zone. This zone extends from the summit of Mauna Kea down to the coast at Kumukahi Point and 40 miles out under the ocean. New islands seem destined to spring from it, in fiery repetition of the southeasterly movement that has brought the chain into being.

Further, seamounts—the peaks of submarine volcanoes—are already pushing up from the ocean floor off the southeastern coast of Hawaii. Their growth can be expected to quicken markedly, if only in terms of geologic time, when the mounting weight of that island's existing volcanoes closes off their intake of magma from the great crack in the Pacific floor, forcing it to find other outlets nearby. If these outlets were to occur in shallow water, Hawaii might very well witness the sudden appearance of a new volcano the size of Oahu's famed Diamond Head. That 761-foot-high mass of basalt, in the opinion of volcanologist J. G. Moore, was the product of a submarine explosion and probably emerged in a matter of days or weeks.

However that may be, one has only to fly over the Big Island, as Hawaii is also called, or drive along the coastal highway to see how extensively the volcanoes have transfigured the existing land. An unending struggle seems to be in process between the explosive volcanoes and the stealthy tropical verdure, the latter overrunning a flow here only to have Mauna Loa or Kilauea recoup the lost acreage in an outpouring somewhere else. Cinder cones, gray-clad and topped with red, tower here and there above lush green fields, dead monuments to past eruptions. Innumerable peninsulas of lava slope away from the mountainsides, extending their miles of glistening black fire rock toward the sea. Some of this is wildly contorted into spines and tendrils—it goes by the Hawaiian name of *aa* (pronounced ah ah) whose literal translation is "torn out by the roots." Some lies in satiny whorls and ropy convolutions, glittering with a patina of volcanic glass—it is *pahoehoe*, the second variety of Hawaiian lava. The impression is one of wild, convulsive movement suddenly arrested. Old flows and new flows, virtually indistinguishable one from another save where the older formations are tinted with the "Hawaiian snow" of gray lichens, lie massive and enduring. The eye is overwhelmed by the incredible intricacy of each square inch of surface and the enormity of the mass. Green gem stones called peridots and clear crystals of feldspar glisten in the dark rock. The ghosts of great trees rise here and there above the tumbled surface, encased in tall tubes of fire rock, molten lava having surrounded the trees during an eruption.

For centuries each eruption has left its own indelible mark upon Hawaii's landscape: the flow of 1801, the dying convulsion of Hualalai volcano, made a track more than three miles wide before plunging into the sea; the flow of 1855 lasted 13 months, longer than any in Hawaii's recorded history, and left a black plateau nine miles across; in 1859 the most voluminous flow in historic time— 405 million cubic yards of lava—started 11,000 feet up the side of Mauna Loa and rolled a glossy ribbon 32 miles to the sea; in 1926 a 13.4-square-mile lake of lava put the fishing village of Hoopuloa to the torch; in 1950 three companion rivers of lava, pouring from a fissure 13 miles long, inundated the land with some 600 million cubic yards of molten rock; in 1960 an eruption at Kapoho destroyed that village and, flowing on a broad front down to the water, added a half square mile of new land to Kumukahi Point. The list could go on and on. Mauna Loa alone has erupted on the average of once every 3.6 years, pouring out a total of more than four billion cubic yards of lava—enough to pave a four-lane highway running nearly 30 times around the world.

In the mind of the ancient Hawaiians, prone as they were to deify any source of adversity, all these great outpourings were the doing of a fire goddess, Pele. As the late William D. Westervelt, an Island historian, noted, "All the eruptions of lava have borne her name wherever they may have appeared. Thus the word 'Pele' has been used with three distinct definitions by the old Hawaiians: Pele, the fire goddess; Pele, a volcano or a fire pit in any land; and Pele, an eruption of lava."

Legend has it that Pele first came to the Hawaiian island of Kauai, driven to look for a new home after defeat in a savage battle with one of her sisters, Namakaokahai, goddess of the sea. She brought with her a magic *paoa*, or spade, for digging the fire pit that would be her home, but the mountain rock was too hard to breach and she was forced to turn to the lowlands of the coast. When she struck the shore with her *paoa*, however, opening a crater there, the waters of her sister, the sea goddess, quickly rushed in and quenched the fires. Fleeing that spot—still known on Kauai as Puu-o-Pele, the Hill of Pele—the fire goddess turned to Oahu. There she was at first successful, digging an enormous crater at Diamond Head, brimful of fire rock, but then the sea welled up and the flames were extinguished in a gigantic explosion. At Maui misfortune was again her lot. She had found a haven in Haleakala, the huge volcano there, when once more the sea goddess swept in upon her. Namakaokahai broke the black lava bones of Pele —the masses of shattered lava, *Na-iwi-o-Pele* (the bones of Pele), are still to be seen along the seacoast at Kahiki-Nui—and left her for dead.

But Pele was far from lifeless, and journeying to the island of Hawaii, she finally dug the fire pit of Kilauea volcano, a home impregnable even to her sister. When she stamped the lava floor there, earthquakes came. When she was angry, eruptions flamed into the sky and burned the forests. So fearful of Pele were the Hawaiians that nobody would cut a tree, eat a berry, move a rock or dig in the earth on the top of Kilauea. And with good reason. Catastrophes which befell transgressors, such as that experienced by Keoua's army in 1790, made a lasting impression on the superstitious.

Keoua, a high chief of Hilo, had amused himself by rolling stones into Kilauea's fire pit while his army rested at the summit on its way to do battle with Kamehameha, the great ruler of the northern part of the island. That night a terrific eruption took place. A curtain of fire rose from the crater. Boulders were blown high in the air. The sky shook with thunder, and lightning played magically in the clouds of smoke. Keoua and his companions spent the next day trying to appease Pele, but the second night there was another eruption and a third during the next night as well. The following day the desperate chief divided his forces into three groups and resumed the line of march. They had not gone far across the rocking earth before a hot sulfurous blast exploded from the crater. The middle group, some 80 men, women and children, was annihilated on the spot. The rest of the army fled. Some time later they found their dead comrades miraculously preserved. As an eyewitness described it, there were "no other marks of decay than a sunken hollowness in their eyes; the rest of their bodies was in a state of entire preservation. They were never buried and their bones lay bleaching in the sun and rain for many years."

The days of the fire goddess, however, were numbered. In 1824 Kapiolani, a noble Hawaiian woman of character and intelligence recently converted to Christianity, decided to wipe out the cult of Pele by defying her to her face. Kapiolani's reasoning was simple. "If I am destroyed," she told her countrymen, "then you may all believe in Pele, but if I am not, you must all turn to the true writings." Much against the entreaties of her friends and the dire predictions of the priests of Pele (who were very numerous at that time) she arrived at the crater one evening after a walk of more than 100 miles from her village. Next morning she began her descent into the volcano.

The fire pit of Halemaumau, the home of Pele, was shaking with explosions and awash in a surf of red-hot lava. A final attempt to dissuade Kapiolani was made by a mysterious personage whose charge it was to feed Pele berries and flowers. "You will die by Pele," he said. But Kapiolani replied: "I shall not die by your god. That fire was kindled by my God." Then, in what justifiably has been called "one of the greatest acts of moral courage ever performed," she descended several hundred feet into the crater and there, after eating Pele's berries and tossing stones into the roaring fires, recited a Christian prayer. The crowd of natives, as much in the grip of terror as curiosity, waited for a death stroke from the fire goddess. It never came. Pele's power had been broken.

Unfortunately, the eclipse of Pele as the fire goddess was purely of theological moment; it left the Hawaiians to cope with "Pele" in the two other meanings of the noun: Pele, "a volcano or a fire pit," and Pele, "an eruption of lava." Volcanic activity on the Big Island still confronts the modern Hawaiians. It exposes them to a physical frontier unlike that faced by the citizens of any other U.S. state. The realities of this situation should not be obscured by the way Hawaiians characteristically run toward rather than away from an eruption of Kilauea or Mauna Loa: despite the magnificent pyrotechnics, there is no record of lava having overflowed their grandstand, the rims of these craters, in the last 150 years. The danger of past activity has been more to property than to life—one man killed by a falling boulder at Kilauea in 1924 is the only such death recorded in the 20th Century. Nevertheless, the manifest destructiveness of lava breaking from the *flanks* of these volcanoes and burning its way through forests, villages and coffee plantations has been enough to keep generations of volcanologists in a state of apprehension. The focal point of their concern is Hilo, the state's second-biggest city (population: 26,360), whose vital harbor is the only one on the island of Hawaii capable of handling the huge sugar cargoes that now move through it.

The potential danger to Hilo from a lava flow has been recognized for more than a century. There have been eight major flows from the northeast rift zone on Mauna Loa's flank, producing a total volume of more than one billion cubic yards. Seven of the eight advanced upon Hilo: one (1881) got as far as an area covered by the present city, another (1935) imperiled the city's water supply in the Wailuku Valley, and a third (1942) stopped only 12 miles short of Hilo Bay. Gordon A. Macdonald, Professor of Geology at the University of Hawaii and formerly director of the U.S. Geological Survey's Volcano Observatory at Kilauea, estimates that between 20 and 25 flows have entered Hilo in the past 2,000 years, most of the city having been built upon them and the whole of Hilo Bay shaped by their incursions. In his view one flow a century can be expected to penetrate Hilo, and one of every three such flows is likely to thrust into the bay.

On the basis of past performance, this works out to an expectation that a flow will enter the city within the next 25 years and go on to the harbor within the next century. Indeed, if the flows of 1881 and 1942 had had the volume of two on the northwest and southwest rift of Mauna Loa (1859 and 1950), they would have been almost certain to enter the bay and undoubtedly overrun much of the city as well. The question troubling Hawaiians, of course, is what, if anything, can be done to avert such a disaster. There is, first of all, the difficulty of preparing in advance for an eruption. Nobody can tell with certainty when one will occur or how severe it will be. For example, the historical spacing of eruptions might have led geologists to believe that after the devastating outbreak of 1955 in the Puna area, some 30 miles south of Hilo, things would be quiet for several decades to come. But only five years passed before there was the violent eruption at Kapoho, half a dozen miles away: an earthquake rolled through the green fields of sugar cane in long undulations, like a tidal wave piling up on the shore; by dusk, lava fountains were roaring from the cloven earth and a river of incandescent rock was driving toward the Pacific, firing the plots of papaya, coffee and orchids along the way. By dawn of the next day the beginnings of a great gray cone were throwing a fire fountain hundreds of feet above the charred plain. Nearly three miles of fertile farmland were buried under the 155 million cubic yards of lava that eventually came from the eruption.

Second, the two types of Hawaiian lava present different handling problems. Both types are chemically the same and, in fact, almost all lava emerges from volcanoes in the form of *pahoehoe*. This type of lava is less viscous than *aa*, gas escapes from it easily, and the surface of a flow therefore remains smooth. But as *pahoehoe* advances down a slope it often thickens, turning into clinkery, jagged *aa*. As a river of *aa* moves, overflow from the main body builds up banks or levees on either side and for several feet above the ground. These contain and channel the successive movements of lava. As a *pahoehoe* flow advances, on the other hand, the top surface often wrinkles over and thickens into a plastic envelope, in effect creating a culvert through which succeeding *pahoehoe* outpourings have been known to flow at speeds of 30 miles an hour. The kind of lava to be contended with—a fact undeterminable until the eruption is actually underway—dictates the nature of defensive measures.

Finally, there is a considerable amount of disagreement among geologists about the effectiveness of these defensive measures. In 1935, when a *pahoehoe* flow threatened Hilo's water supply, the celebrated director of the Hawaiian Volcano Observatory, Dr. T. A. Jaggar Jr., recommended that the Air Corps try breaking the crust and diverting the lava through the rupture in the tube. This novel tactic was successful, though the new channel only partially diverted the flow. In 1942, when a flow of *aa* was headed for Hilo Bay, volcanologist R. H. Finch suggested that this time the bombers try

breaching the channel walls of the lava river. Again bombing was partially successful, the main stream being diminished if not stopped.

Bombing, however, is not the right remedy, as Professor Macdonald sees it, and not because it is said to be an insupportable affront to Pele. The intense smoke covering the area for days or even weeks, plus Hilo's intermittently cloudy weather, makes accurate bombing difficult. Moreover, fast-moving lava could overrun the area before bombing could be carried out; for example, bombs could not have averted destruction of part of the village of Pahoehoe on the night of June 1, 1950, because the flow reached the village so quickly (in about three hours) and because the channel walls were by then insufficiently built up to permit a successful breaching by bombs.

Macdonald's primary solution is to build a stone barrier 17 miles long and 25 to 40 feet high, slanting across the southeastern rift, and so designed as to divert a flow into areas that would lead it away from Hilo, the harbor and the airport. His alternative solution: to have a plan in readiness whereby temporary barriers of brush might be pushed into position by bulldozers *after* the flow has begun its advance on Hilo.

Three government volcanologists—C. K. Wentworth, H. A. Powers and J. P. Eaton—disagree. In a jointly written position paper, they contend that a diversion system would be too costly and "that the hazard of being overrun by lava is one that must be accepted and lived with, perhaps analogous to the acceptance of earthquake hazards by Tokyo and cities in other earthquake areas." And there the subject rests.

"This matter of protective barriers for Hilo is one of the few disagreements I have had with my good friends, Powers, Eaton and Wentworth," mused Professor Macdonald in 1967. "The disagreement as I see it is largely a matter of emphasis. They admit the barriers would work under some circumstances; I admit they would not work under some circumstances. I think we should try to protect Hilo if there is any reasonable chance of success. They apparently feel that we should not try if there is any possibility of failure."

"Well," said Dr. Powers, summing up his thoughts on the ethical problem of having to draw the barrier's demarcation line, leaving one man's land, or life, exposed, while his neighbor is given sanctuary inside, "I just don't want to play God."

The only trouble is, a refusal "to play God," however understandable, leaves the field wide open to Pele's playing goddess.

As his ancestors did before him, a Miloliian hauls a tuna into his outrigger. Tuna average between 20 and 40 pounds, but in these waters a hundred pounder is not unusual and sometimes a villager will land one that tips the scale at 150.

Last vestige of a vanishing society

On the southeast coast of the island of Hawaii, at the base of Mauna Loa volcano, lies the tiny village of Milolii. It has perhaps 65 inhabitants, heirs to an easygoing culture that now seems doomed. Like their ancestors, who lived for 800 years along this shore, they fish for their livelihood and lead an unhurried and uncomplicated life that appears to be light-years away from the pressures of Western civilization.

But slowly the world is closing in on Milolii. Fishing no longer brings in sufficient cash to pay for the villagers' growing wants and needs, and many young people have been attracted to the cities. Although some residents resist the tide of change, their struggle seems hopeless. Sport fishing and a resort planned for construction may well keep Milolii on the map, but its traditional way of life is likely to vanish forever.

Photographed by Michael Rougier

The simple joys
of a Milolii family

In the cold, statistical terms of a government survey the family of
Francis Halena would probably be numbered among America's
underprivileged. The Halenas' cash income is small, and their home
lacks such amenities as indoor plumbing, yet many sophisticated
mainlanders might well envy the Halenas' tranquil existence, for it
contains many of the elements of a tropical idyll.

 While Francis is out fishing during the day, his wife, Dora, tends
the youngest of their six children, shops in the town's only store and
visits with her neighbors. In the heat of the day she may join her friend
Mary Jane Forcum *(above)* in the clear shallows, there to frolic with
their youngsters. In the evening the Halenas' simply constructed house
is cooled by sea breezes while the family sits down to an outdoor
dinner *(left)* that seems more the feast of an island king than the fare
of a plain fisherman. Set under the shade of a palm tree, their table,
decorated with a centerpiece of palm leaves, is lit by the brilliant
Hawaiian sunset. After preparing the evening meal, Dora joins her
family for an ample supper of fresh-caught *opelu,* or mackerel, along
with rice and cooked vegetables. It is this simple and serene existence
that many of the residents of Milolii are trying to preserve.

**Skills inherited
from ages past**

Aki Chang *(above)*, a retired fisherman, puts the final touches on an outrigger he is building. Like many of the men in Milolii, Aki has always built his own canoes, a skill that has been passed from generation to generation in Hawaiian fishing villages. Originally the canoes were dugouts made from koa tree logs that the villagers cut and carried down from the slopes of the Mauna Loa volcano. Now the fishermen buy lighter materials, like plywood, for their outriggers. Until about five years ago, Aki and his wife, Lilly, fished as a team. Over the years they were able to support themselves and their nine children through the sale of their catch. Now Aki receives a government pension and they fish only for the pleasure of being out on the sea or to augment their food supply.

The Changs have lived in a pleasant house by the sea for more than 30 years. Their home is small, but they spend much of their time outdoors, relaxing under a beautiful bower of tree boughs and vines. Here, protected from the hot Hawaii sun, Lilly finds pleasure in pursuing the skills that generations of Hawaiians have perfected. At upper left she is weaving a sun hat for herself out of pandanus leaves; at lower left she sews flowers into a lei. The Changs' children, like many of Milolii's younger people, have all moved away from the village.

A fisherman's paradox of plenty

Two miles offshore Sam Kaupu *(below)*, a husky, hard-working Hawaiian, trolls for such fish as *ahi,* or tuna, and *aku,* or bonito. At about 7 each morning, Sam, like many of his neighbors, goes out to sea in an outrigger, which he has often filled to capacity by noon. Sam then heads back to port, where women and children of Milolii wait in the shallows *(right)* to help him and the other village fishermen unload their catch.

Later in the day Sam's catch will be trucked 70 miles to Hilo, where his fish will be sold at auction. During the summer months, fish are so plentiful that auction prices may drop as low as 12 cents per pound. While Hilo fishermen can make some profit at these prices, Miloliians must pay five cents a pound just to get their fish trucked to market and additional sums for ice to preserve their catch. Too often, Sam and his neighbors find that they have been working for a pittance. A record catch of 550 pounds, for example, netted one Miloliian only about $15.

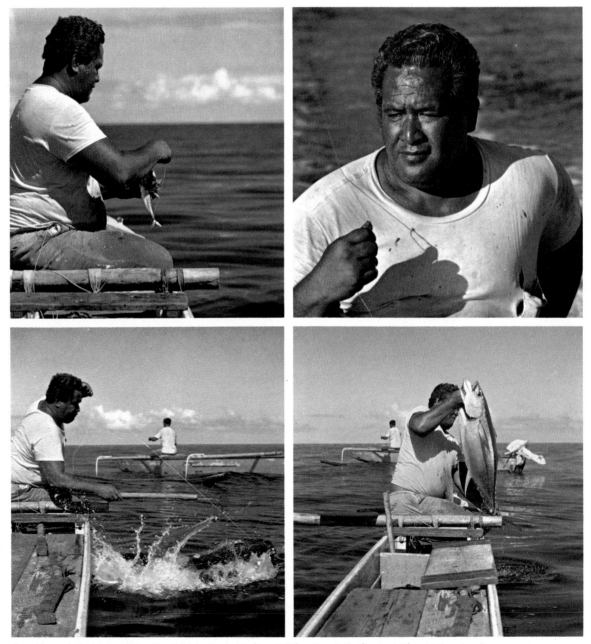

Sam Kaupu baits his hand line *(top left),* trolls slowly *(top right),* gets a strike *(lower left)* and brings in a tuna.

The urgent question of survival

The people of Milolii are aware that their way of life is dying. Fishing has become an increasingly unprofitable occupation, while the need for cash—to buy the children's school clothes or make payments on cars—grows ever more acute. Some of Milolii's citizens accept, and even welcome, the inevitability of change. But others, like Eugene Kaupiko, Milolii's unofficial mayor—shown at right reading to two of his 12 grandchildren—are struggling to maintain traditional Hawaiian values.

The immediate issue in the villagers' debate revolves around the education of their children. Until recently, Milolii had its own schoolhouse, where a single teacher taught all subjects and grades. Today, however, the school-age children go by bus to a consolidated school at Hookena, a round

trip of 40 miles. The youngsters must leave home at 6 a.m. and generally they do not return until late afternoon—a tiring schedule that deeply concerns their parents.

During a recent community meeting at an outdoor shelter near Milolii's harbor *(below)*, Kenneth Asato, the school principal *(facing the camera)*, proposed that the children board near Hookena. He was supported by Sam and Julia Kaupu *(lower right)*, a couple who believe that Milolii's children must be trained to adjust to the outside world. Opposing the proposal was Kaupiko, who fears that boarding would destroy Milolii's close-knit family life. The meeting ended with the problem unresolved, but the debate continues, dividing the town into two contesting camps.

111

A difficult life for the young

Winding its way up the unpaved road to the main highway, a school bus leaves Milolii *(in the distance at upper left)* far behind. The bus carries 16 pupils on the first leg of their daily trek to the consolidated school: 10 hours later, at 4 p.m., the children finally end their long day with the return to their village *(right)*. Someday most, if not all, of these youngsters will leave their village for good. If the experience of those who have already left is any guide, their prospects are likely to be bleak. Raised in an atmosphere where personal property is not important and competition almost nonexistent, native Hawaiians are usually ill-prepared to cope with the pressures of the urban world. Often they find themselves displaced persons—neither equipped to prosper in the city nor able to face returning to the traditional but limited values of the Hawaiian village.

The group of luxury buildings at the base of Honolulu's famed Diamond Head has brought controversy to Hawaii. More housing is needed for tourists and residents, but many Hawaiians argue that further construction would mar the extinct volcano's beauty.

6

The Quickening Pace

Given the series of sweeping changes that have taken place in Hawaii since Captain Cook's arrival in 1778, the Islands may appear to be in a state of chronic flux. And so they are, at least in the sense that their society is continually evolving. But the rate of evolution is something else again, for Hawaii's development has gone by fits and starts. The degree of change experienced has been markedly different from one decade or generation to another. There have been times of intensive change, a series of quantum jumps in many new directions, followed by periods of relative quiescence.

In the 60 years that followed Captain Cook's discovery of the Islands, Hawaii's religious, economic and social structure underwent a complete alteration. Then for roughly half a century things were more or less quiet, if only by comparison, before the onset of another period of sweeping change: the revolution of 1889, which led to the deposing of the monarchy four years later, the setting up of a republic in 1894 and finally annexation by the U.S. in 1898. An era of relative equilibrium followed. Hawaii remained a plantation society for some 40 years—until once again there was a time of explosive change during World War II. Following a slight postwar dip, Hawaii today is in the grip of another surge; the period that opened in the mid-1950s has been one of dynamic evolution.

If, as British historian Arnold Toynbee believes, the whole United States is engaged in a struggle for its very soul, then Hawaii can be viewed as being embroiled in a comparable struggle for its own

Honolulu's spectacular growth into a bustling resort city has been accompanied by a real-estate boom of staggering proportions. As late as the 1930s the area near Waikiki Beach *(above)* was a quiet residential neighborhood. Today, as the picture at right (taken in 1966) reveals, tall resort hotels now crowd the beachfront and behind them expensive apartment houses cater to the city's wealthy. Tourism is responsible for much of Honolulu's prosperity; since 1930 the number of visitors to Hawaii has increased more than 30-fold and land values on Oahu have risen more than 2,000 per cent.

particular soul. The results of this struggle are very mixed indeed and have worked profound alterations in the traditional Island way of life. The "flower children," the hippies, have crowded out the hibiscus as the state symbol in many people's minds; the Hawaiian guitar is considered square by the rising generation; the true native hula is falling into disuse; plastic leis are replacing those of fragrant Arabian jasmine, white plumeria or yellow ginger. Hawaii, once ablaze with birds, now stands unmatched (for its size) as an area of mass extinction of bird life. Even the nene, the state's official bird, whose webbed feet are specially adapted to walking over the Islands' jagged lava fields, was reduced to a few pairs in the 1940s before conservationists stepped in. A poi "famine" occurred on Oahu in the spring of 1967 and many a luau (feast) went without this traditional dish of ground taro root: "Too much of the land has houses on it now," explained a poi manufacturer. "Another thing, too many young people today want to push pencils. They don't want to work and taro farming is hard work."

Other young people manage the Hawaiian *dolce vita* by using sieves to "mine" the hotel beachfronts for lost coins after every weekend. The laughing brown boys who used to dive for dimes off the Matson Line docks have been displaced by older men. Now the diving is done for quarters only, and the take, stuffed in the mouth for safekeeping, is enough to make a typical swimmer's cheeks bulge out like a cornet player hitting high C.

The picturesque Old Hawaii that has largely vanished from the state's busiest island, Oahu, still survives in the wonderful back country of hilly Kauai and along the lava-clad coasts of Hawaii, the Big Island. But in Oahu's Honolulu and its glittering resort area of Waikiki, where as recently as 1958 there was not a single high-rise apartment, office building or hotel, giant structures now transform the entire skyline, pushing back against the mountains, jostling one another at the water's edge. So much concrete and steel has been thrown into the sky that even the climate has undergone a local modification: the trade winds, long prized for their help in keeping Honolulu's temperatures equable, have proved unequal to the task as trees and green space have been displaced by sun-baked parking lots and concrete monoliths.

Pile drivers are now almost as plentiful as palm trees in the Waikiki area, and far louder than the crash of the green Pacific surf. Cloud "cities" still rise magically from the ocean at sunset, making the water off Waikiki seem like a placid lake ringed

about with castles, but Waikiki itself has turned into another Miami Beach. The number of tourists flooding into Hawaii during 1966, mostly to Oahu's resort areas, very nearly equaled the state's population (726,000) at that time and surpassed it by 150,000 people in 1967. "Not only is traffic jammed," lamented the *Honolulu Advertiser*, but "there is a crush on the sidewalks, and the beach itself is often a mass of bodies." One concerned citizen, urging use of a moving sidewalk to ameliorate the traffic paralysis, undertook to prove he could *run* the 10 miles from Pearl Harbor to Waikiki faster than a Honolulu Rapid Transit bus could make the trip. And he did—in one hour and 17 minutes—even though the line's fuming management let their bus jump the gun. A labor leader dourly affirmed: "Only dynamite can solve the problems of a greater part of Waikiki."

So busy were the Hawaiians in trying to keep the hordes of tourists happy that their own happy visages darkened; the traditional friendliness, the personal touch, born in part of a leisurely pace, withered as they strained to cope with an endless succession of quickie tours. The crime rate rose alarmingly—a result, doubtless, of the new dislocations in Hawaii's society. By 1967 Honolulu had the eighth-highest burglary rate in the nation.

So many occurred, in fact—with everything from $16,000 worth of wigs to front-door knockers being lifted—that the *Honolulu Star Bulletin* took to publishing lists of the victims each day like baseball box scores. (Mayor Neal S. Blaisdell declared an Anti-Burglary Week in 1967 and set forth 10 Dos and Don'ts for Honolulu's plundered citizenry.)

The emergence of new trends has been accompanied by a significant accentuation of old trends. Honolulu's grip on the Islands' political, social, economic and cultural life, historically tight, has become even tighter. The City-County of Honolulu, which includes all of Oahu Island, not only boosted its own civilian population from 426,000 in 1958 to 576,000 by 1967, but also raised its percentage of the state's total from 76 to 81; during the same period, the number of people in Maui County increased only by 6,000 and the population of the state's three other counties actually declined. Such an increase, coupled with the political reapportionment ordered by the U.S. Supreme Court, enabled Oahu—already dominant in the House—to wrest control of the State Senate away from the "Neighbor Islands" as well.

In the area of economics, Hawaii's continuous expansion since 1960 set all-time records for visitor arrivals, retail sales, construction, and production of sugar. For the first time, tourism forged ahead of sugar as well as pineapples, Hawaii's longtime money-makers. Military expenditures, with the war in Vietnam making Hawaii an increasingly vital Pacific base, crept upward in the mid-1960s toward World War II levels.

This dramatic expansion of the Islands' economy brought several changes for the better. The proportion of jobless dropped below the national average in 1957, and stayed below. With more and better jobs available, there was a switch away from agricultural labor to jobs in the services and trades (farm workers decreased by almost 11 per cent between 1960 and 1965). The number of people in professional, managerial and technical work shot up 60 per cent in the same period. With more skill, there was better pay: from 1959 on, Hawaiians came to have a higher per capita income than the average American; indeed, from the 1950s to the early 1960s, personal income went up faster in Hawaii than in all but three states of the Union, or for that matter in all but three nations of the Free World. With more to jingle in their pockets, and a little missionary work by the bankers, some of Hawaii's people experienced a virtual revolution in money matters.

"We've had to teach our Oriental citizens that banks are sound and profitable places for the cash they're used to keeping in tin cans and under mattresses," said Rudolph Peterson, a onetime president of the Bank of Hawaii. "The Chinese expect their money to move fast. The Filipinos don't like the idea of having what they own just coming down to some figures in a passbook: they want their wealth where they can handle it. There's no way to get to them except by word of mouth, so we have a Filipino officer of the bank go out in the cane fields and hold a sort of medicine show or camp meeting to get them to open accounts." The results, he added, have often been startling: "One man came in afterward with an oilskin money belt wrapped three times around him. He dropped his trousers to the knees right out on the banking floor to get the thing off, but in it was seventeen thousand dollars. Forty to fifty per cent of our new deposits come from God knows where . . . holes in the ground, under the floor boards." After having experienced only a modest growth between 1950 and 1955, the deposits in Hawaii's banks simply took off: standing at $395 million in 1955, they jumped to $743 million in 1960 and had reached $1 billion by 1967.

Ethnically, Hawaii has continued to be the only American state where citizens of non-Caucasian extraction constitute a majority, but significant changes have taken place in the relative standing of the several races. The Caucasians, flooding in from the United States mainland, now are almost as numerous as the Japanese, who had once outnumbered them by a ratio of nearly 2 to 1. Running virtually neck and neck, each constituted roughly a third of Hawaii's population in 1960, with those of Japanese extraction leading 203,000 to 202,000. (The other third of the population was made up of Filipinos, 69,000; people of part-Hawaiian ancestry, 91,000; Chinese, 38,000; pure or nearly pure Hawaiians, 11,000; Negroes, 5,000.) There was thus, even by 1960, a dramatic shift in Hawaii's ethnic composition, and census estimates revealed that the trend toward a still higher percentage of Caucasians and a lower percentage of Japanese would continue.

This shift in the balance of political power does not mean, however, that the Caucasians will once again dominate the state's other racial groups. Hawaii is committed to maintaining an open society and is far too aware of the advantages of interracial cooperation for that to happen. Moreover, Hawaii's citizens of Oriental descent have come a very long way from the days when Caucasians called the tune. The Japanese have shown an appetite for higher education even beyond that which is characteristic of most immigrant groups. And their young U.S.-educated lawyers, refused admittance to old-line *haole* law firms, have gone into practice—and into politics—for themselves. Today they are firmly entrenched in the civil service and in Hawaii's top elective and appointive positions. In the mid-1960s Daniel K. Inouye was a U.S. Senator; Spark M. Matsunaga and Patsy Takemoto Mink made up the Hawaiian delegation in the U.S. House of Representatives. Six of the 17 heads of the state's executive departments were Americans of Japanese descent; 11 out of 25 state senators; 28 out of 51 state representatives; three of the five-man state supreme court.

The Chinese, for their part, saw Hiram Fong elected to the U.S. Senate in 1959, the first Oriental ever to sit in that body, and have brought their native business acumen successfully to bear in banking, finance and real-estate development. To be sure, as of 1967 few Orientals had risen to a top management post in any of the biggest Hawaiian companies, but this is more a testimony to the fact that few of them have the right sort of executive experience than to racial discrimination.

No, the Islands will not revert to the old way of life; the things that have given them an increasingly open society and an unusual degree of social and economic mobility have been permanently built into the system: universal high-school education in which American standards and expectancies are absorbed, a common language, an expanding urban environment and a long tradition of racial intermarriage. Recently, distinctions between Hawaii's ethnic groups have been further diminished by the emergence of a rapidly growing new component in the population, the cosmopolitans. This relatively youthful group is distinct from the part-Hawaiians —who have typified racial crossings for so many years—in that they represent mixtures of the state's other races (Caucasians with Japanese, Japanese with Chinese, and so on).

What will likely follow, then, from the shift in Caucasian and Japanese percentages will be an increase in voting along ethnic lines in local politics, but no state-wide political rivalry. No one race can command a majority in state-wide elections. Moreover, the people of Hawaii have come to be self-regulating about "plunking" (ethnic-block voting), and the policy of both the Republican and Democratic Parties has been to appeal to all races.

The magnitude of the change Hawaii has undergone since the middle 1950s is perhaps most clearly revealed in an examination of what has transpired in four significant and related areas: improved education; the accentuation of mainland influence, especially on the Hawaiian economy; the impact of tourism; and the inability of some groups, especially the part-Hawaiians, to keep up with the changing environment and the increasingly competitive society that surrounds them.

In education the most dramatic change has occurred in the University of Hawaii. It has been transformed from a fish-and-poi affair with little academic luster to an institution one government report described as being "on the brink of greatness." Statistics tell part of the story. In 1962 the university had an enrollment of 9,500 students and only the most slender financial support. By the end of 1966 the university comprised a state-wide system with an enrollment of 19,000, two academic campuses (the main one in Honolulu, the second at Hilo, on the Big Island), two-year community colleges in operation on three islands and an annual operating budget of $55.6 million.

Since achieving such importance, the university has begun to correct a prime weakness by tailoring its previously inadequate adult-education program to the needs of the community. Its College of General Studies, once criticized within the teaching profession as "limited and unimaginative" in its

preoccupation with on-campus education and rarefied research, is putting new emphasis on state problems (like tourism) and on programs involving Hawaii's ethnic groups, its professions and government employees. As an editorial in the *Honolulu Advertiser* put it: "The University is poised to take on a new dimension—to provide services that can make all Hawaii its campus."

The university has made dramatic progress despite being burdened financially by an increasing number of nonresident students who pay no more for tuition than Hawaiians and whose families, of course, do not help defray the university's expenses by paying Hawaiian state taxes. The number of nonresident students at the university rose from 1,194, or 12 per cent of the total enrollment, in 1961 to 2,912, or 16 per cent, in 1966. The cost to Hawaii's citizens that year was more than $2,000 for each nonresident undergraduate and $4,000 for each graduate student. A bill to abolish the practice, on grounds that Hawaii was the only state in the Union without a tuition differential for nonresident students, passed the legislature in 1967 but was vetoed by Governor John A. Burns. His reasons were notable. "I share the liberal view," he wrote, "that it is desirable to have a composite cross-section of mainland and foreign students at our university for the purpose of stimulating a more catholic atmosphere and to avoid the stultifying provincialism of a closed community."

Hawaii's citizens clearly have placed education high on their list of values. So rapid has been the rise in the number of high-school students going on for more advanced training that Hawaii now stands at the forefront among the states of the Union in this respect, and the university, with its many nonresident students and its broadening curriculum, has been made into an intellectual center whose power reaches far beyond the state.

On the second score—the mainland invasion—it should be said that as recently as 1959 ignorance of Hawaii was widespread and profound. Businessmen from the other states were still writing the Hawaiian Department of Economic Development (when they were not writing the U.S. "Embassy" or "Consulate" in Honolulu) asking what language was used in doing business, what kind of money was acceptable and so on. At the time there were little more than 500 "foreign" (non-Hawaiian) corporations in the Islands (less than half the 1967 figure), and economic control was in the hands of a small, tightly knit group of Hawaiians. The economic, political and social power of this summit group pivoted on the "Big Five," a select set of companies that controlled sugar and pineapples, the dominant industries.

Known today as C. Brewer & Company, Theo. H. Davies & Company, American Factors, Castle & Cooke, and Alexander & Baldwin, all of the Big Five had their origins in the 19th Century when they were the mainstay of the plantation system. Individually or collectively the Big Five financed the plantations, procured their labor, delivered their supplies, provided their financing and transport, and sold their products. Around these five corporate units an oligarchy grew, building up its power from generation to generation, intermarrying and sharing common social as well as business interests. Interlocking relationships pervaded the whole commercial fabric, linking the Big Five with the local banks, trust companies, shipping lines, insurance firms, wholesale and retail outlets, hotels, public utilities, and water and irrigation corporations. At one time, top executives of four of the Big Five firms held offices or directorships in some 40 other Hawaiian enterprises. Even as late as 1960 Big Five companies were linked with the two biggest commercial banks, the Hawaiian Electric Company, the Hawaiian Telephone Company, the Honolulu Gas Company and Matson Navigation.

In this tight system of economic control, power over land was essential, and much of the land was administered by the trustees put in charge of Hawaii's great 19th Century estates. Before statehood, Washington appointed territorial judges agreeable to the oligarchy, and the judges in turn selected the estate trustees—usually from among the oligarchy. Thus many of the leading families had two bases of power, commercial and agricultural, and although they often were philanthropically inclined, the one possession they did not let go of was this power. All the way from land to retail trade, control was exercised in such fashion that the way was smoothed for the insider and made almost impassable for the "interloper."

What caused an irrevocable change in this situation was a sudden increase in the number of tourists who came with statehood. Where tourists had spent some $83 million the year before Hawaii joined the Union (1958), they boosted this by nearly $50 million the year after statehood. With the tourist-primed economy booming, the old-line Hawaiian firms found themselves swept into a new and challenging environment. Although in the main they had enough capital, they were timid about using it, tending to let it lie fallow rather than investing it in new ventures that could take advantage of the opportunities that had come with

statehood. Further, there was not enough managerial manpower in the Islands to meet the expanding situation. Firms that had not already taken on executives from the mainland were faced with the alternative of doing so, with a consequent dilution of local control, or of retaining that control at the price of eventually being trampled to death by competitors with more adventurous managements. An added inducement to abandon the old ways of doing things was produced by the Hawaiian legislature in 1961, when it passed a stiff antitrust law.

The changes resulting from the combination of tourism and an invasion of mainland business were little short of revolutionary. Oligopoly was over and done with. The Old Guard's tight control over marketing and distribution was broken. More and more mainlanders rose to the top of major Hawaiian companies as those who owed their jobs to the old-school lei were replaced with professional managers. Rudolph Peterson, fresh from the customer-pleasing tradition of California banking, took hold of the stodgy Bank of Hawaii and shook it into an awareness of its opportunities (net profits more than doubled between 1956 and 1959). The *Honolulu Advertiser*, a metropolitan daily with a provincial outlook and a plant so antique that all headlines had to be set by hand, was stimulated back to health and usefulness by George Chaplin, who had been editor of the New Orleans *Item*. Oregonian Boyd MacNaughton became the first mainlander to head up C. Brewer & Company— the first mainlander, that is, without family connections on the Islands. His brother, Malcolm MacNaughton, took over the presidency of Castle & Cooke and earned his reputation as one of the two top businessmen in Hawaii. The other businessman sharing that distinction, Lowell Dillingham, who took over as head of Dillingham Corporation from his celebrated father, Walter, runs this diversified Hawaiian enterprise (1966 operating revenues: $160 million) with a predominantly mainland staff; aside from himself, his brother Ben, and a couple of other Islanders, the other top Dilco executives in 1967 were all from other states.

The influx of mainland executives was accompanied by an influx of mainland capital. The Hawaiian investments of out-of-state insurance firms, which stood at a modest $142 million in 1956, soared beyond the $600 million mark in 1966. In addition, mainland companies actually began buying up Hawaiian enterprises. U.S. Plywood acquired Lewers & Cooke, Limited; General Telephone and Electronics bought Hawaiian Telephone.

Understandably, a shiver of apprehension ran

COMPANY NAME	PRINCIPAL FIELDS OF OPERATION	FOUNDING DATE	FOUNDED BY
C. BREWER AND COMPANY, LIMITED	Major income from sugar and molasses. Other interests include insurance, ranching, nut growing and chemicals.	1826	James Hunnewell, a New England sea captain. Company named for another mariner and later partner in the firm, Charles Brewer.
THEO. H. DAVIES & CO., LTD.	Major income producers include sugar, merchandising, foreign investment, insurance, and steamship and travel agencies.	1845	James Starkey and Robert C. Janion, both English merchants. Theodore H. Davies, also English, took over in the 1860s.
AMFAC, INC.	This company, also known by its old name of American Factors, derives much of its income from sugar and merchandising. Other sources include insurance and property development.	1849	Henry Hackfeld, a German sea captain. Name became American Factors after firm was seized by U.S. during World War I.
CASTLE & COOKE, INC.	Controlling the Dole Company, Castle & Cooke derives much of its income from pineapples. Other interests include sugar, food packing, property development and merchandising.	1851	Samuel N. Castle and Amos S. Cooke, both missionaries.
ALEXANDER & BALDWIN, INC.	Major income producers are shipping and "terminal services" (docks, warehouses and such), plus sugar. Other interests include pineapples and merchandising.	1895	Samuel Alexander and Henry P. Baldwin, missionaries' sons, became partners in the 1870s, formally founding the firm later.

The Big Five companies named in the table above dominated Hawaii economically and politically from the second half of the 19th Century to the end of World War II. They are listed in order of their founding; their principal lines of business and the names of the men who founded them are also given. No longer all-powerful, they are still potent factors in the economy of the Islands.

through Hawaii's business community. The price of the stock of many local enterprises on the Honolulu exchange was far below the actual value of a given share, particularly where the assets included large tracts of plantation land that could be sold off for real-estate development. Such a situation was ready-made for raiders, and one soon appeared in the person of Harry A. Weinberg.

A rough-and-ready enterpriser from Baltimore, Weinberg began buying into Hawaiian companies in the late 1950s. The Honolulu Rapid Transit Company, finding itself the object of his attentions, reduced its board of directors from 10 to six members, putting membership beyond the reach of his stockholdings at that time. But Weinberg, who has a reputation for enjoying the panic he produces in management as much as the profit he reaps, kept on buying HRT common. By 1959 he had control. And once in the driver's seat, Weinberg took HRT down a rocky road. He transferred cash assets of the company into a subsidiary (Honolulu Limited) and used $515,000 to buy stock in Texas' Dallas Transit Company. Dallas Transit money in turn was used to buy control of New York's enormous Fifth Avenue Coach Line. In each case Weinberg's action resulted in curtailed service, heavy layoffs, strike threats and a spate of angry charges against

the "outsider" from Maryland. The most common one: he was not in the bus business to stay but intended only to liquidate the lines and exploit their valuable real-estate holdings.

Undismayed by the uproar, Weinberg began buying into other Hawaiian companies. In 1966 one of the Big Five, American Factors, woke up to discover that he had enough shares to support his request for a seat as a director. Once on the board he moved to have three colleagues seated as well. American Factors' board cut its membership from 14 to seven and Weinberg, thwarted but still in a position to make capital of the board's apprehensions, agreed to sell his interest, at a profit. Dillingham Corporation was also put in the position of having to make Weinberg a member of its board, finally did so and then also agreed to buy him out. While some more fortunate Hawaiian companies were able to keep Weinberg at arm's length, he eventually had his way with Hawaiian Rapid Transit. His denial of a wage increase unless it could be tied to a fare boost precipitated the longest transit strike—67 days—in Honolulu history.

Any account of the impact of mainland influence would be incomplete without a summing up of the radical changes in the Islands' power structure. With the partial eclipse of the Big Five there is now no major center of decision making. Decisions are made by the managements of individual companies rather than by members of the oligarchy acting in concert. Corporations are not controlled by major stockholders to the overwhelming degree they once were; professional managers increasingly tend to run the show. Power has come to rest more with labor than with big companies. Business, as Malcolm MacNaughton noted not long ago, has lost much of its influence in the state legislature and can only win its points after "full and persuasive argument and if organized labor [does] not sharply disagree." As for the Big Five, Governor Burns recently observed (with humorous exaggeration) that in today's Hawaii "they've got no more influence than the Cousins Society [the organization of missionary descendants]."

The tremendous increase in tourism was to a significant degree responsible for this dilution of economic power. While a group of men sitting around a table could decide what ought to be done about sugar or pineapple production, decisions in tourism are made by hundreds of entrepreneurs, both large and small. They include the owners of mamma-and-papa eateries and huge hotel chains, and people engaged in such diverse activities as transportation, building construction and basket weaving. But that is only part of the tourist-wrought change. Considered in the round, it is hard to think of any more pervasive influence in the Islands than the physical presence of increasing numbers of tourists and the concomitant outpouring of their dollars. Tourism has vastly accelerated the spread of mainland culture among Hawaiians of all ages, but most significantly among the young; they are attracted to work in Oahu's hotels and restaurants, where they rapidly, and permanently, take on the attitudes of the visitors they serve. "The culture of fun," the ideology of the tourist industry, is hardly healthy for those who live with it on a permanent basis.

Tourism, for all its obvious benefits—income from visitors will reach half a billion annually in the 1970s—has increased the vulnerability of the state's economy, already partly dependent on another changeable source of income, the military. "We could have a bust here if we get overextended in tourism," said James Shoemaker, dean of the Islands' economists, after making a study of the situation. "People don't understand that at the level we've reached, the growth may not look as impressive as when we were doubling our numbers of tourists. There is an enormous difference between going from 250,000 to 500,000 and from 500,000 to 750,000. The jump from 500,000 to 750,000 puts people and facilities under disproportionately heavy pressure. I want to make people understand . . . that tourism is a precarious business and requires the effort of everyone concerned with it. We have only one criterion of success: a pleased tourist. If he isn't pleased he'll go someplace else, and the change can happen very fast."

Tourism has also been a force for significant change in two other areas. It has, first of all, been the prime mover behind the biggest building boom ever to hit the Islands. Construction expenditures stood at $343 million in 1965, three and a half times the 1955 level. Honolulu was fifth among American cities in the volume of building permits although its population ranked only 55th among U.S. metropolitan areas. Construction has been going full blast—and for good reason. City planners in the mid-1960s estimated that Hawaii would need 25,000 hotel rooms by 1970 to accommodate the million tourists expected then, and a whopping 45,000 rooms by 1972-1975, when bigger planes and lower fares could bring two million visitors to the Islands each year.

But inevitably, as more and more high-rise hotels and apartments—all of them big and many of them ugly—have been crammed into Waikiki, the developers have cast a hungry eye at the residential area adjoining Waikiki on the east. Pleading that soaring land values in Waikiki were changing the luxury hotels there into high-volume, fast-turnover establishments, a consortium of developers asked for a zoning variance in order to build a string of luxury hotels and apartments around the base of Diamond Head.

To many outraged Hawaiians the raising of a wall of concrete around this world-famous landmark was akin to obstructing the view of the Statue of Liberty or Mount Rushmore with a ring of incinerators. Orange-colored "Save Diamond Head" stickers appeared on hundreds of automobile bumpers. The Outdoor Circle, a women's organization that has heroically kept Hawaii's natural beauty from being defaced by billboards, loosed a storm of protest on City Hall. The Chamber of Commerce was joined by the International Longshoremen's and Warehousemen's Union in leading an attack on the proposal. Distant newspapers such as *The New York Times* took up the cudgels in behalf of Diamond Head, and letters from their indignant readers joined the chorus of protest that was in full cry in the local letters columns. The Hawaii chapter of the American Institute of Architects entered the fray with an expression of professional disapproval: "We have been told again and again," wrote its president, Edward Sullam, in a letter to the City Planning Commission, "that the deluge of visitors is almost upon us. . . . What will the impact be? Will we have anything left of the fabled beauty of Hawaii? Will the residents have access to beaches and parks? Or will everything of value have been 'deeded' over to the tourist industry?"

Forces opposed to the despoiling of Diamond Head proposed that the 15-acre tract in contention be made into a public park or at least remain zoned for residential use. The developers, for their part, sang the siren song of "progress": "3,500 new jobs" would be created by the hotel-apartment complex, and four million dollars in new tax revenues would come in each year. On the other hand, they warned, taxes would have to be *boosted* if the city made a park of the tract since the cost of buying the land would be formidable. Diamond Head waterfront lots were valued at seven to eight dollars a square foot—more than $300,000 an acre—about as much as the city had paid for an entire park at Kahana Bay on the windward side of Oahu.

In the spring of 1967 the City Planning Commission voted to keep Diamond Head for single-family residential use, several members personally expressing the hope that the city would eventually develop it into a park. And that seemed for the moment to settle the matter. But the threat to Diamond Head, and to all of Hawaii's natural beauties, remained in the air. Apprehensions rose that the developers were going to get their way with Diamond Head as soon as passions cooled. Cynicism about the power of "progress" runs deep in a place like Honolulu, recipient of 80 per cent of the hundreds of millions of dollars that tourists have been spending each year in Hawaii. All too often esthetics have run a poor second in the continual race against "cash and concrete."

In addition to its specific impact on Oahu, tourism, by stimulating the entire economy, has also been a profound force for change in the state's whole attitude toward landownership. Ownership of land has been highly concentrated and jealously guarded ever since the days when the Hawaiian kings controlled it all. In 1967 the state government owned 38.7 per cent of Hawaii's total acreage, the federal government 9.8 per cent and small private landowners less than 5 per cent, while nearly half of all Hawaiian land (47 per cent) was in the hands of only 72 major private landowners. Looking at the degree of concentration in just the *privately owned* land, the statistics are even more startling: in 1967 three estates (originally founded

In a tearful reunion, Sergeant Howard Kiyama of the much decorated 442nd Regimental Combat Team is welcomed home to Hawaii by his father after the close of World War II. Like all Americans of Japanese ancestry who volunteered, Sergeant Kiyama was at first rejected. Later he joined the 442nd, a Japanese-American volunteer unit made up largely of men from Hawaii. The 442nd fought heroically in Italy and Southern France.

by the Bishop, Damon and Campbell families), two ranches (named Parker and Molokai), four of the Big Five corporations and one other firm—only 10 entities in all—possessed roughly two thirds of all the privately owned land in the Islands. Such concentration would have been more bearable had the owners of the land been willing to sell it to satisfy the growing demand for real estate, but they usually refused to sell outright; the holders have preferred to lease it on a long-term basis, retaining ownership. A census of 1960 revealed that only about 25 per cent of the housing units on Oahu were occupied by owners having title to the land.

The attitude of the Hawaiians toward this situation has been somewhat ambivalent. The native Hawaiians have cared little about owning the land their houses were built upon, perhaps because it was not customary in their heritage. The Hawaiians of Oriental descent, on the other hand, were brought up to believe that ownership of land is one with achieving status and success. The Caucasians have also preferred ownership to leasing. The difficulty of instituting a change, however, has increased as the value of Hawaiian land has kept mounting. The point of greatest pressure, of course, has been Oahu, which has become one of the world's most densely populated land masses. Oahu possesses more than half of the best agricultural land in the state, and half of that island's total land area has been in the hands of the big landowners, who have preferred to lease rather than sell.

In 1961 two land-reform measures were introduced in the state legislature with the purpose of making more land available for purchase. The measure originated by the Senate would have freed public land; the House bill would have forced the major private landowners to sell some of their holdings. Needless to say the landowners fought the House bill. The result: the House measure, sent to the Senate, was referred to committee where it quietly died, and the Senate failed to pass its own bill by one vote.

But as the concentration of landownership did not diminish in succeeding years, a Land Reform Bill was finally forced through in 1967. It will make some of the land previously leased by the large estates available for purchase by homeowners, but not by commercial interests. The big landholders, who once again fought against the act, will be permitted to sell their land through "compulsory or involuntary conversion"—a legal device designed to soften the tax bite on all such sales—but if they do not sell, then the state is empowered to take over the land.

The net result of all these many changes has been a period of unprecedented growth. The Bank of Hawaii even goes so far as to declare that "by any measure that might be used (cultural, political, educational, or economic), as of January 1, 1966, Hawaii completed by far the greatest decade in the history of the Islands." Yet, as in any time of rapid development, the pace has exacted its special toll. "Each day in Honolulu," Lieutenant Governor Thomas P. Gill told the Hawaii Psychological Association in 1967, "each of us becomes more a part of the faceless and impersonal human mass. We daily note the loss of family and neighborhood ties, the seemingly greater distance between friends, the growth of impersonality in our daily relationships. We are losing many of those things which have been so important to us in Hawaii—and so much a part of our personal and social make-up." Sad to say, the people most affected have been the descendants of the original Hawaiians.

The Hawaiians and part-Hawaiians are among the least able—or perhaps the most unwilling—to adjust to the changes confronting them. A sort of malaise of the spirit, a sense of frustration and incapacity, seems to have overwhelmed many of them, much as their ancestors reacted to the changes that came hard on the heels of Western contact in the early 1800s. A large number of these native Hawaiians and part-Hawaiians, especially those with better education and training, have moved elsewhere: of the 85,000 pure Hawaiians and part-Hawaiians living in Hawaii in 1950, 20,000 had left the state by 1960. It has been an exodus paralleling that of the 1850s when as many as one fourth of all Hawaiian males between 18 and 53 sailed away on whaling ships.

Many of today's Hawaiians who have stayed have become increasingly alienated from society. How far their alienation has gone was disclosed in a 1962 survey conducted by the Liliuokalani Trust, an organization set up by the last native monarch, Queen Liliuokalani, to look after native children. The survey revealed that although native Hawaiians and part-Hawaiians numbered only 17 per cent of the state's total population in 1962, they accounted for 35 to 40 per cent of all financially destitute families aided by the community, 42 per cent of all children arrested and 51 per cent of all illegitimate births. The school drop-out rate was the highest of any racial group in the Islands. The picture since 1962 has not changed to any significant extent. During 1966, for example, almost half of all Oahu juveniles arrested for major crimes—murder, manslaughter, burglary and automobile theft—were of Hawaiian ancestry.

A belated effort is being made to rectify this situation, particularly in the field of education. However, teachers find that the usual materials and techniques designed for white middle-class pupils simply do not work with many native Hawaiian children. As a result the teacher turnover in predominantly Hawaiian schools is rapid—and dramatically indicates the gap between the conflicting cultures. The *haole* culture, the dominant one, is what is called a "peasant" culture, with emphasis on the private ownership of land and material possessions; the culture of the native Hawaiians, as sociologist Andrew Lind points out, is a folk culture, characterized by openness and the de-emphasizing of private property. It is significant that the native Hawaiians most resistant to changing the traditional values of the old folk culture are the ones at the lowest economic levels.

"Everybody talks about preserving Hawaiian culture," remarked Mrs. Harriet Patterson, a lei seller at Honolulu International Airport and herself Hawaiian, "except the Hawaiians. They seem tired or something. They're not involved." The sad fact is that today, as in the previous century, those at the very vortex of change—the native Hawaiians —once again are the least able to cope with it.

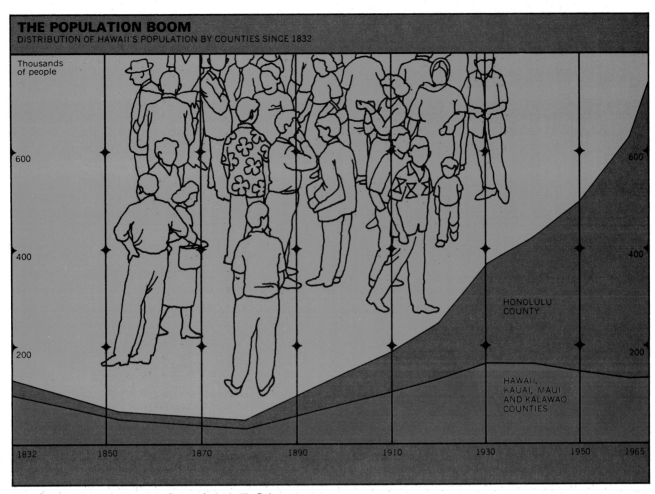

THE POPULATION BOOM
DISTRIBUTION OF HAWAII'S POPULATION BY COUNTIES SINCE 1832

Thousands
of people

600

400

200

HONOLULU
COUNTY

HAWAII,
KAUAI, MAUI
AND KALAWAO
COUNTIES

600

400

200

1832   1850   1870   1890   1910   1930   1950 1965

The population boom in Honolulu County (principally Oahu
Island) contrasts with the irregular growth of the other
Islands. On this graph the county's population is shown in
dark orange. In 1965, the county had 610,101 people.

Progress
in paradise

The very name "Hawaii" conjures up visions of
lovely beaches flanked by swaying palms and
rolling surf. And indeed such places are to be
found throughout the Islands, but most Hawaiians
today find themselves living in a different world
—and one that is continuing to change. Change is
expressed in an economic boom that is rapidly
transforming a once agricultural territory into an
urban society. It is manifested in the shifts of
political and economic power among ethnic
groups. It is revealed in the ever-increasing role in
state affairs played by the island of Oahu and its
rapidly expanding city of Honolulu. By 1966
Honolulu had a population of 343,075 and the
city was growing at the average rate of about
8,000 residents per year. On the following pages,
charts reveal important economic and population
trends both on Oahu and in the entire state.

125

THE MELTING POT'S INGREDIENTS
POPULATION OF THE ISLANDS BY ETHNIC GROUP SINCE 1778

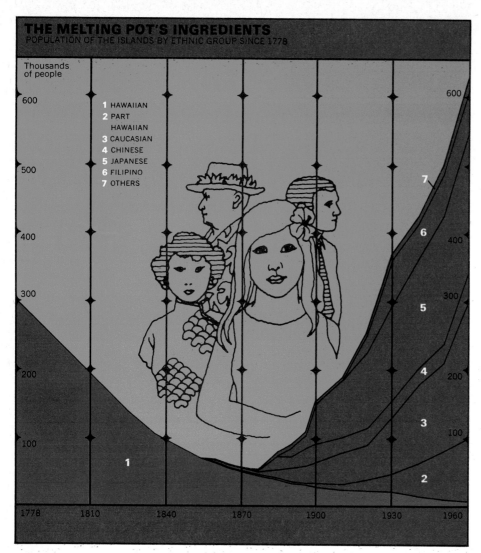

Thousands of people

1 HAWAIIAN
2 PART HAWAIIAN
3 CAUCASIAN
4 CHINESE
5 JAPANESE
6 FILIPINO
7 OTHERS

(y-axis: 100, 200, 300, 400, 500, 600)
(x-axis: 1778, 1810, 1840, 1870, 1900, 1930, 1960)

The ethnic distribution of Hawaii's population has undergone profound changes since Captain Cook's visit in 1778, when an estimated 300,000 natives lived on the Islands. In 1960 only 11,000 residents were classified as native Hawaiians. On this graph the top line indicates total population, and the size of each group is shown by the area between lines. Thus in 1960 Hawaii's Japanese population was 203,000.

Once economically dependent on sugar and pineapples, Hawaii now offers employment opportunities in a wide range of industries. The variety of civilian industries on Oahu, where most Hawaiians live and work, and the percentage of the work force that each employs are shown in the chart at top right. By the mid-1960s the smallest major employers were the once-predominant sugar and pineapple industries. Today, employment bears little relation to ethnic background. The stereotype of the Chinese laborer or the Yankee trader is fast vanishing. The Japanese, for example, who came to the Islands as field hands, have now branched out into every industry on Oahu. The chart at bottom right illustrates this change by showing how the labor force of each ethnic group is divided among Oahu's industries. Each industry is represented by the number labeled on the top chart.

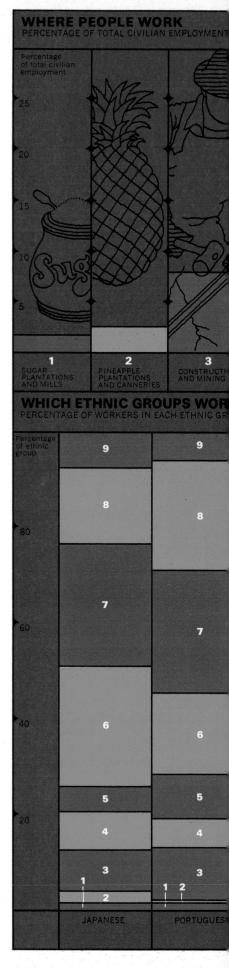

WHERE PEOPLE WORK
PERCENTAGE OF TOTAL CIVILIAN EMPLOYMENT

Percentage of total civilian employment

(y-axis: 5, 10, 15, 20, 25)

1 SUGAR PLANTATIONS AND MILLS
2 PINEAPPLE PLANTATIONS AND CANNERIES
3 CONSTRUCTION AND MINING

WHICH ETHNIC GROUPS WORK
PERCENTAGE OF WORKERS IN EACH ETHNIC GROUP

Percentage of ethnic group

(y-axis: 20, 40, 60, 80)

JAPANESE   PORTUGUESE

ECTED INDUSTRIES ON OAHU, 1964-1966

4	5	6	7	8	9
UFACTURING EPT SUGAR PINEAPPLE	TRANSPORTATION AND COMMUNICATION	WHOLESALE AND RETAIL TRADE	SERVICES	PUBLIC ADMINISTRATION	OTHERS

WHICH INDUSTRIES
PLOYED IN SELECTED OAHU INDUSTRIES, 1964-1966

HER CAUCASIAN　HAWAIIAN　PART HAWAIIAN　FILIPINO　CHINESE

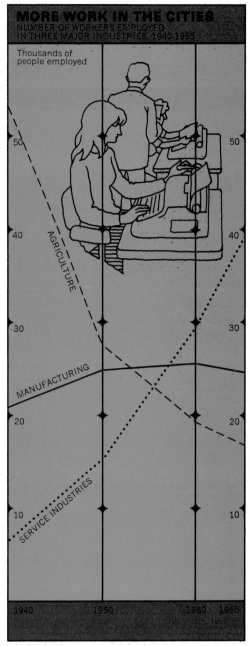

Thousands of people employed

AGRICULTURE

MANUFACTURING

SERVICE INDUSTRIES

1940　1950　1960　1965

Like their mainland compatriots, Hawaiians are migrating to the city in droves. This trend is seen in the sharp drop in farm employment and the rise in activities that are concentrated in the cities, such as services (particularly those catering to the tourist trade). Manufacturing is also more diversified. A few decades ago pineapple and sugar processing plants were the only big factories on the Islands. Today Hawaii can boast an increasing number of manufacturing enterprises in such wide-ranging fields as chemicals, textiles, furniture and printing.

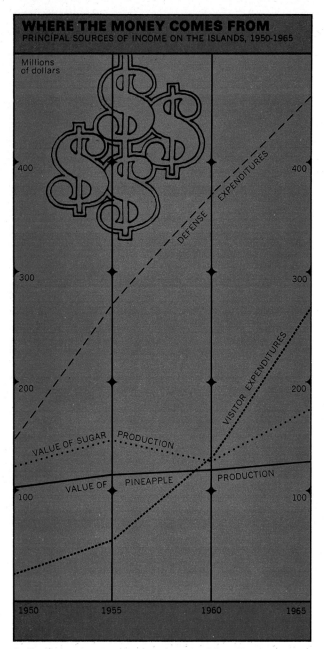

WHERE THE MONEY COMES FROM
PRINCIPAL SOURCES OF INCOME ON THE ISLANDS, 1950-1965

Millions
of dollars

400

300

200

DEFENSE EXPENDITURES

VISITOR EXPENDITURES

VALUE OF SUGAR PRODUCTION

100

VALUE OF PINEAPPLE PRODUCTION

100

1950 1955 1960 1965

As Pacific headquarters for every branch of the military, Hawaii gets more money from the U.S. Defense Department—including the payrolls for about 50,000 servicemen—than from any other source. Sugar and pineapples, once the top money-makers, are today much less important. In 1960 visitor spending became Hawaii's second-largest and fastest-growing source of income.

Hawaii's growing prosperity is revealed by the two related indexes *(right),* reflecting changes in the economy. The top chart shows rising insurance company investments, up some 13-fold between 1950 and 1965. Insurance firms—from Hawaii, the mainland and foreign countries—are financing many of the state's resorts, hotels and apartment buildings. This dramatic rise in investments has been matched by soaring property values *(bottom chart).* Land is particularly precious on Oahu, where most of the construction is taking place. The figures shown, representing assessed values, are little more than half the market prices.

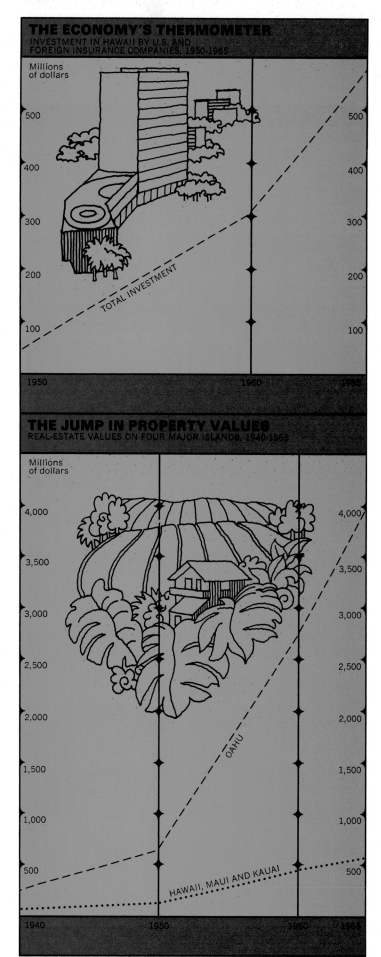

THE ECONOMY'S THERMOMETER
INVESTMENT IN HAWAII BY U.S. AND
FOREIGN INSURANCE COMPANIES, 1950-1965

Millions
of dollars

500

400

300

200

100

TOTAL INVESTMENT

1950 1960 1965

THE JUMP IN PROPERTY VALUES
REAL-ESTATE VALUES ON FOUR MAJOR ISLANDS, 1940-1965

Millions
of dollars

4,000

3,500

3,000

2,500

2,000

1,500

1,000

500

OAHU

HAWAII, MAUI AND KAUAI

1940 1950 1960 1965

Every person, every package, every piece of equipment that enters or leaves Hawaii must be carried by plane or ship. Traffic through the airport and docks of Honolulu—Hawaii's leading port—is vital to the state's economy and a gauge of its progress. In 1965 one and three-quarter million overseas passengers passed through Honolulu International Airport *(graph at right)*, helping to make this Pacific crossroads the 16th busiest air terminal in the United States.

Cargo figures *(graphs below)* reveal that the volume of the state's imports by ship (mostly cars and oil products) far exceeds the volume of exports (mostly sugar and pineapples). On the other hand, volume figures for lightweight goods carried by plane—such as clothing imported and orchids exported—are almost balanced. Despite Hawaii's need to import most of its goods, the state's receipts from the mainland and from foreign countries exceeded its expenditures in 1965 by about $40 million, a favorable balance of payments due to military and tourist spending.

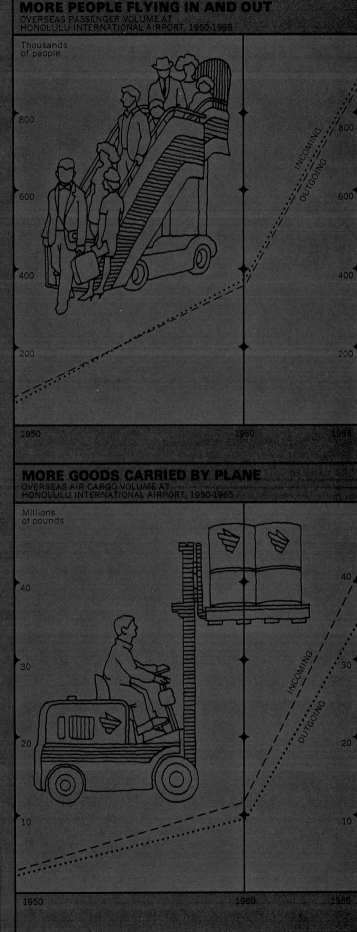

MORE PEOPLE FLYING IN AND OUT
OVERSEAS PASSENGER VOLUME AT
HONOLULU INTERNATIONAL AIRPORT, 1950-1965

Thousands of people

800

600

400

200

INCOMING
OUTGOING

800

600

400

200

1950 1950 1965

MORE GOODS CARRIED BY SHIP
OVERSEAS SHIP CARGO VOLUME AT PORT OF HONOLULU, 1950-1965

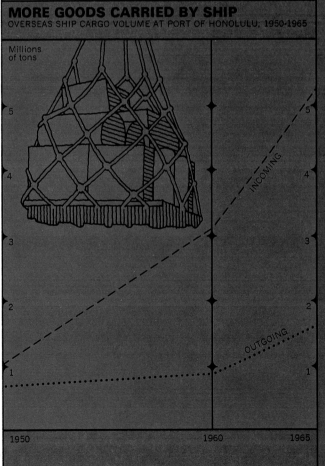

Millions of tons

5
4
3
2
1

INCOMING
OUTGOING

5
4
3
2
1

1950 1960 1965

MORE GOODS CARRIED BY PLANE
OVERSEAS AIR CARGO VOLUME AT
HONOLULU INTERNATIONAL AIRPORT, 1950-1965

Millions of pounds

40

30

20

10

INCOMING
OUTGOING

40

30

20

10

1950 1960 1965

COSMOPOLITAN

FILIPINO

CHINESE

HAWAIIAN

JAPANESE

KOREAN

7

The Aloha
Spirit

The sniper took dead aim at the parked tour bus as its passengers sat enthralled by the splendor of Nuuanu precipice, falling away below them toward the Pacific. Mrs. Cora Montoya, 51, on the second day of the "dream vacation" she had scrimped five years to pay for, was shot through the stomach. Her husband, Peter, a laborer at Swift & Company's Denver packing plant, was shot in the ankle, paralyzing a nerve. At the hospital in Honolulu the cost of intensive medical care and nursing quickly exhausted the Montoyas' slender resources—and kept on mounting until the attending physician explained their desperate situation to a reporter from the *Honolulu Advertiser*. The Montoyas had been against asking for help, he said, because they were such nice people. "I tried to explain to Mrs. Montoya if people helped it would just be an expression of Hawaiian Aloha. They've certainly seen only the short end of it so far. If they were complainers it would be different. I know they have written letters home and not once have they knocked Hawaii. To keep our image up, I thought I'd ask you to

help." An ensuing news item and the *Advertiser*'s sponsorship of a "Montoya Aloha Fund" brought in money so fast—an average of 200 people mailed in a total of $2,000 to $2,500 each day—that within three days Peter Montoya felt obliged to ask that the contributions cease. "We don't know just what it will take in the future," he said, "but we don't want to be hoggish, there will be other people who need help too." In the summer of 1967, two years after their misfortune, Mrs. Montoya and her husband made a happy return trip to the Islands, this time on an expense-free vacation paid for by Hawaiians.

Such spontaneous outpourings of help are not uncommon in the United States, where openhanded aid frequently becomes a smiling successor to violence or adversity. But in the Islands their scope and spontaneity are something special. The word so tellingly used by Mrs. Montoya's physician and by the newspaper in naming the fund—Aloha—is the key. For there is in Hawaii a phenomenon known as the Aloha spirit, and it is far deeper, subtler and more elusive than any rash of sentimental philanthropy. Yet precisely what the Aloha spirit is remains an enigma. Its true nature and significance are as baffling to Hawaiians as its existence is surprising to outlanders. An attempt to

Six beauty queens—each Hawaiian, yet each representing a different ethnic group—are among the 1967 winners of the Ka Palapala Beauty Pageant. Held by the University of Hawaii, this pageant recognizes the state's ethnic diversity by crowning several queens.

understand it—to seek its sources and examine briefly a few of its effects—seems essential to an understanding of Hawaii itself.

Unfortunately, help in clearing up the confusion is hard to come by. Virtually no published material on the Aloha spirit is to be found on the well-stocked shelves of the University of Hawaii's Sinclair Library, nor does Janet Bell, the experienced curator of the Hawaiian and Pacific Collection there, know of any in manuscript. The files of the *Advertiser* are bursting with lore on the Aloha State, but nothing beyond footnotes on the Aloha spirit. Two of these footnotes are somewhat comic and, while pointedly recognizing the existence of the Aloha spirit, suggest that the special warmth and friendliness it is supposed to nurture in Hawaiians is often notable for its absence.

In 1962 students of the University of Hawaii's Marketing and Foreign Trade Department decided to investigate the Aloha spirit as revealed in salesmanship on the Islands. Joined by the Retail Board of the Chamber of Commerce and armed with a commercially oriented definition of the Aloha spirit as "that extra warmth that conveys a personal interest in satisfying the customer's needs," they sallied forth to a cold reception by the salespeople of Honolulu. Sixty-nine of those interviewed were found to have the Aloha spirit, but 87 fell short. Concluded the crestfallen surveyors: "The amount of Aloha spirit to be found in Honolulu stores seems to depend on who the customer is."

The second of these footnotes dates from 1964, when *Advertiser* reporter Joe Carter was shocked into action by reading an account of a New York murder. Some 38 neighbors had watched and had done nothing while a woman was being killed by a thug in the street below. Carter decided to find out if the people of Hawaii would respond any better to another's misfortune: as he put it, "Does the Aloha spirit really live in people's hearts here and are they willing to help the person in need?" Dressed in old clothes and carrying a whiskey bottle full of brown-colored water, he sprawled on the sidewalk in front of Waikiki's busy International Market Place and waited. Some 50 people walked by while his legs were sticking perilously out into the traffic on Kalakaua Avenue. Nobody stopped. Nobody even leaned over to see if he was drunk, ill or dead. Finally, after 15 minutes, he was spotted by three Air Force officers who helped him over to a bench. Wrote Carter: "You can expect help, but frankly, not for quite a time."

The typical tourist is similarly inclined to take a somewhat jaundiced view. A quite understandable skepticism has compounded his confusions about the Aloha spirit. He suspects it may be a kind of cosmetic to cover up blemishes in Hawaiian life, or perhaps a collective version of the "soft sell," designed more to loosen his wallet than enrich the inner man. He cannot fail to note that the conjoining of commerce with "Aloha" is apparent on every hand; in fact, the number of Honolulu enterprises with Aloha in their names makes it possible for him to buy anything from a poodle to a hearing aid without leaving the cozy sanctuary of the word. On top of all this, the notion that a whole state should consider itself a special repository of good will seems preposterous on the face of it. Modern civilization appears to be galloping in just the opposite direction. The trend often seems to be toward factionalism rather than fellowship, toward the rejection of natural warmth in favor of studied "cool" and the stone face.

Recourse to the *Hawaiian-English Dictionary* of Mary Kawena Pukui and Samuel H. Elbert for any lifting of the veil seems at first similarly disappointing. In all the 36 lines devoted to definitions, and to the use of Aloha with other Hawaiian words in stock phrases (like *Aloha aina*, "love of the land"), nothing is even mentioned about the Aloha spirit. However, the dictionary does give a wide range of meanings for the word itself. Among them are love, affection, compassion, mercy, pity, kindness, charity and hello. The general import of Aloha is thus clear, and perhaps if all these various meanings can be kept in the mind at once and the word "spirit" added, we will have a loose working definition of the phrase.

But this is not enough, for in rapidly changing Hawaii, with its multiracial population and its varied attitudes and viewpoints, the phrase has taken on many overtones and colorations. Different people have far different ideas of what it implies; like beauty, it is in the eye of the beholder. Ask "Auntie Katherine" Maunakea, living in the midst of the forlorn houses in the native Hawaiian village of Nanakuli, what the Aloha spirit is and you will get a cynical appraisal born of disenchantment with modern corruptions of the old, true Hawaiian warmth. "It's a kick in the pants," she says. "People take advantage of you." Ask Dr. Stanley D. Porteus, Emeritus Professor of Psychology at the University of Hawaii, and you will find that it has been tinged with materialism: "Personally, I think that we give ourselves far too much credit for the very nice way in which we treat our customers. We have so much to gain by being polite to the people coming here." Dr. Willard Wilson, for many years

The Hawaiian women shown at left, photographed in the 1920s, wear long and rather shapeless dresses known in the Islands as *holokus* —dresses that, oddly enough, were the forerunners of the modern and much shorter muumuus. *Holokus* were first worn soon after the missionaries arrived, but, contrary to legend, they were not forced on the native women by churchmen outraged at their seminudity. Instead, the dresses were made fashionable by the clothes-conscious Queen Kalakua, who had to have the graceful, high waistband of the missionary wives' Empire dresses eliminated to adapt the style to her bulky form. This lack of a waistline gave rise to the loose-fitting muumuu, for the first muumuus were made from the slips worn under the *holoku*. Today both casual and formal versions of the muumuu are popular with Hawaiians and mainlanders alike.

Professor of English at the university, has "a strange misgiving that 'Aloha' is related to climate, warm water and coconut oil massage rather than the deeply mystical and spiritual thing that my friend Abe Akaka makes of it."

And what does the Reverend Abraham Kahikina Akaka, pastor of Kawaiahao Church, believe the Aloha spirit to be? The Reverend Akaka, who is as impressive speaking from the pulpit as he is riding a surfboard off Waikiki, reads profound meaning into the Aloha spirit. He sees in it "the power of God seeking to unite what is separated in the world —the power that unites heart with heart . . . culture with culture, race with race, nation with nation. . . . It is the unconditional desire to promote the true good of other people in a friendly spirit, out of a sense of kinship. Aloha seeks to do good with no conditions attached. . . . There is a correlation between the charter under which the missionaries came—namely 'to preach the Gospel of Jesus Christ, to cover these islands with productive green fields and to lift the people to a high state of civilization'—a correlation between this and the fact that Hawaii is not one of the trouble spots in the world today but one of the spots of great hope. Aloha does not exploit a people or keep them in ignorance and subservience. Rather it shares the sorrows and joys of people; it seeks to promote the true good of others."

Rounding out these observations, one might add that the Aloha spirit is not revealed in any single way nor is it the product of any single thing. It would not be likely to exist without the thrust of materialism, be as moving without spirituality, nor be able to call on so inexhaustible a reservoir of good will without the salubrious influence of Hawaii's unsurpassed climate. However this may be, the Aloha spirit permeates the 50th state like a benign contagion. It can be heard in the timbre of laughter and felt in the simple friendliness of a business contact. Even a short exposure to such good will has a way of turning up the corners of mouths that hostility had clamped in a thin line. All this may strike some as arrant sentimentality; yet the fact is that mawkishness emerges only in efforts to put the Aloha spirit into *words* rather than feelings.

It would be a mistake to assume that all Hawaiians are responsive to the Aloha spirit—they are not, human nature being what it is. Nor do those affected respond in equal measure. But there can be no doubt that what might be called a mainstream of the Aloha spirit flows through Hawaiian life continuously, if variably. The result is a slow

The old Hawaiian straddling a pounding board is mashing the cooked roots of the taro plant to make poi, a popular native food that is eaten with the fingers. The mashed roots are mixed with water to form a paste, and this paste is often allowed to ferment for several days to develop the sour taste favored by most Islanders. Hawaiians grade poi by the number of fingers it takes to scoop up a mouthful. One-finger poi is about the thickness of peanut butter; two-finger poi has the consistency of thick gravy. Though poi is still occasionally made in the traditional manner, it can now be purchased prepared and refrigerated at most Hawaiian supermarkets.

but steady tempering of self-interest, aggression, acquisitiveness, ambition. How else can it be explained that the Hawaiians are not at one another's throats like so many groups elsewhere? After all, they would seem to have good reason to be. The Islands were long in the grip of a kind of agricultural serfdom, which was as certain to harvest resentment as crops of pineapple or sugar cane. The weakening of the old power structure that came with statehood would appear certain to have caused antagonism between the new leaders and the old. And a large part of Hawaii's population is made up of people who are not only hereditary enemies, the Chinese and Japanese, for instance, but are also descended from Oriental forebears traditionally opposed to free association and equality of opportunity across racial lines. The reason must be that there is some special quality of tolerance and forbearance in the Islands' atmosphere.

Just why the people of Hawaii manage to sustain this Aloha spirit is necessarily the result of many things, but foremost among them is the unique combination of traits and background, of customs and beliefs, that make up the character of the native Hawaiians. There is no need in this book to chew the dry bones of the old controversy about whether, in the overwrought prose of one writer,

"God-fearing but life-hating missionaries destroyed the warm, brown souls they came to save," or whether the missionaries threw down the native Hawaiians' god of love and "raised in its stead a god of wrath." Even the Old Testament's gospel of vengeance, reinforced by the rigid Calvinist doctrines of "predestination" and man's "total depravity," would seem to have been an improvement over pagan deities demanding human sacrifice. Suffice it to say, the native Hawaiians were a generous people, traditionally hospitable to strangers, and Christianity appears to have fortified and perpetuated these traits. Nor is it necessary to probe history for the other characteristics that today give flavor and durability to the Aloha spirit; these characteristics can be readily discerned among many modern Hawaiians "of the old blood."

First, the Hawaiian native has always had a firm belief in the *quid pro quo:* the generosity so commonly associated with the Aloha spirit is expected to be returned. The visitor who drops in expects to be accorded hospitality, so he customarily brings a small present—a mango, a papaya or a bit of melon —for his host. By the same token, the Hawaiian will do anything for a friend—that is the meaning of friendship to him—but would expect equal response should occasion demand it.

Hospitality, however, does exist outside of this tit-for-tat exchange in the case of the *hanai*. A Hawaiian term meaning literally "to feed," it designates a stray villager—perhaps a child, perhaps an elderly person—who has been taken in as a permanent "guest" by a Hawaiian family. Drs. Alan Howard and Ronald Gallimore, respectively an anthropologist and a psychologist attached to Honolulu's celebrated Bishop Museum, discovered in their exhaustive investigations of the town of Nanakuli, 30 miles from Honolulu, that between 25 and 30 per cent of the families in this overwhelmingly native Hawaiian community supported a *hanai*.

Second, there is the matter of bringing on evil if hospitality, that essential ingredient of the Aloha spirit, is withheld. The native Hawaiians are an intensely superstitious people and believe firmly in gods, demons and the return of the souls of the dead. The word "spirit," even when benignly modified by Aloha, is not to be taken lightly. Spirits are everywhere in the Islands; one has only to express interest in a feature of the landscape—a rock, a cave, a pinnacle, a tree, even a bird—to be told that it contains the spirit of some warrior or maiden of the long ago. Reports of apparitions are not uncommon, particularly of those appearing on the fog-shrouded road that skirts the volcanoes on Hawaii, the Big Island. A recurrent tale is of a driver who stops to pick up an old woman trudging along with her little white or black dog, only to find on arriving at her announced destination that she and the dog have vanished. Good is said to befall those who have performed such an act of kindness, for the old woman is thought to be Pele, ancient goddess of the volcanoes. Sometimes those who have built houses athwart the old trails crossing the lava fields tell of the sound of footsteps moving through their rooms in the night. Mysterious knockings break the sleep of others who have had the temerity to build upon the stone ruins of a *heiau* (temple).

Louis Kahanamoku, a real-estate operator and brother of Duke Kahanamoku, the world-famous Hawaiian swimmer of the 1920s, is convinced that he encountered the supernatural in another form. One night as he was driving on Oahu a white dog jumped from the side of the road. As it sailed over the hood of his automobile, the animal's head turned toward him and he noticed that its eyes were a flaming red. Shaken and puzzling over how the animal's eyes could be glowing like hot coals when it had passed *between* him and the headlights of his car, he rounded the next curve at a snail's pace. It was well that he did, for at normal speed he could not have escaped plowing into the wreckage of two automobiles blocking the highway.

Another Hawaiian tells of an experience that also occurred at night, but this time along the lonely road that runs in the shadow of Mauna Kea on Hawaii and this time the influence was malign. His car, only three months old and up until then in perfect working order, suddenly went dead. In vain he turned the key in the starter lock; the engine refused to turn over. Then, instinctively, his mind flashed back to the great stock of arcane and primitive lore that he, like all Hawaiian boys of the "old" blood, had been taught by the elders of his community. He particularly remembered how he was told to react when set upon by evil spirits. "In a case like this," he recalled, "the spirits had to be defied, so I got out and cursed them. Then I urinated all the way around the car. When I tried the key again, the motor started instantly."

Caucasians who know the Islands may smile at such episodes, but more from understanding than deprecation. A belief in spirits is the natural response of men faced by the awesome mysteries of nature in Hawaii, mysteries that are hardly less compelling now than they were in the distant past. No one long in the Islands, feeling the mystical menace of the sea magnified and remagnified by the realization that the whole island chain floats on a fiery ocean of lava, can dismiss a belief in the supernatural.

Even the most pragmatic U.S. businessmen are not immune. The writer remembers an incident that took place during a 1960 interview with Henry Kaiser, the tough U.S. industrialist and builder of World War II "Liberty ships" who had moved to Hawaii in 1954. The interview was interrupted by a telephone call from Kaiser's foreman at Hawaii Kai, the enormous Kaiser real-estate development just west of Waikiki. The foreman was troubled by a rock in the path of a bulldozer on the slopes of Koko Head. Some of the men leveling the area said that the rock contained a spirit; if the rock was moved by the bulldozer's blade, they prophesied, there would be a volcanic eruption on Koko Head. The Wild Bull of American Industry listened intently and then said: "Well, of course, I don't believe in that sort of thing." Then he paused and added: "But maybe you'd better build a concrete collar around that rock, just in case somebody might accidentally bump it over."

Alexander Spoehr, former director of the Bishop Museum, tells of an incident that befell one of the museum's early directors. This man was concerned over the apprehensions of several Hawaiians who were building him a scale model of an ancient *heiau.* They murmured that this sort of *heiau* had customarily been consecrated in blood, therefore somebody would die. And somebody did. A workman fixing the roof missed his footing and plunged through a skylight, landing near the model. In such an environment, superstition acts to preserve old ways and attitudes.

A third aspect of native Hawaiian psychology that bears on the Aloha spirit is, paradoxically, the natives' abiding fear of getting involved, of making a commitment. To them, being committed to anything courts the risk of being hurt by that commitment. The owner of a new car, for example, will pretend indifference over what may happen to it in order to spare his feelings should any mishap occur. He would rather let it get dirty and banged up than commit himself to its preservation. More significantly, the natives extend this fear of commitment to personal relations. They shrink from hostility or even the possibility of a snub. As a result, they adopt the pose of taking nothing seriously, for to seem to take a position would be to run the risk of contradiction and affront. It is better to appear to be superficial, to avoid getting involved, even to limiting one's social affairs to a small circle of friends seen repeatedly.

This attitude can have some very pleasant overtones, as Drs. Howard and Gallimore discovered in their study of the town of Nanakuli. In contrast to middle-class Americans, native Hawaiians at a party appear under no pressure to present themselves in the best light or to establish their position, and thus they do not create the subtle tensions characteristic of parties on the mainland. Instead they seem engagingly happy-go-lucky and unaffectedly friendly. What this implies, of course, is that the easygoing attitude of the native Hawaiian, one of the most important roots of the Aloha spirit, derives in part from a studied, self-protective detachment, a seeming lack of commitment.

Founded in the psychology of the original Hawaiians, the Aloha spirit continues in one way or another to affect the attitudes and actions of Hawaiians of every stripe. If, for example, the Islands' Japanese, with 33 per cent of the population in 1960, had occupied the same position of power in some other territory just admitted to statehood, one could reasonably have expected them to try to take over. And in fact some of the more powerful Japanese leaders strove to make up for all their years of second-class citizenship by gaining as much political power as they could. But the Japanese did not choose to turn Hawaii into a battleground of race against race in a battle for supremacy. Instead,

they chose to accept the new opportunities open to them in the post-statehood era and opted to keep Hawaii a place where people of many races could get along in mutual forbearance, cooperative participation and the subordination of group ambitions to general harmony. When asked why there had been no all-out push for power, Mitsuo Takabuki, a leader in Island politics, said: "That's not the way things are done in Hawaii. We are all together here and do not seek special advantage."

Even the most intransigent of individuals—the perennial mavericks—seem in the end to feel the effects of the Aloha spirit. A sort of mellowing appears to take place. Back in the 1930s and 1940s, for example, there was not much evidence that Jack Hall, the tough, militant regional head of the International Longshoremen's and Warehousemen's Union (ILWU), would ever be anything but a thorn in the side of the body politic. Hall had found in first coming to Hawaii that unions there were weak where they existed at all. But he soon changed that, and his organizing tactics were hard-line in every respect. In fact, in testimony before Congressional committees, former members of the Communist Party accused him of belonging to the party in the 1930s.

The feeling that Hall and his aides were not bona fide unionists interested in achieving gains under collective bargaining, but agents of a foreign power out to establish alien control over Hawaii's economy, was if anything heightened by the ILWU's unsuccessful effort to take over the Hawaiian Democratic Party in 1948 and by the great strike of 1949. Two thousand longshoremen went on strike that year and stayed out for almost six months. The economy of the Islands all but went to pieces. Dependent almost entirely on shipping, Hawaiian businesses folded, unemployment rose, tourism faded away, and the pineapple industry, with mounting overhead, was brought to the brink of ruin. "Broom Brigades" of angry housewives, recruited largely from a conservative women's organization, descended on Hall's headquarters bent on "sweeping the rascals out."

Bitterness over the strike had hardly subsided when a new wave of anti-Hall feeling rose in 1953 following the conviction of Hall and six other Hawaiians under the so-called Smith Act for conspiring to advocate the overthrow of the U.S. government by force and violence. The reversal of that conviction in 1958—the Supreme Court had ruled that teaching the violent overthrow of the government could not be made a crime—still did not exonerate Hall in the eyes of some who continued to

Mystifying petroglyphs, or rock carvings, executed by the ancestors of today's native Hawaiians, are found throughout the 50th state. Anthropologists are puzzled by these carvings, which are much like petroglyphs left by other primitive cultures in many parts of the world. No one is certain what these carvings mean, although the one at far right could be interpreted as a woman, the middle one suggests a family *(circle)* and its children *(dots)*, and the central element in the third petroglyph might represent a male because of the stick figure's elongated trunk. Some experts, seeing a similarity between Hawaiian petroglyphs and Hindu religious symbols, postulate a link between the cultures of ancient India and Hawaii. Others maintain that no such link ever existed. There are those who think that the carvings were merely a form of doodling and were without much cultural significance.

feel that Hall was a noxious influence in the Islands.

Given this hostile atmosphere and his past behavior, it would have occasioned little surprise had Hall continued to be a rugged labor boss with an ever-growing animus against those who had so violently castigated him. But strangely enough, he did not. In fact, viewed in retrospect, a subtle change seems to have begun to overtake Hall some years before. In the early 1950s, for example, he showed himself willing to relieve some hard-pressed plantations of wage increases he had initially demanded of the entire industry—in marked contrast to what might be considered the common union practice of seeking to achieve labor's goals by forcing the weaker members of an industry to the wall. Even in the late 1940s many of the Islands' leading businessmen felt that Hall was still a Communist. This alone was enough to have put a big chip on his shoulder, but it did not.

Today Hall is still a tough labor leader—"Anybody who plays me for anything else is going to get his pants clawed off," he says with a half-smile—but in a far different way. His instinct for the jugular, plainly on view during his early years in Hawaii, seems to have been blunted by the realization that he can still bargain hard if in a friendly manner and can still pursue union goals without nailing

somebody's hide to the wall. He is respected as an honest and responsible labor leader—his word is his bond to top businessmen like Lowell Dillingham —and his charitable activities have earned him many accolades. Said George Chaplin, editor of the *Advertiser:* "Jack Hall is one of the half dozen men people call on when they want to get something done."

The mellowing of Henry Kaiser followed a somewhat different pattern, although the workings of the Aloha spirit seemed no less effective. Kaiser's aggressive pursuit of Hawaii had begun in earnest in 1954 when he saw droves of tourists being turned away from the few hotels then on Waikiki. No more room for hotels on Waikiki Beach, he was told, so no more room for tourists. Within a year he and his building partner, Fritz B. Burns, had become Waikiki's biggest private landowners, and the Kaiser-Burns Development Corporation was hard at work turning 20 acres of slums into a resort center with a 2,000-foot-long man-made beach. The *Advertiser* correctly observed at the time that a milestone in Hawaiian history had been "marked by the entry into these Islands of Henry Kaiser."

Within six years Kaiser had built a 900-room $15 million hotel complex, a $13.5 million cement plant, a radio station and one for television, and had started on Hawaii Kai, the huge resort center down the coast from Waikiki. Inevitably Henry Kaiser's zealous and jealous wooing of Hawaii stirred up one storm after another. When a top businessman first heard of Hawaii Kai, he exclaimed in anger and amazement: "My God, he's outflanking all of us at Waikiki!" When the *Advertiser* ventured to ask editorially what was going to happen to the homes and leaseholds of a number of families in the path of the Hawaii Kai development, Kaiser reacted like a Bourbon monarch whose divine right had been questioned; calling the editors cowards, liars and antiprogress, he denounced them as participants in a "stop Kaiser" movement. And, inescapably, Kaiser soon indicated that the Islands were now too small for both himself and Hawaii's Grand Old Man, Walter Dillingham.

At the opposite end of the Hawaiian business world from Kaiser—opposite in temperament, outlook and method—Dillingham was a powerful industrialist in his own right. Born and bred in the Islands, "Uncle Walter" was the son of a first mate on a sailing bark who broke his leg soon after putting into Honolulu and during convalescence became infatuated with Hawaii. Urbane, vigorous and astute, Walter Dillingham had always been a man to reckon with, whether on the polo field (he had played with his sons Lowell, Ben and Gaylord until he was 60) or in business.

Open conflict between Kaiser and Dillingham began when Kaiser learned that a new company, the Hawaiian Cement Corporation, was going to build a $12 million plant using Oahu coral as its raw material. Mainland interests were going to supply the know-how and most of the money; Dillingham and the Bechtel Corporation would build the plant as a joint venture. Kaiser, himself a veteran cement manufacturer, immediately announced that he too was going to build a cement plant. Before very long Dillingham was complaining that Kaiser men were buying up coral outcroppings to deprive his prospective plant of raw material. Kaiser, for his part, accused Dillingham of underhanded tactics in trying to get Kaiser's plant site zoned against "noxious industry." Dillingham, in face-to-face debate, dismissed Kaiser as "a visitor here," only to have the visitor invade Dillingham's preserve, the dredging business, with a million dollars' worth of equipment.

Given so much ill will, a battle to the death seemed to impend. The yearly capacity of the two cement plants totaled 2.7 million barrels, almost three times the amount Permenente Corporation (a mainland Kaiser subsidiary) had been shipping into the Islands and more than double the amount then being absorbed in the state. Kaiser showed himself more than ready to start a price war. "If we have to cut price," he said, "we'll cut it. That's how I broke into the cement business back in the late 1930s."

But what eventually happened? Nothing. There was no price war. The two plants now compete vigorously but amicably, not trying to push each other to the wall but waiting until the market grows big enough to absorb their total capacity. Though the imbroglio with Dillingham reached its height when Kaiser was in his seventies, Hawaii had finally taught him that in business matters he did not always have to fight. Hawaiians felt they could detect a distinct tempering of his thoughts and actions. Until his death in 1967, at 85, the vigorous man in the pink house at Hawaii Kai remained immersed in Hawaii's affairs but no longer with elbows out and teeth bared. Old age? The Aloha spirit!

The troubling question about the Aloha spirit in modern Hawaii is whether it can survive change of the kind already discussed in this book. There is certainly a possibility that it may be simply overwhelmed by alien influences, much as the quality of life in many old New England towns has been impossible to maintain once they were absorbed in spreading exurbs. The hordes of tourists and even new residents from the U.S. mainland can be expected to bring about a dilution of the Aloha spirit. And contact with visitors' attitudes in turn must influence the young Hawaiians coming into Oahu from the Neighbor Islands for jobs in the tourist industry. But even if it is likely to be diminished in the future, the Aloha spirit also seems certain to survive. Even the newest of newcomers sense its presence and respond in kind. In 1965, when Pakistanis and Indians were shooting at one another over Kashmir, an Indian and a Pakistani, both recently arrived students at Honolulu's East-West Center, amiably traveled around the state together while proclaiming the points of view of their warring nations. What is more, on one occasion when the Indian could not be present, the Pakistani delivered his usual spirited advocacy of Pakistan's position and then, at the end, remarked: "My opponent could not be here tonight, but if he were, he would say this." Whereupon he launched into a faithful reiteration of the Indian stance on Kashmir.

Political scientist Lawrence Fuchs once correctly observed that "Hawaii is a spirit, not a place." It seems only necessary to add the spirit continues to be that of Aloha.

Clad in ceremonial robes, an official of the Hawaii Ishizuchi Jinja, a Japanese Shinto sect, waves a paper banner, or *gohei*, over a woman about to enter the sect's shrine. The waving of the *gohei* is a traditional Japanese blessing.

A galaxy of cultures

For almost a century and a half Hawaii has welcomed settlers from every corner of the globe: Asians, mainland Americans and even Europeans have poured into the Islands. Though certainly no one intended it, this influx has brought about an experiment in racial and ethnic relations that has led to the friendly coexistence of a variety of cultures within the Islands. Intermarriage is common—there are more than 60 racial combinations on the Islands—yet it has not dimmed the colorful differences among Islanders, for a number of distinct ethnic traditions still flourish. One need not look far to find a Shinto shrine, a bustling Chinese market, a mainland-style shopping center or a native Hawaiian luau, each one illustrative of a separate heritage. Within Hawaii's cultural mosaic each element sparkles with its own unique brilliance.

Photographed by Farrell Grehan

The persistence
of Japanese virtues

Priests and musicians splendidly attired in the costumes of old Japan give thanks for the blessings of the old year during a centuries-old ceremony at a Shinto shrine on Oahu. The Japanese-Americans—who, with 28 per cent of Hawaii's population, form the Islands' largest non-Caucasian group —generally adhere to the traditional patterns of life established by their ancestors. Even Shintoism, with its

stress on highly formalized, age-old rites, retains the allegiance of many older Japanese. Pride in family and a sense of obligation toward associates are as deeply ingrained in Hawaii's Japanese as they are in the Tokyo workingman. Sometimes, as one American businessman discovered, these qualities can be carried to extremes. In exchange for Christmas cards, his Japanese employees swamped him with chickens and cigars, gifts they could ill afford.

This fierce sense of loyalty has served Hawaii's Japanese well. After Pearl Harbor, Japanese-Americans of the Islands often found themselves hated. Their reaction was not sullen indifference. Instead, thousands volunteered to fight for America, proving their loyalty by making the two units they formed among the most decorated in U.S. military history.

The rich fabric of Chinese life

For Hawaii's 38,000 Chinese-Americans there is much that is reminiscent of their ancestral homeland. Buddhist temples abound on the Islands, as do Chinese restaurants, schools and social organizations. Under the massive canopy of the Oahu market in the center of Honolulu's Chinatown, housewives, such as the one at upper left, can browse through scores of stalls. Here they can find virtually all ingredients that go into the thousands of regional dishes that form the world-famous cuisine of China. Some stalls, like the one at right, specialize in fish; others carry such delicacies as sea turtle and pigs' heads; and some sell mung beans, bok choy and other Oriental vegetables.

Even this Chinatown market reflects Hawaii's role as a meeting place of cultures, for Chinese foods are not the only kinds sold. The cooked octopus *(lower left)* will probably be bought by Japanese, and a host of Western and traditional Hawaiian delicacies are available in the market.

Like other residents of Hawaii, the Chinese have been influenced by their close proximity to peoples of many backgrounds. They have adopted those elements of alien cultures that have seemed useful or attractive, weaving them into the rich fabric of their own heritage. In fact, of all Hawaii's ethnic groups, the Chinese have been the most successful in terms of average income and level of education. And while such events as their annual Narcissus Festival reflect China's ancient arts and amusements—with exhibitions of landscape paintings, fireworks displays and gaudily costumed revelers—these festivities sometimes strike such Occidental notes as the crowning of a beauty queen.

The disappearing native Hawaiians

Dressed in brightly colored aloha shirts and muumuus, the people at right, descendants of Hawaii's original inhabitants, are enjoying their classic native feast, the luau. The traditional main course of this gastronomical marathon, which sometimes lasts eight hours, is a whole roast pig, or *puaa kalua,* that has been cooked in an underground oven.
But food is only part of the luau.
During the course of the feast, guests entertain one another with Hawaiian songs and dances, accompanied by the ukulele's twanging strains.

Today, the luau has become a familiar event for all Hawaiian residents and for tourists visiting the Islands as well. Unfortunately there are very few pure-blooded descendants of the native Hawaiians left to savor its delights. When Captain Cook discovered the Islands in 1778, some 300,000 Hawaiians lived there. But for these simple people, the confrontation with the West was to prove fatal. Within decades tens of thousands succumbed to diseases brought to Hawaii by sailors and missionaries. Others intermarried with immigrants and today there are only about 11,000 Islanders of predominantly Hawaiian stock. Economically these citizens are at the lowest level of the state's population, but they are working to improve their own condition. The proceeds from this luau, for example, went to a scholarship fund for local Hawaiian youths.

Shared memories
of missionary days

In the back room of the Mission House *(below),* one of the oldest buildings in Honolulu, members of the Hawaiian Mission Children's Society meet for tea. Society membership is limited to the descendants of the New England missionaries who came to the Islands in the early 19th Century to preach the Gospel—and stayed to lay the foundations of family dynasties that would control Hawaii's

social and economic life right up to World War II. Photographs of some of these pioneer missionaries appear on the revolving rack at lower left.

Though members of the society are no longer as powerful as they once were, many are still wealthy plantation owners and businessmen. As might be expected, their organization is a bastion of conservatism, more suggestive of yesterday's Boston than today's Hawaii. Members meet to compare genealogical tables or discuss the good old days before mainland money began to challenge their economic sway. Today's descendants of the early missionaries are linked not only by common ancestral memories but often by common ancestors as well. In fact, the popular name for their organization is the Cousins Society.

Filipinos: newest element in a cultural mosaic

To the raucous clang of gongs, Island girls of Philippine ancestry perform the *Binaylan,* a 600-year-old dance traditionally enacted by maidens of the Manobo tribe to announce their eligibility for marriage. The girls are members of the Pearl of the Orient Dance Company, an organization formed by the Filipinos in 1954 in an effort to preserve and exhibit the culture of their ancestors.

Filipinos, who now make up almost 10 per cent of Hawaii's population, were the last major ethnic group to arrive in the Islands. Like most earlier immigrants from Asia, they came to work the sugar fields of the large plantation owners. Though the first large group of Filipinos landed in Hawaii in 1906, only today are their countrymen beginning to move into the mainstream of Island life. In part, the long delay reflected the feelings of many of the laborers that they would someday return to their homeland. A shortage of eligible Filipino women in Hawaii only made them more reluctant to sink roots into alien soil. In recent years, however, this situation has changed. Today, Filipinos are entering a variety of professions, including politics, even as they work to maintain their own unique heritage.

8

Upward, Downward and Outward

The business of predicting the future, a difficult and uncertain exercise with most American states, is deceptively simple in the case of Hawaii. Some things there seem so certain to follow a predictable pattern that the appraising eye is blinded to the less apparent elements in Hawaii's future. With the obvious obscuring the subtle, one is inclined to predict that tourism will simply have taken over the Islands by the mid-1970s and let it go at that.

Certainly, lots of "invisible exports"—the cosmetic phrase for the money tourists drop in Hawaii—will be required to sustain an economy that must import most of the things it needs. Hawaii's Department of Planning and Economic Development has already decided that tourist spending must increase from the $300 million of 1966 to $973 million by 1975 and to $1.8 billion by 1985 if the state's economy is to maintain a satisfactory rate of growth. Its projections put the number of tourists expected to flood into Hawaii at two million by 1975—double the Islands' anticipated resident population for that year. The matter of whether Hawaii

is to be given over to "mass" or "class" tourism will obviously have been settled by then, and in favor of the former, for the early 1970s will see the 500-passenger "Jumbo" jets come winging in. The economics of these enormous planes, each capable of carrying almost as many people as an ocean liner now brings to Hawaii, is such that they must be operated round the clock at close to their capacity; lower air fares, calculated to fill the planes, are bound to ensue, putting a trip to Hawaii in the grasp of many more middle-income people.

It also seems certain that the Neighbor Islands will join Oahu as bustling centers of tourism. Representing 90 per cent of the state's land area and almost three quarters of its sand-beach coastline, they are already winning some tourists from Oahu as the latter struggles with its problems of overcrowding, rising prices and deteriorating recreational areas.

Yet however much the Islands are destined to march to the tune tourism calls, behind that dominant probability lie a number of more unusual and significant elements in the state's future. Hawaiian development appears inextricably linked with movement *upward* (into astronomy and space studies), *downward* (into the ocean) and *outward* (in effecting an economic and cultural conjunction

Precariously balanced in front of the foaming "white water," or wave crest, a surfer begins his ride. During winter, waves run particularly high on Oahu's north shore, and surfers flock to places like Waimea Bay and the "Pipeline" in search of the perfect ride.

of East and West). Development in astronomy and what has come to be called "aerospace" is already well underway. The Islands, surrounded by vast expanses of the Pacific, offer astronomers a dust-free sky. Hawaii's location also makes it a natural, even inevitable, choice of scientists engaged in tracking missiles and measuring space phenomena. In consequence, a "Science City" complex for satellite- and missile-tracking operations has been growing, one new installation after another, on the island of Maui since 1957. The site chosen, atop the brown bulk of a 10,000-foot extinct volcano, now bristles with electronic equipment. The Smithsonian Institution runs the satellite-tracking station there, and the University of Hawaii operates a laboratory for solar studies as well as observatories for the study of the light that glows in the upper atmosphere after the sun has set. The University of Michigan has charge of the Defense Department's ballistic missile and infrared observatory. On Kauai Island the Pacific Missile Range and the Kokee Tracking Station have both been expanded. The former, a Navy facility, is used to track missiles fired from the West Coast into the central Pacific. Kokee, operated by the National Aeronautics and Space Administration (NASA), was designed to follow the Gemini Program's two-man capsules and to serve a similar purpose in Apollo, the program to put men on the moon.

Hawaii is also becoming the Pacific hub for the worldwide communications system using satellites. The military satellite communications system (SATCOM) maintains a ground relay station on Oahu, and it has been joined by a ground station built for the Communications Satellite Corporation (COMSAT). In simplest terms, both systems make use of satellites hovering in a fixed position over the Pacific (because their orbital speed and the earth's rotation are synchronized). The satellites relay signals transmitted from the U.S. mainland, Hawaii or stations in Asia, bouncing them across the Pacific's vast expanse. COMSAT's Pacific satellites, launched in 1967, provide regular telephone, teletype and television communication between the mainland, Hawaii and Japan. Six episodes of a popular Japanese television program were telecast live from Hawaii soon after satellite service began, and these were followed by live coverage of the Hawaiian Open Golf Tournament. COMSAT plans to send other satellites aloft over the Pacific in the future, providing a greatly expanded capacity to handle television signals and other means of communication.

The latest development, however, has come on

Hawaii, the Big Island. There, NASA, with its interest in all aspects of space, has awarded the University of Hawaii a contract to build and operate an 84-inch telescope on a solid lava plateau 13,000 feet up the flank of Mauna Kea. The world's highest observatory, with one of the largest of all telescopes, it will be able to take advantage of the finest nighttime astronomical conditions anywhere: the "twinkling" of the stars, an atmospheric nuisance to astronomers at lower altitudes, is minimal in the clear, cold vault arching over the mountain's summit. "When you go to Mauna Kea at night," says Hawaii astrophysicist John T. Jefferies, "the stars look like diamonds hung on velvet."

Even the outpourings of volcanoes such as Mauna Kea have been harnessed to aerospace: the fields of jagged lava have served to condition groups of astronauts for the kind of terrain that may confront them in a landing on the moon. Overall the result has been so rapid a growth in the study of classical astronomy and the newer field of space exploration that the university's board of regents established an Institute for Astronomy in 1967 with the intent of making the university a major center for teaching and research in these fields.

Hawaii's contributions to the study of the sea also seem sure to increase in the decades ahead. Needless to say, the Hawaiian Islands have had a historic preoccupation with the Pacific, both as a source of an important staple of the native diet, fish, and as the traditional means of interisland travel. In recent times this interest has taken on new dimensions as the infant science of oceanography has begun to grow. Hawaii's position in the middle of a great ocean—the Islands are farther removed from surrounding landmasses than any other archipelago in the world—has made it an ideal center for such studies. "Here, in scarcely charted waters," says Donald L. McKernan, director of the federal Bureau of Commercial Fisheries, "scientists have the opportunity to study the largest ocean expanse of our globe and to do so with the animals of the tropical seas naturally brought close to the shoreside laboratories."

Essentially, however, Hawaii's active role in hydrospace, like its involvement in aerospace, was prompted by federal concern—and money. Even as late as 1958 the U.S. government showed but a cursory interest in oceanography, spending only some $20 million to promote research. Less than a decade later the federal government was spending $310 million a year, primarily in translating its newfound knowledge of the oceans into large engineering projects. Although this represented a

15-fold increase, the total spent on hydrospace was still only a fraction of the vast sums ($5.5 billion in 1966) lavished on the space program. However, the economic reasons for a more equitable apportionment of future funds were compelling. "Money spent learning about the oceans and in developing ocean technology," says Dr. Paul M. Fye, director of the pioneering Woods Hole Oceanographic Institution, "promises a return on our investment through the exploitation of the natural resources available there; whereas the money spent in space has an economic impact only so long as the curiosity of nations remains high. It is unlikely that the space expenditures will prime the economic pump by creating new sources of revenue and thus 'hard' increases in the gross national product."

The natural resources to be found in the oceans are many and varied. The profitable recovery of bromine, magnesium and diamonds has already proved possible and the probability is strong that sulfur, potassium chloride and silver can be economically extracted from sea water with today's technology. World production of oil from beneath the sea has risen markedly; wells located off the coastlines accounted for 8 per cent of the total output in 1960, 15 per cent in 1965. A measure of the sharply accelerated interest in the sea can be found in the fact that industries have applied for the rights to find or exploit solid minerals in more than 500,000 square miles of the world's ocean floor—an area almost as big as Alaska. Money spent by private companies on industrial research in oceanography doubled in only two years (1964-1966); government expenditures for the same purpose were estimated to have tripled between 1963 and 1966.

The oceans' traditional product, fish, has also come in for increased attention because of the worldwide population explosion. It is hoped that improved methods of locating, catching and processing fish will help alleviate the hunger of the 7.5 billion people this planet is expected to contain by the year 2000. The value of food and minerals from the sea has been growing at the rate of 15 per cent per year and is expected to go beyond a level of five billion dollars annually in the 1970s. So important have the seas become that a "wet NASA," to do in the oceans what is already being done in space, has been suggested.

Hawaii's importance to oceanography stems from several significant natural advantages. The state's mid-Pacific position, of course, provides a vantage point to study the major currents in that ocean's vast circulation system—and perhaps explain their dramatic but still mysterious influence

A liquid and lyric language

The Hawaiian language reflects the simple, day-to-day outlook on life held by the ancient Islanders. Words for tangible objects important to the early Hawaiians often are numerous. For example, some 225 separate words denote specific aspects of the taro plant, from which poi, staple of the native diet, is made. Similarly, there are 24 terms concerning waves; the early Hawaiians were great fishermen and mariners and therefore developed many terms to describe subtle variations in the sea. Terms for abstract concepts, on the other hand, are far less numerous and sometimes have to be made up of several words; perhaps the briefest Hawaiian equivalent of "across" is *mai kekahi aoao a i kekahi aoao ae*, which literally translates as "from one side to the other side."

Hawaiian is meant to be spoken; it is liquid with the sound of soft vowels and lyric with the multiple inflections characteristic of a Polynesian dialect. It has the fewest distinctive sounds of any known language; when Christian missionaries devised a Hawaiian alphabet in 1822, they drew on only 12 letters to reproduce the vocal combinations used by the Islanders. Precise inflection is important in a language with so few sounds. For example, the word *"aa"* can have four meanings, depending on its pronunciation. The emphasis on musical sound is illustrated by the native word for a small fish, *humuhumunukunukuapuaa*, which in addition to being melodic translates graphically into "trigger fish with the snout of a pig."

Although this rhythmic, lilting language has been largely displaced among the Islanders by English or a local dialect, "pidgin English," many native Hawaiians battle to preserve their ancestral tongue. In addition, a number of Hawaiian words remain in popular usage because they are so apt. Some of these oft-used words, which are commonly sprinkled into otherwise English sentences, include:

Aloha (ah LOH hah). Love, affection; also used as hello or goodbye.

Huhu (hoo HOO). Angry, anger, wrath; also, to become angry.

Kamaaina (kah mah EYE nah). Native-born Hawaiian.

Kane (KAH neh). Man, husband or boy friend.

Kapu (KAH poo). Taboo, forbidden, prohibited.

Kaukau (KOW KOW). Slang for food: grub, chow.

Keiki (KAY kee). Child, offspring.

Luau (LOO ow). Hawaiian feast.

Mahalo (MAH hah low). Thanks, gratitude.

Malihini (mah lee HEE nee). Stranger, newcomer or guest.

Pau (POW). Finished, ended, completed.

Pilikia (pee lee KEE ah). Trouble of any kind, great or small.

Pupule (poo POO leh). Crazy, insane.

Wahine (wah HEE neh). Woman, wife or girl friend.

on fish migrations, climate and weather. Almost every sea condition that might be required for study can be found within easy reach of its shores. Whereas the nation's continental shelf averages 70 miles in width—and in some cases compels a research vessel to travel 800 miles or more to reach an area where scientists can study the ocean's abysses—Hawaii's offshore area has the advantage of compression. Depths of 18,000 feet lie only 70 miles from the coast, while in between is a band of terraces which, though narrow, contain all the features of the continental shelf. Hawaii is also an excellent jumping-off place for long research voyages. One can cover the length and breadth of this biggest of the world's oceans more cheaply and quickly from Hawaii than from any other base.

As for Hawaii's other special advantages, the waters around the Islands are not only very clear but warm as well, a prime advantage in the training of divers and other submarine workers. Moreover, hurricanes and typhoons occur but rarely, in marked contrast to warm-water bases in the Caribbean area. Finally Hawaii provides access to sea life unavailable elsewhere off U.S. coasts, for most of the species found there are of Southeast Asian origin and the state lies in the migratory path of a number of important fishes.

Interestingly enough, the waters surrounding Hawaii were once regarded as a marine desert by some responsible ichthyologists, and not so many years ago at that. The ocean's intense blue there was taken as evidence that the waters were lacking in plankton, the floating plants and animals which constitute the initial building blocks in the food structure of the sea. But with establishment of a laboratory in the Islands by the federal Bureau of Commercial Fisheries, it became clear, to borrow the analogy of a fisheries official, that the central Pacific is "no marine Sahara, largely devoid of animal life, but something that more closely resembles the high plains of East Africa which may look bleak and barren . . . but which support hordes of lions, wildebeests, and elephants. . . . [The central Pacific] is the habitat of the tunas, animals that in their freedom and power and speed might be called the marine equivalent of the lions of the East African veld." Expressed in economic terms, the seas off Hawaii, especially to the south, constitute one of the world's major fishery resources. Expert opinion holds that they could supply 150,000 metric tons of tuna per year (one metric ton = 2,204.62 pounds) on a sustained basis, substantially more than the entire present U.S. tuna catch.

What Hawaii's share of such a catch might be is a moot question since its tuna fleet seems too outmoded to compete with modern fishing boats such as the Japanese possess. The fleet, which concentrates on catching a variety called skipjack, found in abundance close inshore during the summer months, rarely ventures far to sea. The boats employed are larger than the koa-wood outrigger canoes of the ancient Hawaiians, but the method seems untouched by time: the fishermen still depend upon flocks of birds, which feed on the same small fish the skipjack are after, to guide them to the schools; then the tuna are brought aboard on simple steel hooks. The result has been a commercial catch that as recently as 1964 was only three times greater than the quantity of fish taken in landlocked Arkansas.

Change, however, seems to be in the offing. Thanks to the work at the Bureau of Commercial Fisheries' Hawaiian laboratory, scientists are actually learning how tuna communicate with one another. New insight into how well the fish can see, smell and hear is being applied to methods of locating the schools and concentrating the fish for efficient capture. Refined sonar gear, modeled after submarine detection devices, has been brought into play for finding subsurface schools which the sea birds can never pinpoint. New gear and new methods will likely lead the Hawaiian fleet farther to sea with greater profit.

Hawaii's oceanographic activities have centered around relatively few organizations. The Navy, using Pearl Harbor as the headquarters of both the Pacific Fleet and the Pacific Anti-submarine Warfare Force, has had an obvious stake in oceanographic development within the Islands. The Navy's newest and biggest project has been the construction of the Barking Sands Tactical Underwater Range off Kauai. This $5.6 million installation is designed to track and record the positions of submarines, surface vessels and aircraft, simultaneously checking on the success of their tactics and on weapons performance.

Naturally the Navy's efforts have been a mainstay of oceanographic operations in Hawaii, but the state has been at pains to emphasize the commercial possibilities as well. The Oceanic Institute, founded in 1964 by a young marine scientist named Taylor A. Pryor, is currently involved in the world's largest "sea-farming" operation. A fish-raising project, it combines the latest technology from the institute's laboratories at Makapuu Point with some old tricks learned from the ancient Hawaiians. Pryor is using 18 of a total of 87 fish ponds built by the Hawaiians on the island of Molokai, all just inland from the sea and all kept filled with "fresh" salt water, where fish can be kept to fatten. But where the ancient Hawaiians could get only 150 pounds of fish per acre each year from these ponds, the institute, using new knowledge of fish biology, expects a yield of 2,000 pounds per acre.

In addition to sea farming, the Oceanic Institute is setting up a proving ground for industrial research right on the ocean floor, the three-million-dollar Makai Range. This range has been designed to develop efficient methods of recovering oil, exploiting mineral deposits and other natural resources, and building deepwater construction projects.

Up until now the two prime obstacles to getting at the oil lying beneath the deeper portions of the continental shelf have been (1) the impossibility of completing a drilled well and actually getting the oil flowing without having divers go down to do the job and (2) the inability of even the best of today's divers to stay down long enough to do such work at depths of 200 feet and more. The method which will be used at Pryor's Oceanic Institute to get around these difficulties will be to give divers an undersea habitat to live in, and to train them to work on the sea bottom for lengthy periods.

The habitat, which was being built in 1967, is designed to be lowered to depths of from 230 to 600 feet on the Makai Range and to contain both laboratory and living space. Watertight hatches leading from it will enable its crew, wearing wet suits and aqualungs, to venture forth to work areas that will include—in addition to a simulated oil field with a wellhead, pipelines and a storage tank—an experimental mining section and sites for biological experimentation. The crew will be able to stay down for protracted periods through the use of a new technique called "saturation diving," the scientific basis for which is the fact that once a man's tissues and bloodstream have adjusted themselves during the first few hours of a dive, he can stay down for several days without ill effects.

Should these bold experiments prove successful, the institute's long-range plans call not only for additional habitats, but also for a whole second phase in the oceanographic studies on the Makai Range. This will include placing various kinds of scientific measuring devices on a large section of the ocean floor beginning off Oahu's Makapuu Point and extending for thousands of feet down into the abyss.

Since oceanography is an interdisciplinary science, it is natural that the University of Hawaii, with its wide range of scientific departments, should have become the state's center for it. From a very

slender base in 1964, when there were only three faculty members and 10 graduate students majoring in oceanography, the oceanography department had grown so rapidly by 1967 that it could boast 15 faculty members and more than 50 students. In addition to the support oceanographic studies get from old-line departments like geology, chemistry and zoology, the university has established several agencies that broaden the coverage of marine subjects: the Hawaii Institute of Geophysics, headed by Dr. George P. Woollard, an outstanding scientist in that field; the Hawaii Institute of Marine Biology; and the Pacific Biomedical Research Center. The University of Hawaii's oceanographic operations should expand in the next few years when the federal government's enlightened "sea-grant college" program actually goes into operation. Established by Congress in 1966, this program, as its name implies, is designed to help oceanography in a fashion comparable to the way the old land-grant college scheme has so long aided U.S. agriculture and industry. Money will be given colleges and universities already carrying on oceanographic studies, and it seems reasonable to assume that the University of Hawaii will be a beneficiary. Certainly the university's performance in the sciences generally has been impressive enough for it to qualify: it ranked 32nd out of the nation's 126 state universities in the number of National Science Foundation grants received in 1961; in 1966 it ranked 13th in a field of 187.

The hope of Hawaii as a whole is that by cooperating with, rather than competing against, such established centers as Massachusetts' Woods Hole Oceanographic Institution and California's Scripps Institution of Oceanography, it will find "plenty of room at the bottom." A new era certainly appears to be opening up for the oceans. President Johnson in 1966 signed the Marine Resources and Engineering Development Act, which set up a National Council on Marine Resources and Engineering Development, and a Commission on Marine Science, Engineering and Resources was established later on. Estimates vary widely on what all these developments in oceanography may mean to Hawaii in dollars and cents, but the state's Director of Planning and Economic Development, Dr. Shelley Mark, believes that by 1976 the gross annual product from oceanography and related research activities can go as high as $50 million.

The third influential element in Hawaii's future —its reaching outward to draw the Orient and the Occident closer together—is more difficult to describe since the state has pursued this objective in many fields. It has, for example, established a foreign-trade zone, a duty-free area that will stimulate East-West trade; played host to a center for training Peace Corps volunteers; and brought East and West face to face in a series of international conferences. These conferences explored such world-wide problems and opportunities as urban concentration and conservation, oceanography and aerospace. Among the clearest examples of Hawaii's influence in this great undertaking, however, are the East-West Philosophers' Conferences.

The idea behind these six-week affairs has been outlined by their guiding spirit, Dr. Charles A. Moore, who until his death in 1967 was Senior Professor of Philosophy at the University of Hawaii: (1) to help develop greater mutual understanding between the peoples of Asia and the West at the level of philosophical conviction and (2) to encourage total or global perspective in philosophy. "Mutual understanding," Dr. Moore once declared to the assembled philosophers, "is, in our judgment, based upon open-mindedness and cordiality to alien ideas, rather than mutual criticisms, the trademark, alas, of much of scholarship. Unphilosophically, perhaps, we [at these conferences] have not so much sought solutions of philosophical problems as we have sought the deepest possible mutual understanding and respect." The difficulty always confronting the conferees, he emphasized, was "the common practice of disparagingly comparing one's own *ideals* with the *practices* of others. And . . . the constant danger of falling into the colloquial trap or cliché of thinking of '*the*' East and '*the*' West in utter violation of the great complexity and variety in all the areas and traditions that are our special concern."

The first of these conferences was held in Honolulu in 1939, with others following at 10-year intervals, but at the conclusion of the third meeting, in 1959, Dr. Moore politely suggested that the group might consider holding Number Four somewhere in Asia—at New Delhi, Tokyo or Taipei. The delegates disagreed unanimously and for reasons that Hawaii may be proud of. It was their belief that the essential environment of open-mindedness and cordiality could only be found in Hawaii, where multiracial harmony was a fact of life. "In Hawaii," said one Asian simply, "nobody feels like an outsider or a foreigner." Echoed a fellow delegate: "This is the first conference my Oriental colleagues and I have ever attended where we felt on an equal footing with everybody else."

That 1959 conference was memorable in another respect. At its conclusion a Honolulu businessman named Hung Wo Ching, an enthusiastic observer of its proceedings, had a question for Dr. Moore. Mr. Ching, Board Chairman of Aloha Airlines, wanted to know whether the next conference could take place within five years (instead of 10) provided the $110,000 needed to finance it could be raised in the shorter time period. Assured that money was the only obstacle, Ching issued luncheon invitations to 110 of Hawaii's most important businessmen. Splitting the group into thirds (taking care to see that each third mirrored Hawaii's ethnic composition), Ching gave three luncheons. At each he told the guests they were going to give $1,000 apiece to finance a Philosophers' Conference in 1964—urbanely adding that it would not hurt too much because they could pay at the rate of $250 a year. It goes unrecorded whether all those present responded enthusiastically to Hung Wo Ching, but within six weeks $110,000 was subscribed.

The topic for discussion at the ensuing conference in 1964 was a singularly appropriate one, for if ever a subject was beset with misconceptions by all parties it was "The Status of the Individual in East and West." The most prevalent clichés were described by Dr. Moore at the opening session.

In general, he said, the belief is "that in the East, the entire East, there is no respect or dignity or even autonomy for the individual, who is lost, sometimes said to be annihilated, in an Absolute, in nothingness, in the family, in the State, or in social tradition, whereas in the West . . . the individual is everything, and the group . . . is of relative insignificance. . . ." Dr. Moore concluded that such sweeping generalizations were obviously wrong—and obviously dangerous bars to East-West understanding. Progress comes with glacial slowness in any meeting of minds, and six weeks of deliberation in Hawaii were obviously insufficient to bridge the gap. Yet progress was certainly made. As Chinese-born John C. H. Wu expressed it to his fellow philosophers: "While East is East and West is West, there is East in the West and West in the East. Each instinctively seeks the other for its own completion and fulfillment. Let us therefore treasure their differences; for without differences they would not be able to enrich each other."

While Hawaii's gap-bridging role is necessarily intermittent in the case of the Philosophers' Conferences, the state does possess an important instrumentality for daily dialogues in Honolulu's Center for Cultural and Technical Interchange between East and West. Colloquially known as the East-West Center, this pivotal organization was set up in 1960 by the U.S. government, which picked up the $8.1 million tab for its six handsome buildings on the University of Hawaii's Honolulu campus as well as for its successive yearly budgets ($5.8 million for fiscal 1967).

The center itself has neither curricula nor faculty, both being supplied primarily by the university, to which it is bound by close administrative and academic ties. Nor is it able to confer degrees or academic honors, for these too are the province of the university. What it does, essentially, is to establish an international community of scholars where students drawn from 31 nations in Asia and the Pacific area, along with participants from the United States, can study on full scholarships. In the appraisal of its chancellor, Howard P. Jones, the center "crosses national frontiers, bringing together from different countries groups concerned with identical problems, exposing them to their opposite numbers in other lands. It crosses boundaries within societies, drawing together countrymen formerly separated by sectarianism, geographical distances and occupations. It generates ideas as useful to Americans as to Asians, shattering ethnocentricity, combatting condescension, and ordering the traffic in ideas along a two-way street."

All students at the center are committed to two major undertakings—and expected to succeed in both. The first is the pursuit of a specific field of study or technical training in some area of interest not only to Asia and the Pacific Basin but to the U.S. as well. Technical training courses have run the gamut from electrical engineering to supermarket management. Other studies have included such professional fields as law and agricultural economics, but have also stretched to embrace languages and religions.

The second of the two major undertakings required of students at the center goes by the mouth-filling term of cross-cultural interchange. Americans are required to live and work with Asians and other students from the Pacific. Asians are thrown with Asians of other nationalities, often for the first time. To its great credit, the center takes a down-to-earth view of cultural interchange, expecting no instant utopia. "Familiarity does not necessarily breed affection," one of its publications cautioned incoming students. "Passions may be heightened rather than decreased as men of different nationalities meet face to face." Surprisingly, Asians and Pacific Basin students often discover they know less about one another than they do about their American confreres. The Australians, given to full-lunged criticism of their government and society, are astonished at the apprehensions that tie the tongues of some Orientals. The gregarious Koreans are dismayed to find in Japanese students an unwillingness to socialize (they tend to concentrate exclusively on their studies).

This is not to say, of course, that students from Asia and the Pacific Basin are letter-perfect in their knowledge of Americans. A Korean, composing a letter to his family back home, asked his American roommate in all seriousness whether the phrase "Wash up" was not the customary greeting in the U.S.; whenever he had been invited to an American home, he had always been greeted at the door with "Wash up?" (A more knowledgeable Thai, so greeted before lunch, confounded his host by taking a shower; after all, it was not an unusual thing to do on a hot day in his native Thailand.)

How effective a job the East-West Center did in five years of operation from 1962 to 1967 may be told statistically. At the end of these five years it had turned out almost 7,000 alumni. Of this number all of the technical trainees and more than half the student grantees were from Asia or the Pacific. Most important, they took their skills and knowledge back to their native lands. Ninety-five per cent of them returned home upon completion of their center courses. Many filled key jobs. One became deputy administrator of the Micronesian Congress, another chief of an agricultural experimentation station in Taiwan; a third took office as dean of women at a Japanese university. Polled about the effectiveness of their center training, 75 per cent of the American students and 82 per cent of those from Asia and the Pacific declared it had been *very* effective.

Hawaii's contribution to East-West affairs, however, is also a business matter. Hawaiian companies have been reaching out beyond the confines of the 50th state to set up shop all over the world. The activities of Dillingham Corporation (construction, mining, real estate, transportation) now range from Australia to Canada to the Persian Gulf. In 1966, for the first time, its overseas business matched the volume generated within Hawaii. As for Hawaii's old-line companies, the Big Five, they are exporting their enormous expertise in land management and the growing of sugar. American Factors has contracts to act as technical consultant in India, Pakistan, Taiwan and South America; its most ambitious project is the development of 1.4 million acres of land for agriculture in Australia. C. Brewer and Company has won research, development and management contracts (primarily in agriculture) in Iran, Iraq, Ecuador, Peru and Colombia. Theo. H. Davies & Company is engaged in manufacturing, trading, insurance and sugar services throughout the Philippines. Castle & Cooke, for its part, has pursued abroad the diversification it began in the Islands: a joint venture in Thailand (the Thai-American Steel Works Company); banana, brewing and shipping operations in Honduras and Costa Rica; controlling interest in a Philippine glass company and a concrete plant in Malaysia's Kuala Lumpur. Hawaiian enterprises are also operating abroad in banking, insurance and finance. Significantly, Hawaii had only 11,000 eastbound travelers from Pacific and Asian countries in 1955, but by 1966 the number passing through on their way east was more than 100,000.

To be sure, the future potential of Hawaii both economically and culturally needs qualification. Much of the Pacific's trade bypasses the Islands now and will undoubtedly do so in the future. Great as the growth of Asia is expected to be in the next 50 years, Hawaii can be expected to participate in the expanded economic activity only to a relatively small degree. The Islands are, after all, no more populous than a good-sized mainland city, and the population projected for 1985—1,165,000 —does not alter this comparison. At the same time, if Hawaii were simply to preserve its relative position vis-à-vis the anticipated growth of economic activity throughout the Pacific, the Islands' continued prosperity would be assured. The present economic plan for the state reflects Hawaiian confidence in being able to do just that: projections for 1985 are based on the assumption that the private sector should be producing $7.3 billion worth of goods and services by then, more than triple the figure for 1965.

Hawaii's effectiveness in its cultural role of bringing East and West closer together has also been discounted in some quarters. Abbott Kaplan, former director of the University of California's extension division at Los Angeles, declared in his 1967 study of the University of Hawaii: "Despite the talk of Hawaii becoming the great bridge between the East and the West—at the moment it is that only geographically, certainly not culturally or intellectually. Little has been done, outside the degree programs in the University, to deepen the knowledge of Hawaiian citizens and ethnic groups of their own and of others' rich cultures. . . . It would be too bad if Hawaii followed the pattern of the mainland with regard to ethnic cultural differences—where our notion of Americanizing people was essentially to de-foreignize them, and to develop a bland, conformist, least common denominator mass-culture. The goal should not be the . . . development of a

pallid, largely Anglo-Saxon 'low cult,' but cultural diversity and pluralism. . . ."

Unfortunately, Kaplan's remedy—that Hawaiians of Oriental origin build upon an already reawakened interest in their roots and backgrounds, with the university helping out—seems unequal to the task. A common language (English) and the relentless vulgarization of even that by television and radio is a powerful force for continued "Americanization." But even if Hawaiians of Oriental extraction seem destined to have fewer differences and more things in common with the typical American from the mainland, does this then presage a weakening of Hawaii's role as a bridge between East and West? Hardly. In the last analysis, the most convincing proof that Hawaii is a bridge is its rate of intermarriage between people of Eastern and Western extraction. Every marriage between Japanese and Caucasian or Filipino and Portuguese testifies to the acceptance of a foreign culture in the most complete way possible.

Furthermore, Hawaii's unequivocal reconciliation of the races has the faculty of making even the most insensitive Asian or mainland American realize we are all partners in the vast world of the Pacific. Nowhere else is it possible to feel so at ease among the races bordering that great ocean. And nowhere else is there so marvelous a mixture of Yankee ingenuity and grit, Oriental industry and perseverance, and native Hawaiian good will and good humor.

Someday, perhaps, the ethnic groups in Hawaii may attain a knowledge of their origins that will enable them, as Dr. Moore once wrote, "to glimpse what belonging means to a Chinese; to understand how a Hindu can regard his personality as only a mask overlaying and obscuring the infinite beneath; to crack the paradox of the Zen monks in Kyoto. . . ." Should they gain such knowledge, it would allow them the enriching experience of living in two worlds at once, in the world of their cultural heritage and in the world of modern Hawaii. As grand a prospect as this is, it should not cloud the fact that Hawaii's people have already made a contribution to the world they in fact do live in. It is still a revolutionary idea, as social scientist Daniel W. Tuttle Jr. has put it, "to judge a man on what he can contribute, not where he was born or what color his skin is or the religion he professes."

Despite imperfections and shortcomings, when all is said and done, Hawaii may justly claim that its achievements on this, the sociological frontier, are the equal of any wonders worked against the physical frontier by modern science.

Jagged green precipices mark the pali, or cliff, coast on Molokai, which runs the entire length of the island's windward side. The steep wall of rock is pierced by deep coastal valleys that are isolated by high cliffs and rough seas.

Islands forged in fiery caldrons

No other land could so longingly . . . haunt me sleeping and waking," wrote Mark Twain after he visited the Hawaiian Islands in 1866. Like millions of more recent visitors, the author was enchanted by the landscape's serene beauty. But this impression of serenity has always been deceptive, for the islands were born and matured in the fiery violence of volcanic eruptions. Time and again the mountains have shuddered, and from caldrons in their bellies have come rivers of lava to lay waste to the land. And time and again the islands have been reborn, as lush greenery sprouted from the ash-strewn desolation. Even today the people of the island of Hawaii keep watch on their temperamental mountains, and though the volcanoes on the other islands are silent, other foes—tidal waves and earthquakes —hold the land hostage to nature's whim.

Photographed by Farrell Grehan

Clouds floating lazily over the forbidding windward coast of Molokai *(above)* move toward the steep slopes of the island's central mountains. Water released by such clouds has a scouring effect on the slopes, carving deep ravines in the palisades. On the island of Kauai almost perpendicular cliffs *(right)* jut skyward, their deep green foliage nourished by low-lying clouds that create a humid atmosphere.

Protected by towering cliffs laced with slender waterfalls, Waipio Valley *(left),* on the Big Island (Hawaii), once harbored prosperous native villages. Here many Hawaiian kings built residences. Other native communities thrived in the region of Wailua Falls *(right),* on the island of Kauai. The cascade is located at the head of the Wailua River, one of the few navigable waterways on the Islands. At the base of the 50-foot-high falls lies a deep pool rimmed with hala trees and tropical flowers. Here visitors can take a refreshing dip, just as Island chiefs did in centuries past.

Amid the greenery of a tropical rain forest on the island of Hawaii *(far left)* a bright red flower stands out. Called a lobster claw because of its resemblance to the crustacean, the plant is a relative of the banana and is a Central American species brought to Hawaii for ornamental purposes. The Big Island's rich soil, its year-round warmth and its moist air combine to create a lush region of flowers. Even periodic volcanic eruptions only temporarily halt the irrepressible growth of vegetation. The amaumau fern *(left),* one of the first plants to take root on lava beds, is shown flourishing in a spot that only 10 years previously was a desolate sea of steaming rock.

The peril from volcanoes on the island of Hawaii is startlingly revealed in a farmer's field of cultivated orchids *(left)*, which grow near cinder cones created when Kilauea Volcano erupted in 1960. Spewing lava 1,000 feet in the air, the eruption destroyed the town of Kapoho and buried much valuable land near this field. But the orchid farmers were undaunted, and despite the threat of new eruptions they refuse to leave their land. Even while they farm, the volcano remains active, for farther up its slope *(above)* the earth is covered with sulfur that constantly steams up through fissures in Kilauea's crust.

Desolate and remote, a string of craters winds up the side of a sleeping volcano called Haleakala, or House of the Sun, on Maui Island. Along the lip of the crater wall are two observatories and a satellite tracking station *(center background)* that sparkle against the bleak terrain. High altitude and clear air make this mountain a perfect site for the study of the heavens. U.S. astronauts have also tested equipment on Haleakala for a lunar landing, using a gigantic depression within the mountain's 10,000-foot-high crest *(upper right)* as their proving ground. Large enough to swallow Manhattan, this basin was formed by the erosion of several craters, and its floor may be the closest thing on earth to a lunar landscape.

No part of Hawaii is very far from the sea, and the sea is rarely far from the lives of Hawaiians. It has been long the Islands' highway to the world, a storehouse of food and a playground. But the encircling ocean is something more: an ever-present force that establishes much of the Islands' ambience. Whether rushing between Maui's offshore boulders *(left)*, shimmering beside Oahu's bold promontories *(center)* or pounding against the Big Island's lava rocks *(right)*, the sea adds to the atmosphere a strong element of languor and a hint of barely suppressed violence.

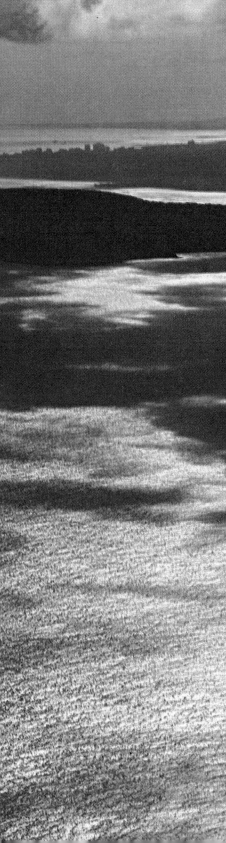

In the twilight's calm a group of Oahu
fishermen cast their lines into the Pacific from
Kahe beach, just 15 miles from downtown
Honolulu. The dedication of the Islanders to
ocean sport is legendary. It was the Hawaiians
who invented surfboarding, and many residents
delight in the dangerous pastime of riding the
crests of a turmoil of breakers. Others prefer
the quieter joys of sailing or skin diving, and
some, like these anglers, take pleasure in
fishing at sunset when the soft light on the hills
and the lapping of the water against the shore
combine to make a world of contentment.

Suggested tours

On the following pages six maps show sections of the two Frontier States that are of particular interest to the tourist. No attempt has been made to show every road and town. Instead, scenic routes, parks, historic sites and other special features have been emphasized. The text accompanying each map gives a description of the area. Opening dates and hours, especially for tours of businesses, should be confirmed locally, since they may vary with the season of the year. The six areas covered are shown on the small maps at left, along with a key to the symbols used. Some of the more remote points of interest can be reached only by plane or ship, but transportation can generally be arranged in cities. Although the Alaska Highway is open the year around, travelers are urged to avoid driving it during the winter, when temperatures may drop to 60 below zero, and during the spring thaw, when the unpaved sections are extremely muddy.

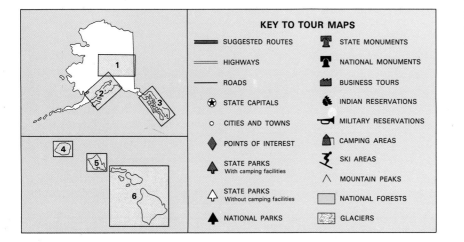

KEY TO TOUR MAPS

- SUGGESTED ROUTES
- HIGHWAYS
- ROADS
- ★ STATE CAPITALS
- ○ CITIES AND TOWNS
- ◆ POINTS OF INTEREST
- ▲ STATE PARKS With camping facilities
- △ STATE PARKS Without camping facilities
- ▲ NATIONAL PARKS
- STATE MONUMENTS
- NATIONAL MONUMENTS
- BUSINESS TOURS
- INDIAN RESERVATIONS
- MILITARY RESERVATIONS
- CAMPING AREAS
- SKI AREAS
- ∧ MOUNTAIN PEAKS
- NATIONAL FORESTS
- GLACIERS

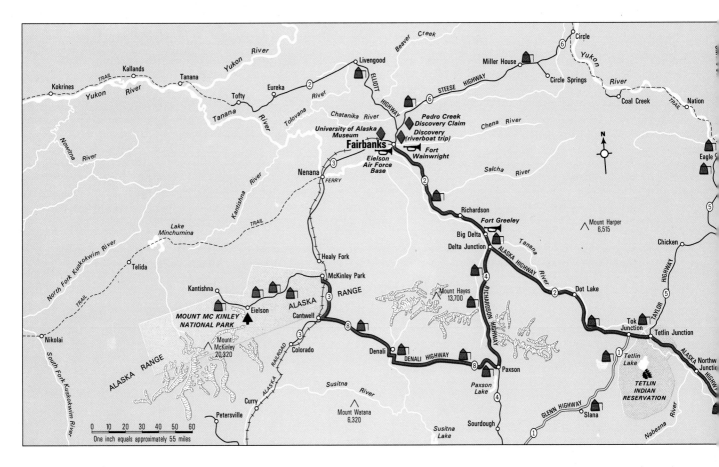

One inch equals approximately 55 miles

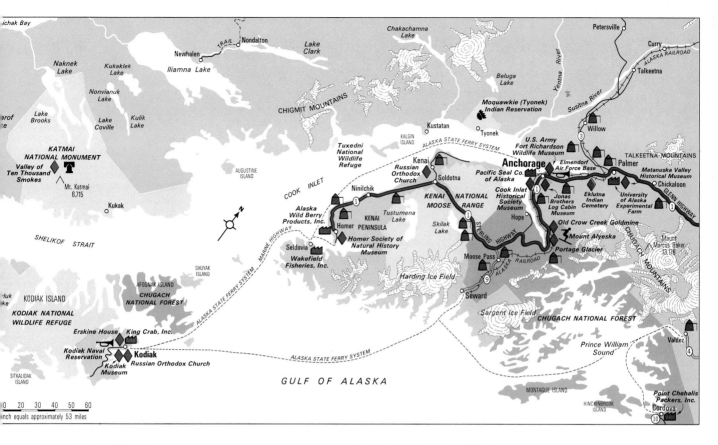

1. Interior Alaska

Deep in the heart of Alaska (*left*), but easily accessible by plane, train or automobile, lies the state's second-largest city, Fairbanks. Set in the fertile Tanana River Valley, which spreads to the foothills of the massive Alaska Range, Fairbanks is a good starting point for tours through some of Alaska's most majestic scenery. In town a few buildings from the early gold-rush days still stand, and visitors are reminded of the gold-rush era every July when residents observe the Golden Days Celebration with parades, art exhibits and a gold-panning contest.

Northeast of Fairbanks via the Steese Highway is the town of Circle, on the storied Yukon River. This is the northernmost point accessible by a highway in North America. The road passes the site of the region's first gold strike, made on July 22, 1902, by an Italian immigrant prospector named Felix Pedro. A few miles west of Fairbanks, on the highway to Nenana, is the University of Alaska, with its museum of Eskimo and Indian artifacts. The most spectacular of the area's attractions, the 3,030-square-mile Mount McKinley National Park, is a relatively short trip of 122 miles from Fairbanks by rail. The trip by road, however, is much longer, and tourists who wish to drive to the park from Fairbanks must go roundabout by way of Delta Junction, Paxson, Denali and Cantwell, a total of 340 miles. In the park, grizzly bears, moose and other wild animals roam free in the shadow of majestic Mount McKinley, North America's highest peak (20,320 feet), which the Indians called Denali (The High One).

2. South Central Alaska

South Central Alaska is the state's most heavily populated region, with bustling fishing villages, thriving farms, and Alaska's largest city, Anchorage. Set on a bluff overlooking Cook Inlet, Anchorage has far outgrown its origin as a small tent town staked out in 1915 for railroad workers. Downtown, the Cook Inlet Historical Society Museum houses relics of pioneer days as well as examples of Eskimo handicrafts. In February the city stages Alaska's largest winter festival, the Fur Rendezvous, with sled-dog races, parades and dances.

About 50 miles northeast of Anchorage is Palmer, in the fertile Matanuska Valley, where long hours of summer sunshine produce mammoth 50-pound cabbages, seven-pound turnips and three-pound potatoes. South of Anchorage, the Sterling Highway passes the Mount Alyeska ski resort, where a mile-long chair lift operates all year long, carrying visitors above the tree line for a view of eight glaciers winding among the barren mountains. From Mount Alyeska the road leads across the rugged Kenai Peninsula. Salmon abound in the area, and each August the coastal town of Seward—south of Anchorage along Route 9—stages a contest for the largest salmon taken from the adjoining bay.

Ferries run from the mainland to Kodiak Island, site of the first Russian settlements in Alaska, established in the 1700s. The island is also notable for its Kodiak bears, the world's largest carnivores, and for the giant king crabs that sometimes weigh as much as 25 pounds.

175

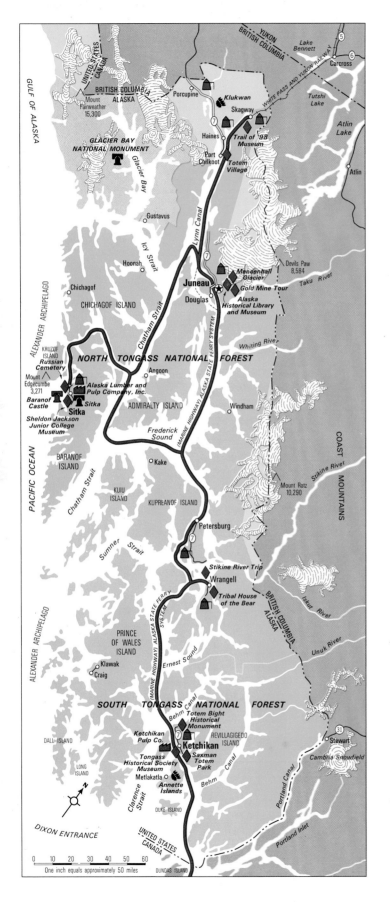

3. The Alaskan Panhandle

Southeastern Alaska, the famed Panhandle consisting of forested islands off a glacier-studded mainland, is a scenic setting for the heavily traveled Marine Highway, an inland waterway. Throughout the year ships of the Alaska State Ferry System make the 490-mile run between Prince Rupert, British Columbia (*just off the map at the bottom*), and the northwest terminus of Skagway, Alaska. Ferry tickets from Prince Rupert to Skagway cost $36.25; automobiles are carried for $105.

The first port of call of the journey northward is Ketchikan, nestled on a narrow shelf between steep, green mountains and the sea. Like other coastal towns, Ketchikan prospers on fishing and logging. The Ketchikan Pulp Company shows visitors how timber is processed into pulp ready for shipping to American and foreign markets. South of town, Saxman Totem Park displays one of the world's largest collections of totem poles.

Wrangell, 102 miles farther north, is also rich in Indian lore. A Tlingit Indian community center, Tribal House of the Bear, contains totem poles 200 years old. The island town of Petersburg, the next stop, was settled largely by Norwegians, and every year a festival commemorates Norway's Independence Day, May 17. Charter planes and boats are available for hunting and fishing trips or for sightseeing to nearby glaciers.

Twice a week during the summer the ferry goes from Petersburg to Baranof Island and the town of Sitka, once the capital of Russian America. A monument marks the site of Baranof Castle, home of the leader of the early Russian settlement, which overlooks the island-dotted sound and a huge extinct volcano, Mount Edgecumbe. The next port is Juneau, largest town in the Panhandle and the capital of Alaska. At one time gold mining was one of Juneau's major industries, but today only the mine railway is in use, carrying tourists to a spectacular lookout high above the town. A short drive away is massive Mendenhall Glacier, where a visitor's center overlooks the face of the ice flow as it plunges into a deep lake formed by the meltwater.

Near the end of the ferry journey are the adjoining towns of Port Chilkoot and Haines, at the southern terminus of the road leading north to the Yukon and the Alaska Highway. In Port Chilkoot a popular attraction called Totem Village displays totem poles, a pelt-drying rack, a reproduction of a tribal house and a replica of a fur trapper's cabin. The ship's final call is at Skagway, once the main gateway to the Yukon's gold fields. The town is quiet now, with a population of about 700 instead of the 20,000 it had in 1898, but its citizens relive the Gold Rush days several nights a week during the summer with a restaging of the "Shooting of Dan McGrew."

4. Kauai

The east and west coasts of Kauai present entirely different façades. Because of this topographical dissimilarity, Kauai—the oldest of the Hawaiian Islands—contains the state's most varied scenery, from white beach and lush valley to arid plain and rocky canyon.

Daily flights from Honolulu bring visitors to Lihue, on Kauai's southeast coast. From Lihue, the road north runs past fields of sugar cane to Wailua, where a motor launch follows the jungle-lined Wailua River to an exotic, fern-covered grotto and a waterfall that splashes onto rocks tinted emerald with moss. Just west of Wailua is the Holo-Holo-Ku Heiau, a temple where princesses went to bear their royal young. Continuing north and then west, the road circles the island to Lumahai Beach and Haena. Both so epitomize tropical beauty that they were used as locations for the motion picture *South Pacific*.

The road west of Lihue leads to some of Kauai's most rugged terrain. Near Koloa, 10 miles away, is a striking shoreline of black lava, where the incoming waves rush through a lava tunnel and spew out in a geyserlike spray called the Spouting Horn of Koloa. At Waimea a monument marks the site where the English explorer Captain Cook landed in 1778. The road then turns inland and leads through thick forests to Waimea Canyon, carved through rich red and brown earth by the Waimea River as it flows from the flanks of Waialeale mountain, one of the wettest spots on earth. At the end of the road, in the Kokee State Park, the Kalalau Lookout stands above a deep, green valley with jagged cliffs that plunge 4,000 feet to the magnificent but forbidding Na Pali Coast.

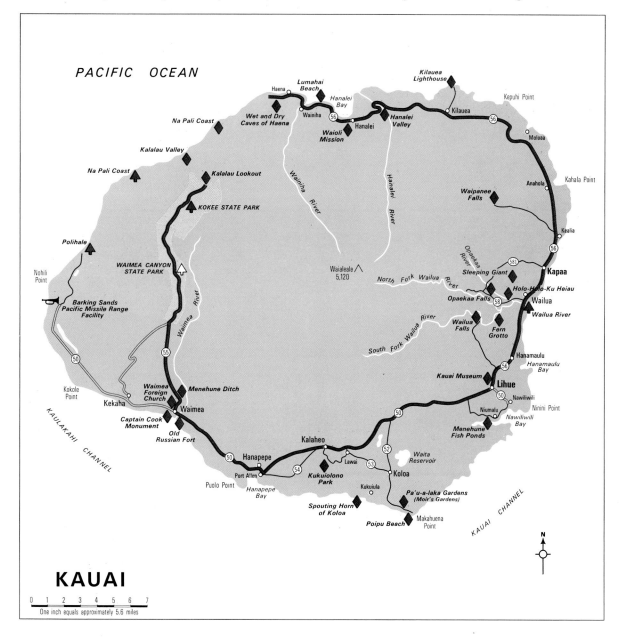

KAUAI

0 1 2 3 4 5 6 7
One inch equals approximately 5.6 miles

5. Oahu

The name "*Oahu*" in Hawaiian means "the gathering place." It is an appropriate name for this part of the 50th state, for though it is only the third-largest island in the Hawaiian chain, 82 per cent of the state's population and most of its major commercial enterprises are on Oahu.

The island's major city, Honolulu, also the state capital, is an important stopover for many aircraft flying the Pacific route to Asia. Among the city's interesting sights are the Honolulu Academy of Arts, which houses a fine collection of American, European and Oriental art; Iolani Palace, once the home of Hawaiian monarchs and now the seat of state government; and the Bernice P. Bishop Museum, repository of the world's foremost collection of Hawaiian and Polynesian artifacts.

Southeast of Honolulu's center, along a road that hugs the coast, one comes first to the famous Waikiki Beach and then Diamond Head, the extinct volcano that is perhaps Hawaii's most celebrated landmark. Farther east, along Route 72, is Sea Life Park, where many marine animals can be viewed in simulated ocean settings. The road then loops northward, forming, with Route 83, a coastal highway that passes a number of excellent campsites. Coral Gardens, along this highway, offers rides in glass-bottomed boats over colorful coral formations, and farther north at Laie is the Polynesian Cultural Center with a display of the arts and crafts of Pacific Islanders.

Many visitors to Oahu will be interested in seeing the U.S.S. *Arizona* Memorial at Pearl Harbor, where 1,100 sailors, who died when the *Arizona* sank at her mooring on December 7, 1941, lie buried beneath the waters.

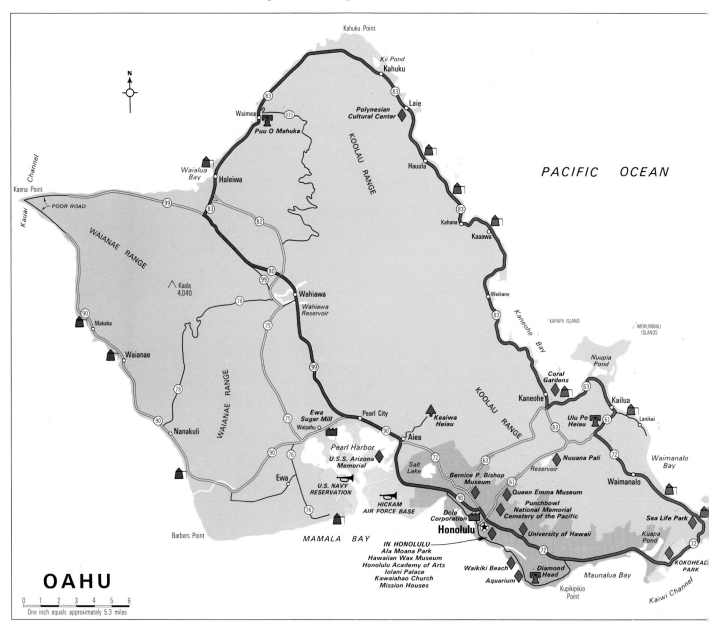

OAHU

0 1 2 3 4 5 6
One inch equals approximately 5.3 miles

178

6. The southeastern Islands

Southeast of Oahu is a cluster of islands that include the island of Hawaii, the largest land mass in the Hawaiian chain. The Big Island, as Hawaii is also called, is the only part of the state still threatened by active volcanoes; the most famous is towering Mauna Loa, more than 13,000 feet high. Route 11, running southwest from Hilo —the Big Island's largest city—passes close to Mauna Loa in Hawaii Volcanoes National Park. Within the park, visitors can walk along trails through some of the most desolate, yet starkly beautiful, areas in the state. Beyond the park, Route 11 turns northward along the western coast to pass by Hulihee Palace at Kailua, the summer home of Hawaii's royal family in the 1800s.

Across the Alenuihaha Channel from Hawaii Island lies the second-largest land area in the state: Maui. On its northwestern coast, along Route 30, is Lahaina, once the capital of the Hawaiian Empire that extended from the island of Hawaii to Kauai. Much of the town has been restored as it was in the 19th Century, when it was a center for whalers and missionaries as well as Island royalty. In Wailuku, the county seat, the Maui Historical Society Museum houses some of the first books written in the Hawaiian language.

Lanai Island, to the west of Maui, is often called the Pineapple Island, for its fields are planted exclusively in this one fruit; at the Dole plantation, visitors can tour the fields. To the north lies Molokai Island, home of a number of the state's remaining Hawaiians and the site of another reminder of former times, Hansen's Disease Settlement, a station set up for the treatment of leprosy.

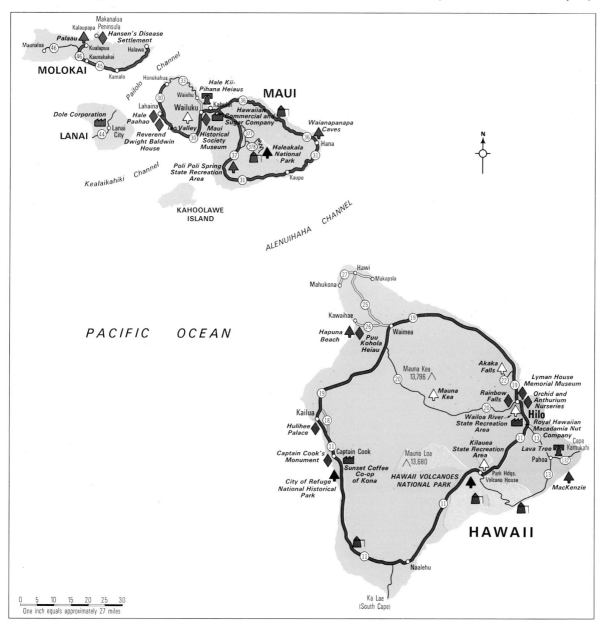

Museums and galleries

Alaska

Anchorage
Anchorage Log Cabin Museum, 700 Fifth Ave. Natural history collection of stuffed animals (including big-game trophies), minerals and Alaskan furs. Mon-Sat 9-6.

Cook Inlet Historical Society, 630 Fifth Ave. Eskimo, Indian and pioneer artifacts. Collection of historical photographs. Sat-Wed, hols 1-5; Fri, Sat eves 7-9:30.

College (near Fairbanks)
University of Alaska Museum. Broad and excellent collection, including biological, archeological, ethnographic and historical exhibits emphasizing Alaska and the Far North. Winter: daily 1-5; Fri eves 5-8; summer: daily 9-6; Fri eves 6-8.

Fairbanks
Exposition Grounds. Various special exhibits, including photographs, paintings, antique mining equipment. Summer: daily 10-10.

Haines
Sheldon's Museum, Lynn Canal Bldg. Indian artifacts, ivory carvings and local historical items. May-Sept: on tour days; other times by appointment.

Juneau
Alaska Historical Library, Capitol Bldg. Excellent collection of books, maps, documents and photographs dealing with Alaska, plus newspaper files from 1868. Mon-Fri 8:30-12, 1-5.

Alaska State Museum. Displays of Indian, Eskimo and Aleut artifacts, Russian and Gold Rush mementos, rocks, minerals, photographs. Winter: Sun-Fri 8:30-5; Sat 1-5; summer: Mon-Fri 8:30-5, 7-10; Sat 1-5, 7-10; Sun 1-5.

Kenai
Restoration of Fort Kenay, American Army post built in 1869. Contains local historical items, photographs, artifacts of Indian and Eskimo cultures. Hours to be announced.

Ketchikan
Tongass Historical Society Museum, Barney Way. Indian artifacts, rocks and minerals; photograph collections and local historical mementos. Mon-Fri 2-5, 7-9; Sat-Sun 2-4.

Kodiak
Kodiak Historical Society Museum, Mill Bay Rd. Archeological items from the Kodiak and Aleutian Islands. Sun 1-4 and by appointment.

Port Chilkoot
Totem Village. Faithfully executed reproductions of a tribal house, pioneer trapper's cabin, several totem poles. Always open.

Sitka
Sheldon Jackson Junior College Museum, Lincoln St. Alaska's oldest museum, it contains Russian Orthodox religious objects and such Indian and Eskimo artifacts as Haida slate carvings, Tlingit relics, totem poles, Eskimo implements, ivory carvings, masks and shaman charms. June-Sept: Mon-Sat 10-12, 2-4; Sun, hols 2-4; Oct-May: by appointment.

Sitka National Monument. Totem pole collection and Indian center with craftsmen doing carvings. Mon-Fri 8-12, 1-5; Sat-Sun by appointment.

Skagway
Trail of '98 Museum, McCabe College Bldg., Spring St. Collections depict Alaskan history and native culture, including Klondike Gold Rush relics. May-Sept: daily 3-5, 7-9.

Hawaii

Hawaii Volcanoes National Park (Island of Hawaii)
Thomas A. Jaggar Memorial Museum. Natural history exhibits emphasize volcanology, but include ethnology, zoology and botany. Daily 7:30-5.

Hilo (Island of Hawaii)
The Lyman House Memorial Museum, 276 Haili St. Missionary relics in a house built in 1839. Exhibits also include Hawaiian artifacts, lava specimens, shells. Tues-Sat 10-4; Sun 1-4.

Honaunau (Island of Hawaii)
City of Refuge National Historic Park. Restored temple site. Daily 7:30-5.

Honolulu (Island of Oahu)
Archives of Hawaii, Iolani Palace Grounds. The most important collection of Hawaiiana existing; old prints, photographs, journals, books, treaties and other documents that re-create the history of Hawaii. Mon-Fri 7:45-4:30; Sat 8-noon. Closed Sat July-Aug.

Bernice P. Bishop Museum, 1355 Kalihi St. Founded in 1889, this museum has since achieved world fame as a center of research into the archeology, ethnology and natural history of Hawaii and other Pacific islands. Mon-Sat 9-4:30; Sun, hols 1-5.

Children's Museum of Natural History, 1201 Ala Moana Blvd. The outstanding feature among the natural history and science exhibits is the shell collection. Mon-Fri 9-4; Sat 9-noon.

Foster Botanic Gardens, 180 N. Vineyard Blvd. Nine-acre oasis of ancient trees and rare plants; orchid greenhouse. Daily 9-4.

Gima's Art Gallery, Ala Moana Center. Commercial gallery that displays work of the better Island artists as well as Japanese scrolls and screens. Mon-Sat 9:30-5; Mon, Thurs, Fri eves open to 9.

Hawaiian Mission Children's Society, 553 King St. Three old Mission Houses maintained as one museum: clothing, furniture, utensils and china used in early Protestant missionary homes; portraits of missionaries. Mon-Fri 9-4; Sat 9-1.

Honolulu Academy of Arts, 900 S. Beretania St. The only art museum of a general comprehensive nature in the Asian-Pacific world. Included in the museum are such Chinese masterpieces as the 100 Geese Scroll of Ma Fen; one of the most distinguished collections of Korean ceramics outside the Orient; a Japanese collection; and the Kress Collection of Italian Renaissance paintings. Tues-Sat 10-4:30; Sun 2-5.

Honolulu Zoo, 151 Kapahulu Ave. Includes a collection of tropical birds as well as pandas, zebras and gibbon apes. Daily 9-5.

Iolani Palace, King and Richards Sts. Only royal palace in U.S. Throne room and other items of Hawaiian historical interest. Mon-Fri 8-12, 1-4; Sat 8-11:45.

Queen Emma Summer Palace, 2913 Pali Hwy. Royal relics housed in the delightful former summer home of Kamehameha IV's queen. Mon-Fri 9-4; Sat 9-noon.

Tennent Art Foundation, 201 Prospect St. Houses the paintings of one of Hawaii's foremost artists, Madge Tennent. Tues 10-noon; Fri, Sun 3-5.

Ulu Mau Village, Ala Moana Park. Re-creation of an old Hawaiian chief's village; demonstrations of skills of ancient Hawaiians. Tues-Sat 9:30-4.

Waikiki Aquarium, University of Hawaii, 2777 Kalakaua Ave. Hawaiian and Indo-Pacific fishes, mollusks and crustaceans. Tues-Sat 10-5; Sun, hols 1-5.

Kailua-Kona (Island of Hawaii)
Hulihee Palace, Alii Dr. Originally the summer home of Hawaiian royalty, now a museum. Mon-Sat 8:30-4:30.

Kokee Park (Island of Kauai)
Kokee Natural History Museum. Exhibits of local plants, wildlife, rocks, and examples and pictures of petroglyphs. Winter: Tues-Sun 10-3:30; summer: daily 10-3:30.

Lahaina (Island of Maui)
Lahaina Restoration Foundation. Hawaii's Williamsburg, with a prison from 1851; a stone courthouse built in 1857; the old Baldwin House, built by missionaries in early 19th Century; Lahainaluna High School (founded 1831); and the Printing House, where Hawaii's first paper was printed. Most exhibits open Mon-Sat 10-4.

Laie (Island of Oahu)
Polynesian Cultural Center. Villages built in styles of various Polynesian peoples; exhibits of their arts and crafts. Mon, Wed, Fri, Sat 10-7; Tues, Thurs 10-5.

Lihue (Island of Kauai)
Holo-Holo-Ku Heiau, Kings Hwy. A restored temple of the god Ku with a sacrificial stone where victims were placed to appease this bloodthirsty deity. Beyond the enclosure of the temple are the royal birth stones, on which the royal wives bore their children. Always open.

Makapuu Point (Island of Oahu)
Sea Life Park. Aquarium with reef fish and performing porpoises. Winter: Tues-Sun 10-5; summer: Tues-Sun 10-6.

Wailuku (Island of Maui)
Maui Historical Society (Hale Hoikeike), on road to Iao Needle. A museum abounding in Hawaiiana: fine koa calabashes, silver punch bowls, and furniture carved from native wood; stone implements of war and peace recall early Hawaii. Mon-Sat 10-3:30.

Local festivals and events

Alaska

Beaver Roundup, Dillingham. Presentations of Eskimo games and dances; dog races and other winter festivities. Feb.

Fur Rendezvous, Anchorage. Largest of Alaska's winter events, featuring three-day World Championship Sled Dog Races. There are also parades, car races, Eskimo dances, and the Miners and Trappers Ball. Feb.

Homer Winter Carnival, Homer. Sports and other entertainment. Early Feb.

Ice Worm Festival, Cordova. Dances, art show and a rodeo. Early Feb.

North American Championship Sled Dog Races, Fairbanks. Racers come from as far as New England to compete in this biggest of dog-racing contests. Mar.

State Championship Dog Races, Soldotna. Includes weight-pulling contest between teams of Huskies. Mar.

Alaska Arts and Crafts Show, Juneau. Works of contemporary Alaskan artists and craftsmen. Mid-Mar.

Russian Easter, Sitka. Impressive service at St. Michael's Russian Orthodox Church conducted by the Bishop of Alaska. Mar, Apr or May.

Copper Basin Spring Festival, Glennallen. The season is hailed with baseball, exhibits and a parade. May.

King Crab Festival, Kodiak. This carnival, which honors the shellfish so important to Kodiak, includes plays and skin-diving contests. May.

Chilkat Indian Dances, Totem Village, Port Chilkoot. Traditional native dances are performed by a renowned Indian troupe on days when cruise ships come in. May—mid-Sept.

Days of '98 Show, Skagway. Skits, dancing and a re-enactment of "The Shooting of Dan McGrew" are performed every night a boat arrives, to commemorate the days when Skagway was the port of entry to the gold fields. May—mid-Sept.

Little Norway Festival, Petersburg. The town's largely Norwegian population celebrates Norway's Independence Day with traditional costumes, dances and smörgåsbords. May 17.

Alaska Music Festival, Anchorage. One month of concerts, recitals and lectures. June.

Whaling Festivals, Point Hope, Wainwright and Barrow. Eskimos participate in dances, blanket-tossing contests and, when the whaling has been good, in a whale-blubber feast. June.

Midnight Sun Baseball Game, Fairbanks. The game is played at midnight without the benefit of artificial lighting. Mid-June.

Midnight Sun Festival, Nome. To celebrate the absence of darkness, a raft race is held on the Nome River starting at midnight, plus a carnival and "days of '98" dance. Mid-June.

Sitka Salmon Derby, Sitka. Prizes given for the largest salmon and halibut caught over two successive weekends. Late June.

Strawberry Festival, Haines. This annual event marks the ripening of the famed, large strawberries grown in the area. Usually July.

All-Alaska Loggers Championship, Sitka. Log sawing, chopping and rolling plus tree-climbing and ax-throwing competitions. Other carnival festivities to celebrate Independence Day. July 4.

Golden Days, Fairbanks. The city's birthday is honored with costume parades, contests and the Eskimo "Olympics." July 22.

Golden North Salmon Derby, Juneau. Oldest and largest salmon derby in Alaska, lasting three days. Late July or early Aug.

Harvest Fair, Skagway. Displays of the jumbo fruits and vegetables produced by the area's long, sunny summer days. Aug.

Homer Fair, Homer. Displays of locally raised fruits and vegetables; arts and crafts, and other typical "county fair" features. Aug.

Kenai Days, Kenai. Beluga whale hunting is a feature of this festival. Also a carnival and exhibits. Aug.

Silver Salmon Derby, Seward. Anglers compete during height of salmon season. Aug.

Sitka Garden Fair, Sitka. Local produce, flowers and crafts are displayed. Sept.

Alaska Day Festival, Sitka. Indian dances, a costume ball and a traditional pageant commemorate the formal transfer of Alaska from Russian control to that of the U.S. Oct. 18.

Hawaii

Chinese Narcissus Festival, Honolulu. Five weeks of Chinese New Year festivities including feasts, fireworks, street dances, and fashion, art and flower shows. Early Jan—early Feb.

Cherry Blossom Festival, all Islands. The largest of Japanese celebrations, with three months of activities, including trade and flower shows, cooking demonstrations, and judo and karate exhibitions. Feb—late Apr.

Sea Spree, Haleiwa-Waialua, Oahu. The time of Queen Liliuokalani commemorated with surfing contest and canoe races. Early Feb.

Opening of State Legislature, Honolulu. Music, dancing and presentation of leis at Iolani Palace. Third Wed in Feb in even-numbered years.

Kamehameha School Song Contest, Honolulu. Annual children's choral contest at Honolulu International Center Arena. Mar.

Kuhio Day, all Islands. State holiday celebrating the birth of Prince Kuhio, Hawaii's first delegate to the U.S. Congress. In Honolulu there is a band concert, formal ball and performances of ancient chants. Mar 26.

Buddha Day, Honolulu. The birth of Buddha celebrated by tea ceremony, Buddhist Choir concert and Japanese dances in Kapiolani Park. Closest Sun to Apr 8.

Pan-Pacific Festival, Honolulu. Fair at University of Hawaii presenting foods, music and costumes of Pacific nations. Finals of the Ka Palapala Beauty Pageant. Late Apr or early May.

Hibiscus Show, Honolulu. Specimens of some of the 5,000 varieties of the state flower are shown at Ala Moana Park. May.

Lei Day, all Islands. Everyone wears leis to greet spring. Specially designed leis are exhibited and there are programs of dancing and music like the hula pageant at Waikiki Shell in Honolulu. May 1.

Captain Cook Festival, Kailua-Kona, Island of Hawaii. Hawaiian games, music, fishing derby and canoe races. Early May.

Lahaina Whaling Spree, Lahaina, Maui. Costumed pageant, canoe race and beard-judging contest, commemorating the whaling days of the 19th Century. Early May.

Fiesta Filipina, Honolulu. Dances, sports, fashion and handicraft shows, and celebration of Philippine Independence Day. Mid-May—mid-June.

Kamehameha Day, all Islands. State holiday in honor of the great leader and warrior king. In Honolulu it is celebrated with a parade, canoe races and pageants. June 11.

Festival of the Arts of This Century, Honolulu. Two weeks of concerts, dance programs, art exhibits and films presenting modern works by Oriental and U.S. artists. Late June—July.

50th State Fair, Honolulu. One week of exhibits of industry, agriculture, arts and crafts, foods and flowers. The Miss Hawaii Pageant is part of the fair. Late June or early July.

Bon Odori Season, all Islands. Japanese *bon odori* dances honoring the dead are held outdoors at different schools and Buddhist temples. Each weekend during July and early Aug.

Hawaiian International Billfish Tournament, Kailua-Kona, Island of Hawaii. Anglers compete for marlin and tuna. Late July or early Aug.

Hula Festival, Honolulu. Hundreds of dancers of all ages perform ancient and modern versions of the state dance in Kapiolani Park. First two or three Suns in Aug.

Aloha Week, all Islands. To usher in the fall, everybody wears a muumuu or brightly colored shirt during a week of parades, cultural programs and general gaiety. Mid-Oct.

Honolulu Orchid Society Show, Honolulu. Biggest orchid show of the year, at Honolulu International Center. Demonstrations of lei and corsage making and Oriental flower arranging. Late Oct.

International Surfing Championships, Makaha Beach, Oahu. The world's top surfers ride the five-to-20-foot waves. Late Dec.

Wildlife of the Frontier States

A sampling of the natural life found in the Frontier States is given on this and the following pages. In each case both the common name and scientific name of the plant or animal are given. The information supplied is not intended to be comprehensive; for additional material on the region's fauna and flora the reader should refer to specialized books on wildlife. Useful works containing such information are listed on page 188.

ALASKA

Mammals

Kodiak bear

Ursus middendorffi, the largest of all carnivores, stands as tall as 12 feet and weighs as much as 1,500 pounds. It is named for Kodiak Island, where it flourishes.

Wolverine

Found throughout Alaska, *Gulo luscus* will attack animals far larger than itself. The water-repellent fur of the wolverine is used for making parka hoods.

Alaska fur seal

Prized for its pelt, *Callorhinus ursinus* once was hunted almost to extinction but is now protected by law. It comes ashore only to breed between May and August.

Walrus

Odobenus rosmarus lives in shallow waters and on ice floes. This marine mammal's meat is an important staple in Eskimo diets and its skin is used for clothing.

Brown lemming

Lemmus trimucronatus, a rodent, is best known for its periodic mass migrations, during which thousands of them die in attempts to cross large bodies of water.

Barren ground caribou

This deer travels in herds that often number in the thousands. *Rangifer tarandus granti* has thick fur to protect it from the cold, broad hoofs for moving in snow.

Dall's sheep

Ovis dalli is a wild white sheep that inhabits mountains and uplands. It lives in rugged terrain where it can use its agility and balance to escape predators.

Dall's porpoise

Phocoena dalli, whose white underside shows when it leaps from the water, is often seen from ships taking the inland waterway through the Panhandle.

Birds

Emperor goose

This goose *(Philacte canagica)* breeds and stays within Alaska's borders, wintering only as far south as the Aleutian Islands. It is usually found near salt water.

Rough-legged hawk

Buteo lagopus, a bird of prey, is the most common hawk of Alaska's interior, frequenting the Yukon and Kuskokwim Valleys. It is often a gray-brown color.

Willow ptarmigan

This small arctic grouse *(Lagopus lagopus)* is the state bird of Alaska. A popular game bird, it has brown feathers in the summer and white in the winter.

Arctic tern

Sterna paradisaea completes the longest migration known, flying some 25,000 miles a year from the Arctic to the Antarctic and back. It breeds in all parts of Alaska.

Least auklet

Called the least auklet because it is the smallest of all auks, *Aethia pusilla* breeds in great numbers on the Pribilof Islands off the west coast of Alaska.

Snowy owl

This large arctic owl *(Nyctea scandiaca)* hunts during the day. It inhabits the northwest coast and tundra of Alaska, nesting on the ground instead of in trees.

Steller's jay

A nonmigratory inhabitant of Alaska's southern coastal forests, the jay *Cyanocitta stelleri* is much admired by bird watchers for its rich blue-black color.

Lapland longspur

Of the same family as sparrows and finches, *Calcarius lapponicus* is a widely distributed Alaskan land bird. It migrates south to Western states during the winter.

Fish

Chinook salmon

Oncorhynchus tschawytscha, also known as the King salmon, is the largest Pacific salmon. Averaging 15 to 25 pounds, it is a mainstay of the Alaskan fishing industry.

Dolly Varden trout

Found in salt and fresh water, *Salvelinus malma* is Alaska's most abundant trout. Commercial fishermen dislike it because it eats the eggs and young of salmon.

Arctic grayling

The largest of all graylings, *Thymallus signifer* is a prized game fish and lives in the major river basins north of the Gulf of Alaska. It has a large dorsal fin.

Inconnu

Living in remote northern rivers, *Stenodus leucichthys* is called the inconnu (unknown) because so little is known of its habits. It is an excellent game fish.

Trees and flowers

Sitka spruce

The predominant lumber species of Alaska, *Picea sitchensis* grows in the state's southern coastal forests. This spruce generally attains heights of 200 feet.

Sitka alder

Alnus sinuata is a small tree whose usual height is less than 10 feet. It can be found south of the Arctic Circle along mountain streams and in wet lowlands.

Arctic poppy

Papaver radicatum is a yellow flower found in the arctic tundra. This poppy has hairlike growths on its stems and leaves that protect it from the cold.

Mountain harebell

One of the most widely distributed wild flowers in Alaska, the mountain harebell *(Campanula lasiocarpa)* has small blue-violet flowers that are shaped like bells.

HAWAII

Mammals

Hawaiian bat

Hawaii's only indigenous land mammal, *Lasiurus semotus* is thought to have flown there from either North or South America long before the first Polynesians arrived.

Hawaiian monk seal

Its oil and smooth fur made *Monachus schauinslandi* a prize for hunters, who nearly killed off the entire species. Barely 1,500 of these now-protected seals survive.

Hawaiian rat

Rattus exulans, a small rodent, probably came to Hawaii with the first Polynesians. Its body measures some four to six inches long, and its tail is as long or longer.

Humpback whale

An awkward-looking, 50-foot giant, *Megaptera novaengliae* is the most common large whale found near Hawaii's coast. Despite its size, it can leap fully out of the water.

Birds

White-tailed tropicbird

Also called the bos'n bird because it follows ships for long distances, *Phaethon lepturus* usually nests in cliffs along the shore. Its white tail streamers grow to 16 inches.

Nene

Hawaii's state bird, *Branta sandvicensis* is a native goose that lives away from the water on arid lava slopes. Now protected, it is one of the world's rarest birds.

American golden plover

A migratory shore bird that breeds in the Arctic, *Pluvialis dominica* lives in Hawaii nine months of the year. Once settled, the birds do not fly far from their new nests.

Sooty tern

This tern *(Sterna fuscata)* is one of Hawaii's most common sea birds. Islanders, annoyed by its cries, call it *ewaewa*, which means "looked at with disfavor."

Short-eared owl

Known as a migratory bird in North America, *Asio flammeus* is a permanent resident in Hawaii. A day flyer, it ranges from mountains to open grasslands and towns.

Omao

The omao *(Phaeornis obscura)* is the only thrush native to Hawaii. Already extinct on some islands, it lives both in dense forests and in the scrub on lava flows.

Elepaio

Kauai, Oahu and Hawaii each have their own variety of *Chasiempsis sandwichensis*, a flycatcher found only in this state. The birds live in high forests and feed on insects.

Apapane

Himatione sanguinea, most common of the Hawaiian honey-creepers, faces extinction as the forests of ohia-lehua trees, where it feeds on nectar, are cut down.

Fish and reptiles

Moray eel

Although *Gymnothorax eurostus* is one of Hawaii's most dangerous types of fish—its vicious bite can mangle an arm—it is also the eel most commonly sought for food.

Dolphin

Not to be confused with the mammal dolphin, *Coryphaena hippurus* is a fish, caught for both food and sport. Called *mahimahi*, it is popular in Hawaiian restaurants.

Moorish idol

Common in warm reef waters as shallow as five feet, *Zanclus canescens* stands out with its broad black and white stripes. Its length rarely exceeds seven inches.

Convict tang

The convict tang *(Acanthurus sandvicensis)* gets its name from its vertical black stripes. A reef dweller about nine inches long, it is found only around Hawaii.

Wahoo

A slender mackerel weighing up to 150 pounds, *Acanthocybium solandri* is a favorite food fish in Hawaii. Its Island name, *ono,* means "delicious."

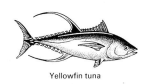

Yellowfin tuna

Named for its bright yellow fins, *Thunnus albacares* is the most abundant of the tropical tunas. It is a great sport fish and commercially one of the most valuable.

Green turtle

Chelonia mydas is prized for the delicate flavor of its tender meat and is named for its green fat. Constant hunting has drastically reduced its numbers off Hawaii.

Mourning gecko

Lepidodactylus lugubris, the most common lizard in Hawaii, uses minute hair-covered plates on its feet to crawl up walls and across ceilings in search of insects.

Trees and flowers

Screw pine

A small tree 20 feet in height, *Pandanus odoratissimus* has long, slender leaves used for weaving baskets. Its stiltlike roots give it the nickname "walking tree."

Koa

Acacia koa grows to 100 feet with wide-spreading branches toward its top. Its fine lumber, called Hawaiian mahogany, is used for furniture and ukuleles.

Candlenut

Strung on bamboo slivers, the oily nuts of Hawaii's state tree (*Aleurites moluccana*) were once used as candles. Roasted and spiced, they make a popular snack.

Ohia-lehua

Metrosideros collina, a tree believed sacred to the goddess Pele, bears bright red blossoms— the official flowers of the island of Hawaii—that are used in leis.

Ti plant

A symbol of good luck, *Cordyline terminalis* has many uses. The leaves are used for thatching and hula skirts, and brandy can be made from the fermented roots.

Yellow ginger

The fragrant *Hedychium flavescens,* brought from India for ornamental gardens, now grows wild in low, damp forests. This herb has delicate, pale yellow petals.

Ilima

Sida fallax, a variety of the hibiscus, has bright yellow-orange flowers that were once reserved for the royal leis of Island chiefs. It is the official flower of Oahu.

Beach morning glory

Ipomoea pes-caprae has roots and runners that anchor themselves in sand. The roots have been eaten during famines, although they are poisonous in large amounts.

Statistical information

State nickname, date of admission, capital

Alaska: Last Frontier; admitted January 1959 (the 49th state); Juneau.

Hawaii: Aloha State; admitted August 1959 (the 50th state); Honolulu.

Population

Alaska: 292,000 (1970 Bureau of Census estimate).
Hawaii: 756,544 (1967 *State of Hawaii Data Book* estimate).

By city (the states' 10 largest cities are listed in order of size: figures for Alaska are estimates from the 1970 *Editor and Publisher Market Guide;* those for Hawaii are 1966 and 1967 estimates from the *State of Hawaii Data Book*):
Honolulu: 343,075.
Anchorage: 53,000.
Kailua-Lanikai: 31,500.
Hilo: 26,360.
Kaneohe: 24,200.
Pearl City: 19,600.
Fairbanks: 19,468.
Wahiawa: 16,600.
Aiea: 15,100.
Waipahu: 12,600.

Land areas

Alaska: 586,400 square miles.
Hawaii: 6,424 square miles.

Hawaii, by islands, in square miles:
Hawaii: 4,021.
Maui: 728.
Oahu: 602.
Kauai: 553.
Molokai: 259.
Lanai: 141.
Niihau: 72.
Kahoolawe: 45.
Others: 3.6.

Coastlines

Alaska: 34,000 miles.
Hawaii: 1,052 miles.

Principal Alaskan rivers (length in miles)

Yukon: 1,875.

Kuskokwim: 800.

Porcupine: 555.

Koyukuk: 554.

Tanana: 531.

Colville: 428.

Stikine: 335.

Copper: 300.

Susitna: 300.

Major ranges and mountain peaks

Aleutian Range: Runs 1,600 miles along the Alaska Peninsula and westward through the Aleutian Islands; highest peak is Mount Redoubt (11,200 feet).

Hawaiian Chain: Runs 1,600 miles, mostly underwater, in the North Pacific Ocean (the Hawaiian Islands are the peaks of a part of this range); highest peaks (above sea level) are Hawaii Island's Mauna Kea (13,796 feet), Mauna Loa (13, 680 feet) and Maui's Haleakala (10,023).

Alaska Range: Runs 600 miles through south-central Alaska; highest peaks are Mount McKinley (20,320 feet), Mount Foraker (17,400 feet) and Mount Hunter (14,573 feet).

Brooks Range: Runs 600 miles across northern Alaska; highest peak is Mount Michelson (9,239 feet).

Kenai-Chugach Mountains: Run 450 miles through south-central Alaska; highest peak is Mount Marcus Baker (13,176 feet).

St. Elias Mountains: Run 250 miles in southeast Alaska and the Yukon; highest Alaskan peak is Mount St. Elias (18,008 feet).

Wrangell Mountains: Run 100 miles in southeast Alaska; highest peak is Mount Blackburn (16,390 feet).

National parks, forests and monuments (Alaska)

Tongass National Forest: 16,015,912 acres.

Chugach National Forest: 4,726,080 acres.

Katmai National Monument: 2,697,590 acres.

Glacier Bay National Monument: 2,274,595 acres.

Mount McKinley National Park: 1,939,493 acres.

Sitka National Monument: 54 acres.

National parks (Hawaii)

Hawaii Volcanoes National Park (Island of Hawaii): 220,345 acres.

Haleakala National Park (Maui): 26,403 acres.

City of Refuge National Historical Park (Island of Hawaii): 182 acres.

Some world and U.S. superlatives

World's tallest mountain, base to peak: Mauna Kea, Hawaii, 32,000 feet (some 18,200 feet of it is underwater).

Highest point in North America: Mount McKinley (20,320 feet).

Largest state, U.S.: Alaska.

Least densely populated state, U.S.: Alaska (0.4 per square mile).

Northernmost point, U.S.: Point Barrow, Alaska.

Westernmost point, U.S.: Attu Island, Alaska.

Lowest mean annual temperature, U.S.: Barrow, Alaska (9.6° F.).

Pronunciation glossary

Alakanuk (a luh KA nuck). A village in western Alaska near the Bering Sea.
Aleutian Islands (a LOO shun). An archipelago extending southwest from the Alaska Peninsula.
Athabascan (ath uh BASS ken). A member of a people speaking the Athabascan language.
Bethel (BETH el). A village in southwest Alaska.
Bodega Bay (bo DAY guh). A shallow inlet of the Pacific Ocean west of Santa Rosa, California.
Diomede Islands (DIE a meed). Two islands in the Bering Strait, one belonging to the Soviet Union (Big Diomede) and the other belonging to the U.S. (Little Diomede).
Foraker, Mount (FOR uh ker). A

mountain in central Alaska.
Gastineau Channel (GAA sti no). A navigable channel in southeast Alaska between Douglas Island and the mainland.
Haida (HIGH da). A member of a North American Indian people inhabiting islands off British Columbia and Alaska.
Haole (HOW lee). A white person in Hawaii, formerly any foreigner.
Hilo (HEE lo). A seaport on the Island of Hawaii.
Juneau (JOO no). The capital of Alaska.
Kahoolawe (kuh hoe LA vay). One of the Hawaiian Islands.
Kauai (kow WHY). Fourth largest of the Hawaiian Islands.
Kenai Peninsula (KEE nigh). A peninsula extending 150 miles

southwest from Anchorage into the Gulf of Alaska.
Kobuk River (ko BOOK). A river in northwestern Alaska.
Kotzebue (KOTT seh bew). A village in northwestern Alaska.
Kuskokwim River (KUS koe kwim). A river in western Alaska.
Lanai (luh NIE). One of the Hawaiian Islands.
Maui (MOW wee). Second largest of the Hawaiian Islands.
Mauna Loa (MOW nuh LO uh). An active volcano on the Island of Hawaii.
Molokai (MO lo KIE). An island in central Hawaii.
Niihau (NEE how). One of the Hawaiian Islands.
Oahu (o AH hoo). Third largest and most populous of the Hawaiian Islands.
Seward (SOO ard). A town in southern Alaska.

Shumagin Islands (SHOO muh gin). A group of about 20 islands and islets in the North Pacific off the south coast of the Alaska Peninsula.
Talkeetna (tal KEET nuh). A village in southern Alaska.
Tlingit (TLING git). A member of an American Indian people of the coastal regions of southern Alaska and northern British Columbia.
Tsimshian (CHIM she an). A member of an American Indian people of the coastal region of British Columbia.
Tyonek (tie O nik). A village in southern Alaska.
Waialeale, Mount (WHY a lay a lay). A mountain in central Kauai.
Waikiki (WHY kee kee). A beach on southeastern Oahu.
Wrangell Mountains (RANG gel). A mountain range in southeast Alaska.

Credits and acknowledgments

Maps for front and back end papers by Jeppesen & Company, Denver, Colorado. Maps on pages 174 through 179 © by The H. M. Gousha Company, San Jose, California. Maps on pages 11 and 13 by Lothar Roth.

The sources for the illustrations that appear in this book are shown below. Credits for the pictures from left to right are separated by commas, from top to bottom by dashes. Cover—Farrell Grehan. Front end papers—Drawings by Richard Boland. Chapter 1: 8, 9—Gordon Tenney. 15—Eric A. Hegg, courtesy University of Washington Library. 19 through 31—William Garnett. Chapter 2: 32—Ralph Crane. 34—Woodcut by Dale B. De Armond. 36—E. W. Merrill, Sitka, 1899. 38—Culver Pictures, Inc. 41—Alfred A. Blaker from *Eskimo Masks: Art and Ceremony* by Dorothy Jean Ray, University of Washington Press, 1967 (3). 43 through 46—Lee Friedlander. 47—R. W. Kelley (3), Lee Friedlander. 48 through 53—Lee Friedlander. Chapter 3: 54, 55—Ralph Crane. 56, 57—Cook Inlet Historical Society, Anchorage. 61—Map by Lothar Roth adapted from U.S. Department of Commerce and Geodetic Survey. 63 through 73—Lee Friedlander. Chapter 4: 74—Ralph Crane. 81 through 85—William Garnett. 86, 87—Map by Jerome Kuhl. 88, 89—Joseph S. Rychetnik. Chapter 5: 90—R. Wenkam. 92, 93—Bernice P. Bishop Museum, Honolulu. 97—Hawaiian Mission Children's Society, Honolulu, Bernice P. Bishop Museum, Honolulu (2)—Hawaiian Mission Children's Society, Honolulu, Bernice P. Bishop Museum, Honolulu. 98, 99—Map by Vic Kirishjian. 103—Farrell Grehan. 104 through 113—Michael Rougier. Chapter 6: 114, 115—Fred Maroon. 116, 117—Pan Pacific Press Photo, Bob Bone. 123—*Honolulu Star Bulletin.* 125 through 129—Art by Graham Percy. Chapter 7: 130—Farrell Grehan. 133—Bernice P. Bishop Museum, Honolulu. 134—Hanalei Museum, Kauai, Hawaii. 137—Michael Rougier. 139 through 149—Farrell Grehan. Chapter 8: 150—George Silk. 159 through 173—Farrell Grehan. 182 through 185—Drawings by Rudolf Freund. Back end papers—Drawings by Richard Boland.

The editors of this book wish to thank the following persons and institutions for their assistance: Russell Apple, Pacific Area Historian, National Park Service, Island of Hawaii; Robert Atwood, Publisher, *Anchorage Times;* Richard Bader, Professor of Oceanography, University of Hawaii; Charles Braden, Pacific Regional Director, Eastern Airlines, Honolulu; William Byler, Executive Director, Association on American Indian Affairs, New York City; Harry Chuck, District Superintendent, Hawaii Schools, Hilo, Hawaii; Jack Culbreath, Branch Chief, Information and Education, U.S. Forest Service, Juneau; Victor Fischer, Director, Institute of Social, Economic and Government Research, University of Alaska; Fred and Joan Fisher, Bureau of Indian Affairs School, Kotzebue, Alaska; the Reverend James Flynn, Teller, Alaska; Sam Gilstrap, Deputy Chancellor for Administration, East-West Center, University of Hawaii; Senator Ernest Gruening, Alaska; Dr. Thomas Hitch, Vice President and Director of Economic Research, First National Bank of Hawaii, Honolulu; Chinn Ho, Chairman, Capital Investment Company, Ltd., Honolulu; Gerrit P. Judd IV, Chairman, Department of History, Hofstra University; Charles J. Keim, Dean, College of Arts and Letters, University of Alaska; Michael Krauss, Associate Professor of Linguistics, University of Alaska; Ed Ladd, Supervisory Archeologist, National Park Service, Island of Hawaii; Dr. Margaret Lantis, Department of Anthropology, University of Kentucky; Arthur D. Lewis, Senior Vice President, Eastern Airlines, New York City; Richard Lyman, Chairman, Board of Trustees, Bishop Estate, Honolulu; James and Dorothy Magoffin, Interior Airways, Fairbanks; Louise Martin, Librarian, Department of Planning and Economic Development, State of Hawaii, Honolulu; Fred Kalani Meinecke, Instructor, Anthropology and Hawaiian, University of Hawaii; Nina of "Nina's Originals," Juneau; Mary Nordale, Special Assistant to Senator E. L. Bartlett, Alaska; Al Phelps, Editor, *Nome Nugget;* Congressman Howard Pollock, Alaska; Dr. Howard Powers, Head Scientist, Hawaiian Volcano Observatory, Island of Hawaii; Joyce Roberts, Pineapple Growers Association of Hawaii; Robert Schmitt, Department of Planning and Economic Development, State of Hawaii, Honolulu; C. W. Snedden, Publisher, *Fairbanks News-Miner;* Margaret Titcomb, Librarian, Bernice P. Bishop Museum, Honolulu; James Tobin, Superintendent, Volcanoes National Park, Island of Hawaii; Carl von Hake, U.S. Coast and Geodetic Survey, Rockville, Maryland; Dr. William R. Wood, President, University of Alaska.

Bibliography

*Available also in paperback.
† Available only in paperback.

Alaska

General and historical reading

Alaska. Editors of *Sunset* Magazine. Lane Publishing Company, 1963.

Atwood, Evangeline, *Anchorage: All-America City.* Binfords and Mort, 1957.

Barbeau, Charles Marius, *Totem Poles.* National Museum of Canada Anthropological Series #30, Vol. I, 1950.

Benedict, Ruth, *Patterns of Culture.* * Houghton Mifflin, 1959.

Butler, Evelyn, and George A. Dale, *Alaska: The Land and the People.* Viking Press, 1957.

Chaffin, Yule, *Alaska's Southwest, Koniag to King Crab.* Chaffin, 1967.

Chevigny, Hector, *Russian America.* Viking Press, 1965.

Colby, Merle, *A Guide to Alaska.* Macmillan, 1950.

Dockstader, Frederick, *Indian Art in America.* New York Graphic Society, 1966.

Drucker, Philip, *Indians of the Northwest Coast.*† Natural History Press, 1955.

Eide, Arthur Hansin, *Drums of Diomede.* House Warven, 1952.

Freuchen, Peter, *Book of Eskimos.*† World Publishing Company, 1961.

Gruening, Ernest, *The State of Alaska.* Random House, 1954.

Gruening, Ernest, ed., *An Alaskan Reader (1867-1967).* Meredith Press, 1966.

Heller, Herbert L., *Sourdough Sagas.* World Publishing Company, 1967.

Hughes, Charles Campbell, *An Eskimo Village in the Modern World.* Cornell University Press, 1960.

Hulley, Clarence C., *Alaska: Past and Present.* Binfords and Mort, 1958.

Keithahn, Edward L., *Monument in Cedar.* Roy Anderson, 1954.

Macdonald, Ronald St. John, ed., *The Arctic Frontier.* University of Toronto Press, 1966.

Nichols, Jeanette, *Alaska.* Russell and Russell, 1963.

Ray, Charles K.:
Alaskan Native Secondary School Dropouts. University of Alaska, 1962.
A Program of Education of

Alaskan Natives. University of Alaska, 1959.

Ray, Dorothy Jean, *Eskimo Masks: Art and Ceremony.* University of Washington Press, 1967.

Rogers, George W.:
Alaska in Transition. Johns Hopkins Press, 1960.
The Future of Alaska. Johns Hopkins Press, 1962.

Sherwood, Morgan B., *Exploration of Alaska 1865-1900.* Yale University Press, 1965.

Sherwood, Morgan B., ed., *Alaska and Its History.* University of Washington Press, 1967.

Steffanson, Evelyn, *Here Is Alaska.* Scribner's, 1959.

Tompkins, Stuart Ramsay, *Alaska: Promyshlennik and Sourdough.* University of Oklahoma Press, 1945.

Weyer, Edward Moffat, Jr., *The Eskimos: Their Environment and Folkways.* Anchor Books, 1962.

Wherry, Joseph H., *The Totem Pole Indians.* Wilfred Funk, 1964.

Williams, Howell, ed., *Landscapes of Alaska.* University of California Press, 1958.

Special topics

Eppley, R. A., *Earthquake History of the United States.* U.S. Government Printing Office, 1965.

Fitzgerald, Joseph H., *Report to the President's Review Committee for Development Planning in Alaska,* Vols. I and II. Federal Field Committee for Development Planning in Alaska, 1965.

Institute of Social, Economic and Government Research, University of Alaska, *Industries of Alaska.* University of Alaska, 1966.

Morgan, Murray, *One Man's Gold Rush: A Klondike Album.* University of Washington Press, 1967.

Parran, Thomas, *Alaska's Health: A Survey Report to the U.S. Department of Interior.* University of Pittsburgh Press, 1954.

Rogers, George W., and Richard A. Cooley, *Alaska's Population and Economy.* University of Alaska, 1963.

Spurr, Stephen H., and others, *Rampart Dam and the Economic Development of*

Alaska. University of Michigan Press, 1966.

Transportation Consultants, Inc., and Smith, Wilbur and Associates, *Alaska Highway Study.* U.S. Department of Commerce, 1965.

U.S. Congressional Commission on Interior and Insular Affairs, *Mineral and Water Resources of Alaska.* U.S. Geological Survey, 1964.

U.S. Department of the Interior, *Natural Resources of Alaska.* U.S. Government Printing Office, 1966.

Natural setting and wildlife

Gabrielson, Ira N., and Frederick C. Lincoln, *The Birds of Alaska.* Wildlife Management Institute, 1959.

Palmer, Ralph S., *The Mammal Guide.* Doubleday, 1954.

Peterson, Roger Tory, *Field Guide to Western Birds.* Houghton Mifflin, 1961.

Rhode, Clarence J., and Will Barker, *Alaska's Fish and Wildlife.* U.S. Department of the Interior, Circular 17, 1953.

Guidebooks

The Alaska Travel Guide. Lake Advertising Agency, 1967.

Fodor, Eugene, Robert C. Fisher and Barnett D. Laschever, eds., *Fodor Shell Travel Guides U.S.A.; Pacific.* * David McKay, 1966.

Henning, Bob, ed., *The Milepost— Guide to the Land of the Midnight Sun.* Alaska Northwest Publishing Company, 1967.

Lou Jacobin's Guide to Alaska and the Yukon. Guide to Alaska, Inc., 1967.

U.S. Department of the Interior, *Natural Resources of Alaska.* U.S. Government Printing Office, 1966.

Hawaii

General and historical reading

Borden, Charles A., *Hawaii, Fiftieth State.* McCrae Smith, 1950.

Clark, Sydney, *All the Best in Hawaii.* Dodd, Mead, 1960.

Davenport, William W., and others, *Hawaii 1966.* David McKay, 1966.

Day, A. Grove, *Hawaii and Its People.* Little, Brown, 1955.

Fuchs, Lawrence H., *Hawaii Pono.* Harcourt, Brace and World, 1961.

Gessler, Clifford, *Hawaii: Isles of Enchantment.* Appleton-

Century, 1937.

Hawaii, A Guide to All the Islands. Editors of *Sunset* Magazine. Lane Publishing Company, 1965.

Kuykendall, Ralph S., and A. Grove Day, *Hawaii: A History.* Prentice-Hall, 1961.

Lee, W. Storrs, *The Islands.* Holt, Rinehart and Winston, 1966.

Lind, Andrew W., *Hawaii's People.* University of Hawaii Press, 1955.

Loomis, Albertine, *Grapes of Canaan: Hawaii 1920.* Hawaiian Mission Children's Society, 1951.

Porteus, Stanley D.:
Calabashes and Kings. Pacific Books, 1945.
A Century of Social Thinking in Hawaii. Pacific Books, 1962.

Pukui, Mary Kawena, and Samuel H. Elbert, *Hawaiian-English Dictionary.* University of Hawaii Press, 1957.

Stearns, Harold T., *Geology of the State of Hawaii.* Pacific Books, 1966.

Weaver, Samuel P., *Hawaii: U.S.A.* Pageant Press, 1959.

Natural setting and wildlife

Dunmire, William, *Birds of the National Parks in Hawaii.* Hawaii Natural History Association, 1961.

Kuck, Loraine E., and Richard C. Tongg, *Hawaiian Flowers and Flowering Trees.* Charles E. Tuttle, 1958.

MacDonald, Gordon A., and Douglass H. Hubbard, *Volcanoes of the National Parks of Hawaii.* Mid-Pacific Press, 1966.

Munro, George C., *Birds of Hawaii.* Charles E. Tuttle, 1960.

Neal, Marie C., *In Gardens of Hawaii.* Bishop Museum Press, 1965.

Peterson, Roger Tory, *Field Guide to Western Birds.* Houghton Mifflin, 1961.

The Wondrous World of Fishes. National Geographic Society, 1965.

Guidebooks

Bob Krauss' Travel Guide to the Hawaiian Islands. Coward-McCann, 1963.

Davenport, William W., and others, *Hawaii, 1967, Fodor's Modern Guides.* * David McKay, 1966.

Hazard, Patrick D., *The Dolphin Guide to Hawaii.* * Doubleday, 1965.

Thrum's Hawaiian Annual. Star-Bulletin Printing Company, 1967.

Index

Numerals in italics indicate an
illustration of the subject mentioned.

189

The Frontier States: the works of man

ALASKA

Economic activities in Alaska revolve around federal defense expenditures and the state's natural resources. Commercial fishing—mostly for salmon, halibut and king crab—is the state's leading industry. The exploitation of Alaska's vast forests is a key to growth, as is the development of mineral resources. The discovery of oil and natural-gas deposits has drawn much capital investment.

Historical monuments in Alaska include numerous Indian totem poles *(above)* and the Russian-built Orthodox Church at Kodiak. Parts of Fairbanks recall the gold-rush era of the early 1900s.

HAWAII

Economic activities in Hawaii are strongly oriented toward national defense, tourism and agriculture. Catering to visitors is now Hawaii's largest industry; the number of tourists has multiplied more than six times since 1955. Agriculture, however, remains a vital element of Hawaii's economy with sugar and pineapple the leading crops. Light manufacturing is also developing rapidly.

Historical monuments in Hawaii include Oahu's Iolani Palace *(above)*—home of the Islands' last monarchs—and ruins of sacred temples built by native Hawaiians before the missionaries arrived.

Scale of map: one inch to 143 miles

INTERNATIONAL DATE LINE

Poin

Shishmaref

Ignaluk

Wales   Tayl

Teller

Nome   Sole

Gambell
Savoonga

Alak

Mo

Scammon   Va
Bay

Hooper Bay   Ma

Be

Tanunak   Napa

Mekoryok

Kipnuk

Quinhaga

Platinum

Saint Paul

Saint George

Attu

Fort Randall   Sand F

False Pass   Belko

Akutan

Dutch Harbor

Nikolski

Adak   Atka